Teacher appraisal

C000161455

EDUCATIONAL MANAGEMENT SERIES
Edited by Cyril Poster

Teacher appraisal

Training and implementation

Second edition

Cyril and Doreen Poster

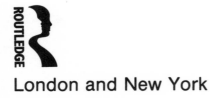

London and New York

First published 1991
Second edition published 1993
by Routledge
11 New Fetter Lane, London EC4P 4EE

Simultaneously published in the USA and Canada
by Routledge
29 West 35th Street, New York, NY 10001

© 1991, 1993 Cyril and Doreen Poster

Typeset in 10 on 12 point Garamond by Witwell Ltd, Southport

Printed in Great Britain by Mackays of Chatham PLC, Chatham, Kent

Copyright
It is normally necessary for written permission to be obtained
in advance from the publisher. Because *Teacher Appraisal*
contains resource material, those pages which carry the wording '© Routledge 1993' may be photocopied. The normal
requirement is waived here and it is not necessary to write to
Routledge for permission.

British Library Cataloguing in Publication Data

A catalogue record for this book is available from the British Library

Library of Congress Cataloging in Publication Data has been applied for

ISBN 0-415-095778 (pbk)

Contents

Figures

Training materials

Introduction to the second edition

The second edition of *Teacher Appraisal: a Guide to Training* is radically different from the first edition, for a number of reasons. Its predecessor was completed in the late summer of 1990 and published in March 1991, before the publication of the Department for Education (DFE) regulations and guidelines. While these had been fairly accurately forecast in the National Steering Group (NSG) report of 1989, and even more accurately by the draft regulations of the following year, we had been unable to deal in fine detail, as we now have done, with the regulations and, more importantly, their implications. Much that previously appeared in the chapters that followed, both training material and commentary, has had to be updated and modified. There are also two completely new chapters, one on the regulations as they affect grant-maintained schools, the other on developments in the two countries of the United Kingdom, Northern Ireland and Scotland, not subject to the education act that introduced appraisal into England and Wales.

There are other, even more cogent reasons for a second edition. We know that the first was widely used for local education authority (LEA) training in the hectic days that followed the announcement of 1 September 1992 as the date on which appraisal would be introduced nationally. We ourselves have been involved in running as many appraisal workshops since the publication of our book as in the four years preceding it. Although there will still need to be central training as new headteachers and senior staff are appointed, we believe that the emphasis has now shifted to consortium- and school-based training, and even to self-study. The training material in the book has been much revised and extended to reflect this. We wish here to reaffirm our determination to avoid sexist language at all times. We dislike the use of he/she, and prefer instead sometimes to use the masculine form and sometimes the feminine form for the senior post in any given situation. For most case studies we have chosen forenames which can be either male or female; and Vicky Hoyle and Andrea Bull can easily become Victor and Andrew if the reader wishes.

We like to think that we too have learnt during the two years since the first edition was published. One innovation that has met with widespread approbation on workshops has been that we have taken two case studies, one primary, the other secondary, through all stages from job specification to appraisal statement.

Every training session of any worth improves the performance of the trainers by showing up weaknesses and inconsistencies, and by providing new insights. One such, the School Management Competences Project, came to our attention only days before we completed the text, and we were so impressed by its implications for appraisal that we burnt midnight oil to introduce it. We are much indebted to a fellow trainer, Gill Cleland, and to the project staff at the University of Wolverhampton, for permission to make extensive use of material only now being published. Almost all the previous training materials that reappear here – some we have jettisoned as not sufficiently answering the needs of teachers – have in some way or other been improved since the first edition and there is a wealth of new materials. Most of the text has also been rewritten, and we believe that the book will be even more useful than its predecessor.

As ever, people have been most generous with their help and advice. In Dudley LEA, where over a period of four years we have run residential and one-day workshops for one in four of the teaching staff and all the inspectorate, Ian Cleland, LEA chief inspector, and Clive Burns, LEA senior secondary inspector, and Phil Lucas, Jill Hart, Trevor Taylor, Anna Smith and Pearl White have been unstinting in their support. The last two deserve special mention for their critical reading of our text and their helpful comments in the very final stages. Margaret Burslem, Walsall appraisal coordinator, Ian McGough, her Sandwell counterpart, and Mary Williams, headteacher, and Angela Flynn, appraisal coordinator, of Gwent have shared with us information and guidelines data prepared for their LEAs. Eric Macfarlane, author of *Education 16–19* (1992), gave us invaluable advice on the state of play in the new corporate colleges. Lesley Anderson, co-author with Brent Davies of *Opting for Self-Management* (1992) and John Wilkins, Principal of Stantonbury Campus, Milton Keynes, gave us much help as we sought to clarify apparent anomalies in the DES regulations as they applied to grant-maintained schools.

Marian Shaw of Oxford Brookes University was a valued critic when we were preparing the outline of the book. Pamela Munn of the Scottish Council for Research in Education and editor of *Parents and Schools* (1993) and Stewart Wilson, Rector of Banchory Academy, sent us valuable information and documentation on developments in Scotland. John Leonard of the Department of Education of Northern Ireland gave us useful, recent information for Chapter 14, which we were happy to incorporate.

There were in the first edition chapters on appraisal in tertiary institutions and on appraisal in the USA. Pressure on space has forced us to omit these as freestanding chapters and we offer our apologies to our friends Maurice Benington of the University of the West of England at Bristol and Shirley

Hord of Texas whose contribution to them was considerable. Some of the salient points have been included elsewhere in the book.

There is also a host of friends and acquaintances, for reasons of space unnamed, who have sent us a newspaper cutting here, a comment there, all of which have helped to make this book what we sincerely hope it is: useful to a teaching profession too little regarded by the public and politicians alike, overworked, underpaid, but remarkably resilient for all that!

Cyril and Doreen Poster
Bristol, 1992

Chapter 1

What is appraisal?

All organisations, whether they are factories, businesses, hospitals or schools, exist to provide a product or service to the satisfaction of their clients or customers. Appraisal is a means of promoting, through the use of certain techniques and procedures, the organisation's ability to accomplish its mission of maintaining or improving what it provides while at the same time seeking to maintain or enhance staff satisfaction and development. For employees in any concern to perform effectively, they must be well motivated, have a sound understanding of what is expected of them, have a sense of ownership and possess the abilities and skills to fulfil the responsibilities they are charged with.

In most organisations there takes place at regular intervals, usually annually, a formal review of some kind between staff members and their immediate managers. There is little conformity over what this review is called: performance review, performance appraisal, staff development review, staff appraisal are among the terms most commonly in use. There are two distinct trends in appraisal: the one focuses on performance, the other on development.

Performance review (or appraisal) focuses on the setting of achievable, often relatively short-term goals. The review gives feedback: on task clarification through a consideration of the employees' understanding of their objectives set against those of the organisation; and on training needs as indicated either by shortcomings in performance or by the demonstration of potential for higher levels of performance.

Staff development review (or appraisal) focuses on improving the ability of employees to perform their present or prospective roles, through the identification of personal developmental needs and the provision of subsequent training or self-development opportunities.

In sum, the former is concerned with the task, the latter with the individual.

This distinction is, of course, an over-simplification, since the performance of any organisation depends on both the delivery system and those who deliver it. There are many variations in the marriage of these two views of the purpose of appraisal, and it is difficult to conceive of any appraisal system that can wholly ignore the one or the other.

For simplicity and brevity we intend throughout this book to use the word *appraisal*, glossing it only when it is necessary to make our intention and meaning absolutely clear. Readers in England and Wales will be well aware that there has been much antagonism in their educational circles to the use of this word: the next chapter, on the history of the introduction of appraisal, explains why. There are LEAs which have fought shy of the word to such an extent that they have sought to employ the term *staff development review*, or some such phrase, exclusively even though it is clear that the system that has been established by the DFE does not confine itself to this aspect. Others have sought to establish the use of *staff development and appraisal*, a term which accurately reflects the concern of administrators and teachers alike, but which is too cumbersome for repeated use. In general, although there are LEAs which seem determined to perpetuate in their documentation the use of their chosen phrase, the single word *appraisal* now has widespread currency.

INDIVIDUAL AND ORGANISATIONAL NEEDS

Appraisal is one of a number of techniques designed to promote the integration of the individual into the organisation. Each individual comes into the organisation with a unique set of needs and objectives, preferences for ways of performing and expectations of a wide range of personal satisfactions. One is ambitious, keen to achieve well in a short time and move rapidly up the career ladder; another may wish to do no more than perform competently, gaining personal satisfactions elsewhere, in activities unconnected with the workplace. The problem for individuals is to make a contribution within organisations set up by others, in such a way as also to satisfy their personal needs. The problem for organisations is to harness the unique talents of individuals and coordinate their activities towards the achievement, by effective and efficient means, of organisational objectives. This process of matching the needs of individuals to the objectives of the organisation can best be described as 'integrating the individual and the organisation'. That bland phrase may serve to hide the pressures that an organisation may put on individuals to subordinate their own interests to those of the organisation, or, alternatively, the devious ways whereby the individual may seek to subvert the organisational objectives.

Organisations have at their disposal many interactive procedures whereby they may monitor and control the integration of their employees. These include:

- recruitment selection, placement, induction
- training, coaching, delegation, mentoring

- promotion, pay and reward systems, including bonuses
- performance review and appraisal
- counselling, grievance and disciplinary procedures
- exit interviews.

Since it is unlikely that there will be a perfect match between the interests of the individual and the organisation, there will always arise the need to find ways of reconciling the differences. The strategies for handling these differences will vary from one organisation to another: in one, the differences will be papered over; in another, they will be fully explored and every attempt will be made to negotiate a mutually satisfactory solution; in a third, the organisation will impose its solution. The approach to the resolution of differences will also colour the organisation's choice of, or specific approach to the use of, any of these integrating processes.

All organisations have become aware that the accomplishment of a task is not solely a matter of individual ability or motivation, but is often also dependent on the support of co-workers. A small team of cooperating colleagues working on a common task will usually handle higher levels of stress and better maintain confidence and morale in the face of problems than an individual working in isolation. Similarly, as was first discovered in the automotive industry in the USA many decades ago, teams work better if they have knowledge and understanding of the objectives and performance of other teams. Both for the satisfaction of the social needs of individuals and for the achievement of institutional objectives a supportive climate, with a high level of collaboration and communication, is desirable.

The needs of individuals have been extensively analysed by sociologists and occupational psychologists. Not surprisingly, it has been found that, while there are differences based on age, culture, personality and social class, there exists a fairly common set of wants and needs. For middle managers and professionals these include a need for responsibility, relative autonomy, a sense of achievement, interesting and challenging work, opportunity for personal growth and development and the occasion to use specific skills (Vroom, 1964; Herzberg, 1966).

Additionally, individuals need to be provided with essential information if they are to achieve the organisational objectives. They feel they have a right to know:

- what is expected of them, what objectives they should be trying to achieve, whether they have a right to share in the shaping of these objectives
- what are their areas of responsibility, authority and discretion
- the extent to which they are achieving their objectives and meeting performance requirements
- how they may correct any shortfall between their objectives and their performance.

These requirements suggest certain desiderata for any effective integrating process, including appraisal.

ORGANISATIONAL MANAGEMENT STYLES

McGregor (1960) posited two polarised sets of assumptions about the way organisations regarded their employees: the well known Theory X and Theory Y. A bureaucratic, hierarchical organisation will act on the assumption that its employees:

> dislike work, have little ambition, want security and require to be coerced, controlled or threatened with punishment. In contrast, theory Y holds that staff will seek responsibility if the conditions are appropriate, exercise self-direction and control if they become committed to organisational objectives, and respond to rewards associated with goal attainment.
>
> (Dennison and Shenton, 1987)

In real life organisations rarely conform wholly to either polarity. It is now widely accepted that organisational behaviour, while to some extent predetermined by the organisation's self-image, will swing on a sector arc between these two polarities according to the demands of the situation and the response of management to those demands. Burns and Stalker (1968) produced such a model in which the terms *mechanistic* and *organic* represent those polarities. The mechanistic type of organisation is defined as one:

> suitable to stable conditions, to a hierarchical management structure in which there is a clear definition of assigned roles, formal and mainly vertical communication, and a built-in system of checks and supervision. The organic type of organisation, on the other hand, is designed to adapt to a rapid rate of change, to situations in which new and unfamiliar problems continually arise which cannot be broken down and distributed among the existing specialist roles. Relationships are therefore lateral rather than vertical, and form and reform according to the demands of the particular problem.
>
> (Poster, 1976)

While there has been an observable swing in the management of schools in the past half century towards the more participative organic style of management the rate of change currently imposed on all educational institutions impedes them from developing a holistic style. Managers are forced to make situational responses to a welter of demands from the DFE and from society which appear to be in conflicting and contradictory styles but which may merely be a reflection of the pressure put upon them and the institution they manage. Appraisal, properly implemented, both helps to make staff more understanding of the cause of these variations in style while encouraging management to make more tempered judgments about the style required by a particular set of demands and to be less inclined to bend to whatever wind blows hardest.

ORGANISATIONAL CLIMATE AND APPRAISAL

Organisational climate is a concept that refers to the different cultures or qualities possessed by organisations regardless of whether the structure is hierarchical and bureaucratic or informal and dynamic, or whether risk-taking and the use of individual initiative is encouraged or frowned upon. Every school:

> has a particular culture, determined by the individual values and experiences which each person brings to it, the ways in which people act and interact and the footprints they leave behind them.
>
> (Beare *et al.*, 1989)

The differences in organisational climate and culture will both determine and be determined by the processes used to integrate the individual into the organisation. The hierarchical institution is likely to regard the induction process, for example, as one in which the newcomer is given a thorough grounding into the organisation's operational system. The dynamic institution will use induction as an opportunity to demonstrate the breadth of discretion and responsibility available to the newcomer. It follows, therefore, that appraisal in the one organisation will be concerned with assessing the extent of the individual's conformity to the organisational ethos and with meeting targets; in the other, with the development of initiative, self-development and goal achievement.

There may well be some variation between the wants of the individual and the climate of the organisation. This variation becomes highlighted on each occasion when the individual makes formal contact with any of the organisation's procedures, appraisal above all. The dynamic organisation may seek to accommodate the individual's wants within the climate of the institution. It will not alter its culture to suit the individual; in doing so it might well disturb the equilibrium of other members of staff. It will, however, be prepared to study suggestions and criticisms, make them available, if helpful, to wider discussion, and absorb them into its culture if this can be done with profit. The organisation which is rigid in its unwillingness to explore any mismatch between the individual and the institution will create a climate of intense frustration, demotivation, low effectiveness and adaptability, poor morale, low job satisfaction, high staff turnover and the rest of the ills that beset a sick organisation.

We have postulated that appraisal is one of a number of procedures for integrating the individual into the organisation, and that the desired outcome is achieved in part by meeting the individual's social and psychological needs. Failure to meet those needs will result in organisational ill-health. However, an organisation which bases its appraisal processes solely on the meeting of these needs will not necessarily produce the intended or desired result. Appraisal must be to the benefit of *both* the individual *and* the organisation. As we will show in later chapters the appraisal system, in addition to promoting the wellbeing of the organisation's members, must contain the hard characteristics of clear goalsetting, sound appraisal data and purposeful review.

THE RANGE OF THE APPRAISAL PROCESS

Appraisal may have, provided its procedures are geared to recognising this, a range of purposes, some centred on the needs of the organisation, some on those of the individual, some on both. While unquestionably concerned with personal professional development, appraisal will also include procedures for assessing the individual's performance in discharging specific and agreed responsibilities. These will derive from the job specification and the goals set at the previous appraisal interview or on a new teacher's arrival at the school.

Thus appraisal, as we view it, brings together both staff development and performance review. If it does not, we can see no merit in it: it will be merely a cosmetic exercise. To review performance is not to be judgmental. Indeed, if performance is not reviewed there is only hearsay evidence on which to base staff development needs. How can teachers be helped to become better teachers if nobody in the school knows how they are performing? How can the school become a better school unless there is an awareness, not of the statistics of its academic achievement and truancy rate, as is currently bruited as the panacea, but of what the school's teachers are doing to maintain and improve their performance in the interests of the students?

Performance appraisal must not be confused with merit rating. Appraisal, properly used, will provide the organisation with far greater benefits than any mechanical procedure for assessing eligibility for merit payments. Those who may find the case for performance-related pay attractive should study the arguments mustered in the wide-ranging contributions to the book edited by Tomlinson (1992). If it were to be introduced, then those tempted to find in the appraisal process a ready mechanism for their decision making would do well to heed the many expert researchers from the USA, who are unanimous in stating categorically that appraisal should not be used for this purpose.

THE POTENTIALITIES OF APPRAISAL

It is widely claimed that a well-run appraisal system will benefit . . .

. . . individual members of staff by:

- giving them a greater sense of purpose through the provision of clear objectives
- encouraging self-development and personal initiative
- enhancing their self-esteem and self-confidence
- reducing alienation and resentment, by providing the opportunity for free discussion
- providing opportunity for the dissemination of career advice

. . . the organisation by:

* enhancing the communication of organisational aims to all staff and facilitating the coordination of effort
* channelling individual effort into organisational goals
* providing the opportunity to initiate problem-solving and counselling interviews
* contributing to the institutional audit or review
* giving managers greater control through the setting of objectives within a school development plan

. . . both individual members of staff and the organisation by:

* helping to build morale
* encouraging better communication, both vertical and lateral, and the creation of a more open style of management
* providing the means whereby the individual can influence the organisation
* facilitating the identification of talent
* providing a mechanism whereby individual effort may be recognised even when no financial reward can be given
* integrating the individual and the organisation.

No one system will ever achieve all these potential benefits of an appraisal system: the climate and circumstances of the organisation will determine which of the potential benefits might realistically be achieved and which could not be accommodated. In one organisation, the climate might be favourable primarily to the support and encouragement of the individual; in another, to entrepreneurialism and self-development; in a third, the required focus might be more narrowly conceived, on achieving specific objectives within tight resource constraints.

Again, the nature of appraisal as seen by one organisation may be developmental: to review and plan those steps which will best contribute to the personal and professional development of individual members of staff. Another organisation may see the purpose of appraisal as mainly concerned with maximising staff performance: to involve and develop each member of the institution in such a way as to create the maximum benefit for the organisation.

Any single system which sought to be so comprehensive that it combined all the possible benefits of appraisal would almost certainly create such a confused multi-targeted approach that it would fail. It is necessary to remind oneself that appraisal has to be resourced in terms of time and expertise; and the more conflicting its objectives the greater the resource needs are likely to be. The designers or adapters of any appraisal system – and it must be recognised that, even within a national system, there will be adaptation to the particular needs and circumstances of the school – must be clear about their priorities. Once

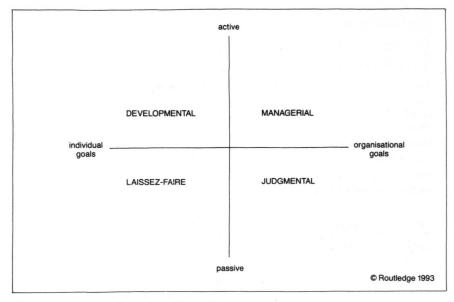

Figure 1.1 Types of appraisal interview

they have established their appraisal objectives, they must not grieve over the absence of other, no doubt valuable, potential outcomes.

MODELS OF STAFF APPRAISAL

There are four ideal types of appraisal interview. The implication of *ideal*, we hasten to add, is that you are unlikely to meet any appraisal process that wholeheartedly and exclusively has the characteristics shown for any one type. What one can say is that one of these types, broadly speaking, represents the appraisal style that is being adopted by a particular organisation, although it may borrow from any of the other types some aspect that it finds suited to its conditions or requirements.

In Figure 1.1 the horizontal axis denotes whether the emphasis is on individual or organisation goals: that is, whether the main concern is for the growth of the individual as a means to organisational development or whether the interests of the organisation predominate. The vertical axis indicates the extent to which management sees itself as having a proactive role: that is, whether its main concern is with the setting of objectives or performance targets, with the identification of training needs, with reaching agreement on developmental tasks, or with taking or sharing of responsibility for developmental growth and the achievement of objectives. The salient features of the four basic types are indicated in Figure 1.2.

Developmental

Assumes professional, collegial and collective authority to lie within the profession

Has as its main concerns truth, accuracy, the maintenance of moral, ethical and professional values

Works through peer appraisal of colleagues

Has a bipartite approach towards enabling self-improvement

Seeks to produce agreed programme with shared responsibility for the achievement of objectives

Is concerned with longer-term, professional development

Managerial

Assumes right to manage: hierarchical position confirms authority

Is concerned with doing and achieving, with efficiency and effectiveness

Appraises through line management

Makes strong use of incentives and praise and reproach from superior

Sets targets in order to maximise organisational objectives

Is concerned with shorter-term assessment of performance

Laissez-faire

Recognises the importance of self-development

Allows managerial abdication from responsibility

Encourages subordinates to raise issues

Demonstrates a lack of focus, direction and purpose

Has a belief in the importance of self-motivation

Allows appraisee to decide on the need for follow-up

Judgmental

Uses appraisal to maintain social control

Assumes managerial authority to make judgments

Collects data for the assessment of the subordinate

Rates individuals against one another

Assumes the necessity of extrinsic motivation

Uses system for merit rating and performance-related pay

© Routledge 1993

Figure 1.2 Key features of the four basic types

There are clear strengths and weaknesses in all four systems. The left-hand polarity of the horizontal axis of Figure 1.1 emphasises individual responsibility but may place excessive reliance on the ability of all individuals to make sound judgments at all times. It also gives too little recognition to those occasions when the needs of the organisation may override those of the individual. The right-hand polarity may be highly effective in setting institutional goals and making objective judgments, but may fail to capitalise on the knowledge and inner strengths that the individual has to offer.

The emphasis on objectives and yardsticks characteristic of the managerial type of appraisal has been criticised on several grounds: the rapidity of the rate of change may well invalidate or modify the goals that the managers have set; lower echelon staff have little control over the factors that affect goal achievement and therefore little motivation to take responsibility; and, particularly true of education, despite the present emphasis on the identification of performance criteria, there are large areas of activity in which specific targets cannot be identified and which may be undervalued in any review of this kind.

The growing influence from the 1970s onwards on management theory and practice of humanistic psychology has promoted the recognition of the value of individuals within organisations, and of their autonomy and self-actualising potential. Today individuals take and are willingly given far more responsibility for managing their own career progression, for determining their own goals within the broad limits of the organisational aims and objectives, and for assessing their own capabilities and developmental needs.

Nevertheless, while recognising and commending this, it must be accepted that few people are wholly capable of judging their own capacities, strengths and weaknesses without some form of catalyst. In some organisations, and increasingly in schools, that catalyst may be a *critical friend*, a peer or superior who acts as a sounding board for a colleague's assessment of his own abilities, progress and worth. In some few schools this provision may be built into the management system, sometimes by making it part of the role of the line manager, sometimes by the appointment of a senior manager as staff development officer, usually with a strong element of counselling and even trouble-shooting in the role.

Yet the movement towards formalising and universalising a system of personal and professional staff development, rather than relying on hit and miss procedures that have a habit of becoming less available and apparent as other pressures on resources of time and expertise grow, has led to the institution of compulsory teacher appraisal in England and Wales. Teachers have accepted appraisal for staff development, recognising that any increase in personal skills and self-understanding leads also to the improvement of the effectiveness of the institution as a place of learning. Government, blown first by this wind then by that, has changed its mind more than once about both the importance of appraisal and the kind of appraisal it wants; this the next chapter will disclose. Nor, indeed, can we be sure that the uncertainty is ended. At the time of writing there are straws in the wind, such as the possible use of appraisal to determine performance-related pay, that may yet become sticks to beat the backs of teachers.

Chapter 2

The evolution of appraisal

The main concern of this chapter is to chart the path by which appraisal has come about in England and Wales in order to inform and illuminate the practical issues and training considerations which follow. The widely accepted starting point is 'The Great Debate', initiated by James Callaghan in 1976 which called for higher standards and greater accountability in education. There was little response, other than some sage head-nodding, until well into the 1980s, although it was evident that a national programme of teacher appraisal was viewed increasingly as essential to the achievement of Callaghan's demands. It was obvious that there would be a need for much careful negotiation with the teacher unions and associations if an innovation of this magnitude were to be introduced into a profession which had for decades shielded itself from anything which might smack of outside interference. Headteachers had been known to refuse access to their schools to LEA advisers: the island fortress mentality was still with us in some places even as late in the century as this. This was a situation to handle with diplomacy, then.

There could have been no more unfortunate approach to the topic of raising standards than the statement which appeared in *Teaching Quality* (DES, 1983):

> Concern for quality demands that [where] teachers fail to maintain a satisfactory standard of performance, employers must . . . be ready to use procedures for dismissal.

Not surprisingly this statement roused the ire of the teaching profession and the resultant hubbub drowned out the many excellent features of that publication. At a time when the fall in pupil numbers was beginning to lead to expectations of better conditions and resources, teachers, rightly or wrongly, saw appraisal as a means by which the teaching force would be drastically reduced. How is 'a satisfactory standard of performance' to be assessed? What percentage of teachers would be adjudged to have failed to achieve it? And the cynics suggested 'Why, that percentage which would obviate the extra expenditure to reduce class size!'

For teachers and LEAs alike, the first priority at a time of considerable turbulence in the educational atmosphere was the in-service training of all staff to improve their skills and knowledge, not the weeding out of so-called incompetents. By what criteria is incompetency to be judged? LEA officers maintained that they already had at their disposal the machinery for ceasing to employ unsatisfactory teachers. Advisers were skilled in indicating to no-hopers that they were in the wrong profession and in helping them to leave it with dignity; and, indeed, dismissal procedures could if necessary be invoked for those who were unwilling to heed advice. Those procedures were, and still are, lengthy and cumbersome; but that is because they are circumscribed by conditions and rights of appeal that ensure that no teacher is wrongfully dismissed.

The statement by the then Secretary of State Sir Keith (now Lord) Joseph, in a speech in January 1984 to the North of England Education Conference may have been intended as a palliative but did little to mollify teacher outrage:

> I attach particular importance to the interesting and innovative work . . . in the important area of teacher assessment and in the schemes of collective self-assessment within the schools.

His use of the term 'assessment' is worthy of note. There was in the early days a disturbing confusion between assessment, which is both judgmental and summative, and appraisal, which is developmental and formative. Quite what his reference to 'schemes of collective self-assessment' was intended to convey has never been clear.

This confusion over terminology was to continue for some years and to bedevil relationships between the Department of Education and Science (DES) and the teachers' unions. It was not a matter of mere semantics: underlying the choice of words were major differences of intention over the fundamental purposes of appraisal. Indeed, many of those who were supportive of a strategy for school improvement and personal professional development for teachers became chary of using the word 'appraisal' lest its misuse nullified their good intentions.

At a time when confusion and argument were at a peak, the DES belatedly but wisely commissioned from Suffolk LEA, one of the few then with first-hand experience of the introduction of appraisal, a report which was later to be published under the title of *Those Having Torches* (Suffolk LEA, 1985). While there was much criticism of that report's excessive reliance on the outcomes of a fact-finding tour in the USA – where each state is responsible for setting up its own scheme of appraisal and where much is made of somewhat mechanistic check sheets and computerised statistics of teacher performance – it nevertheless contained much that was valuable and thought-provoking. Above all, it contained two categorical statements that set the agenda for much of the discussion that was to follow. The first was in the form of what is increasingly being described as a 'mission statement':

> The corner-stone of appraisal schemes is the belief that teachers wish to improve their performance in order to enhance the education of pupils.

The second might well be called a shot across the bows of those who had commissioned the report, the remit for which had been typically vague:

A precise definition of the purposes of the appraisal system is imperative: failure to do this can not only be inhibitory but is also downright disastrous.

The fact that an appreciable number of schools were already engaged in staff appraisal – whether or not they chose to call it that is irrelevant – was not something of which the DES appeared to be aware. Certainly they showed no signs of taking account of, for example, the well-documented three years' experience of a voluntary scheme that had been introduced stage by stage, with the full support and cooperation of the staff of a Hertfordshire comprehensive school (Bunnell and Stephens, 1984). The stance of that school had been: 'If we want an appraisal scheme to match our needs and principles we must involve ourselves in the making of it.'

This was the approach of a number of schools, some of which documented the development of their schemes, though few with the thoroughness and objectivity of Bunnell and Stephens. Turner and Clift (1985) published as the first stage of an Open University project begun in October 1984 a register and review of schemes developed in over fifty schools. Newman (1985) conducted a survey 'to establish the pattern and practice of staff appraisal in secondary schools in the south and south-west of England'. Of over 200 schools in the seven LEAs of the survey – a response rate of over 88 per cent – nearly one in four was in November 1984 operating a staff appraisal scheme.

There is no means of knowing whether or not this pattern was being replicated on the same scale in other regions and in primary schools – indeed one suspects that it was not – but there is ample evidence that appraisal schemes were mushrooming, mainly as a strategy for school improvement. Newman thought it wise to warn that:

While there are many common features in appraisal schemes operating in different schools, there is no single universal arrangement that will work for all. Experience has shown that there may be difficulties if a school 'borrows' a scheme from another school and tries to use it without any attempt to see whether it is suitable or not.

That warning needs to be heeded even now, when we have a national scheme of appraisal. If schools and LEAs are not given sufficient flexibility to adapt their appraisal process to meet their needs of different management styles and structures, different approaches to learning, different staff experiences, then it may well become a straitjacket and not a strategy for improvement.

In the same year Her Majesty's Inspectorate (HMI) produced a report *Quality in Schools: Evaluation and Appraisal* (HMI, 1985) which was the outcome of a two-year survey of a number of LEAs and schools where appraisal was taking place. In the report, HMI offered just such a definition as the Suffolk team had called for:

Staff appraisal involves qualitative judgments about performance and, although it may start as self-appraisal by the teacher, it will normally involve judgments by other persons responsible for that teacher's work – a head of department or year, the headteacher, a member of the senior management team or an officer of the LEA. This appraisal may well (and usually does) include the identification of professional development needs.

The statement, well intentioned though it might have been, was flawed in two respects: it confuses appraisal with assessment, invoking 'judgments by other persons'; and, oddly, the language in which it is cast clearly has secondary school management structures in mind, even though primary schools outnumber secondary schools by over six to one.

LEGISLATION

The Secretary of State may by regulations make provision for requiring LEAs or such other persons as may be prescribed, to secure that the performance of teachers to whom the regulations apply . . . is regularly appraised in accordance with such requirements as may be prescribed.

(DES, Education (No. 2) Act, 1986)

Like so much else in this piece of legislation, enactment was to be through regulations hereinafter to be made and, important to bear in mind, are subject to revision or reformulation without parliamentary debate. 'Such other persons as may be prescribed' we now see from the regulations as providing alternative procedures for grant-maintained schools; but equally the same phrase may be used to provide the grounds for the further reduction of the authority of the LEA. The open-endedness of 'such requirements as may be prescribed' has made many educationists fearful that the appraisal process which we have now might, in the period of monitoring and review required by the regulations, be radically altered or even wholly replaced by a 'tick-a-box' system of appraisal, not unknown in some branches of the civil service.

The discussions which followed the legislation, and in particular the report of the Advisory, Conciliation and Arbitration Service (ACAS) Appraisal/ Training Working Party (ACAS, 1986) gave rise to a pilot study which began in January 1987. The DES selected six LEAs representing a geographic and demographic cross-section, a wide range of experience of appraisal, and, so it seemed, an even wider range of expectation of the nature and purpose of a national appraisal scheme. The six LEAs were Croydon, Cumbria, Newcastle, Salford, Somerset and Suffolk. The National Development Centre for School Management Training (NDC) was appointed national coordinator and the Cambridge Institute of Education (CIE) national evaluator.

Many of the misgivings and suspicions of the teaching profession were dispelled by the open behaviour of the pilot authorities and particularly the NDC. The National Steering Group (NSG) which was set up to oversee the project was representative of teacher unions and associations, LEAs, the DES and HMI. Although there occurred from time to time the withdrawal of one or other of the two largest teacher unions, for reasons unconnected with the project, harmony largely prevailed. An interim report was presented to a national conference in May 1988, and the definitive report *School Teacher Appraisal: A National Framework* (HMSO, 1989) set out the findings of nearly two years of intensive work.

A NATIONAL FRAMEWORK

The NSG report was circulated in October 1989 to all chief education officers (CEOs) along with a survey (DES, 1989b) by HMI of their view of developments in appraisal in the six pilot schemes and other LEAs. In a covering letter the DES indicated that the new Secretary of State, John MacGregor, had decided that:

> in view of the far-reaching reforms on which schools are now engaged it would not be right to make Regulations in the near future which required *all* schools to introduce appraisal within the next few years.
>
> (DES, 1989a)

What led to this *volte face* we will never know, though it is likely that the problem of resourcing this innovation lay at the heart of the change of attitude: the NSG and HMI had independently estimated the cost of appraisal at £40 million a year in the initial period. There is also the possibility that this Secretary of State, like his predecessor, was attracted to practices in the USA or in the Civil Service: simpler, undeniably less costly, but far less effective.

The reaction of teachers and LEA officers and advisers was, despite the fact that all were justifiably suffering from 'innovation fatigue', broadly one of disappointment, for several very cogent reasons. First, this was one innovation – possibly *the* one innovation – in the planning of which teachers' representatives at national and local level had been scrupulously involved. Secondly, the NSG had skilfully steered appraisal away from being a judgmental process, and it was widely seen by headteachers and teachers alike as developmental, helpful to their personal professional development, to improved school management and effective learning. Thirdly, increasingly during the previous two years, teachers and administrators in forward-looking LEAs had begun to grapple with the evolution of a strategy for the introduction of appraisal and had set up their own pilot training schemes in collaboration with consultancies and higher education establishments. Finally, there was a growing realisation that appraisal could well be the key to the growth of skills in the management of other innovations.

In January 1990 MacGregor denied that he had gone cold on appraisal and announced that he proposed:

to issue guidance to schools and LEAs [to] be followed, as soon as practicable, by regulations requiring the introduction of schemes of appraisal across England and Wales within a fixed period.

(MacGregor, 1990a)

Yet, in the event, he issued no regulations. At the British Education Management and Administration Society (BEMAS) conference in September 1990 he announced that he had decided against making appraisal obligatory:

Appraisal is essentially a management issue. Our general policy is that decisions about the way schools and teachers are managed should be taken locally.

(MacGregor, 1990b)

As for funding, he authorised £9 million a year for three years beginning in 1991–2 for *both training and implementation*. Thereafter funding specifically for appraisal was to cease. His argument ran thus:

In most walks of life appraisal schemes, once bedded in, are not specifically funded at all – they are a normal part of good personnel management. The time which they require is more than repaid through the greater effectiveness of the staff appraised.

(MacGregor, 1990b)

This was flawed logic, and showed an appalling ignorance of how schools operate. In other walks of life – the Civil Service, industrial management, banking, for example – it is relatively easy to free both appraiser and appraisee for the appraisal interview with no detectable interference with the normal running of the department or organisation. The NSG report had made it clear that classroom observation must be a central feature of appraisal, a view fully endorsed by the guidelines and regulations that his successor in office was to introduce. In both primary and secondary schools, but particularly in primary schools, there is little likelihood of the appraiser being free to observe unless cover can be found. Appraisers are, after all, teachers. Teachers, in small primary schools even headteachers, have classes. Cover has to be paid for from the school's budget and the cost will be at the expense of books and other materials: children's learning, in other words. Is this how standards are to be raised?

After more than a year of dither, contradiction and procrastination, MacGregor's successor in office, Kenneth Clarke, wasted no time. The Education (School Teacher Appraisal) Regulations 1991 (HMSO, 1991) were made and laid before Parliament in July 1991 and came into force the following month. These, accompanied by extensive guidelines, were in the hands of CEOs by the beginning of the Autumn term. In the next chapter we look closely at the regulations and, most importantly, at their implications.

Chapter 3

The regulations and their implications

The Education (School Teacher Appraisal) Regulations (HMSO, 1991) were not open to parliamentary debate: the Education (No.2) Act of 1986 gave the Secretary of State powers to make these regulations 'after consulting . . . such associations of local authorities and representatives of teachers as appeared to be concerned'.

The regulations were distributed together with a circular of explanation and guidance. Those not likely to be concerned with legal niceties have undoubtedly found the circular easier to follow, more 'user-friendly' to use the present-day jargon. It indicated a number of areas where LEAs or governors have discretion, and it also clarified the policy over aspects of appraisal which had caused concern among teachers at the draft stage.

In this chapter we intend to cover what we regard as the key issues, and particularly to comment on those which affect decision making within the LEA or the school. For ease of reference we have in the main used the same sub-headings as appear in the circular. Regulations specific to grant-maintained schools are covered in Chapter 13.

TEACHERS TO WHOM THE REGULATIONS APPLY

All qualified teachers, now including those teachers who have just completed their professional training since the probationary requirements have been withdrawn, are covered by the appraisal regulations, provided they are on at least a one-year contract, full-time, or, if part-time, teaching at least 40 per cent of full-time at a single school (Guidelines §7). There follows a long list of teachers outside this category where 'those responsible for managing such teachers may wish to consider how far [comparable] appraisal arrangements can be applied to them'. There is a distinction between 'those responsible for managing' and the term widely used elsewhere in the regulations, the 'appraising body'. The latter is, for LEA-maintained schools, the LEA itself. While for those groups listed which operate from a central base – advisory and specialist/peripatetic teachers in particular – any discretionary decision is likely to be made by the LEA, there are some situations where the decision might well be made by the governors on the advice of the headteacher.

Some schools, for example, have supply teachers who are 'on call' to that one school only, for geographical reasons or because of crèche facilities made available to them there. Some teachers may for personal reasons have temporarily dropped below 40 per cent of full time, but desire to continue within the appraisal cycle. A number of primary schools have expressed the wish to introduce voluntary appraisal of NNEB assistants, on the very valid grounds that their contribution to class management in early years' learning is inextricably bound up with that of the qualified teacher.

For those who operate under LEA control as subject advisory teachers, as peripatetic music teachers or within a race relations centre, for example, there is a strong argument for some form of appraisal. Subject advisory teachers and those involved in time-limited projects, in particular, usually expect to return to the classroom after a few years and will feel professionally disadvantaged if they are then introduced for the first time into the appraisal cycle. Indeed, many of these will be relatively senior and might reasonably expect to be appraisers by virtue of their line management role within a school. Not only will they not have had training as appraisers; they will otherwise have had no experience at all of the appraisal process.

APPRAISAL AND SCHOOL DEVELOPMENT PLANS

The document wisely draws attention to the relationship between appraisal and the school development plan. Indeed, it goes so far as to say: 'appraisal should support development planning *and vice versa*' (Guidelines §11) (our italics). We make the case elsewhere that there must be a symbiotic relationship between the goals of the individual teacher and those of the school as an institution and that this relationship continues through the planning-for-delivery process (Figure 4.3) and into the evaluation of outcomes (Figure 9.2).

Nevertheless, there can be dangers in too close an identification between appraisal and development planning. There was a time when development planning could be thought of as a three-year rolling programme, in which the current year was 'fully fledged', the second year detailed but open to modification in the light of the previous year's experience, and the third year in outline only. Senior managers in schools are today only too well aware that external pressures, in particular the excessively rapid rate of change – and sometimes of counter-change – often make a mockery of even a one-year development plan. Good practitioners are becoming accustomed to a monitoring process which seeks to identify, almost by extra-sensory perception, changes of policy and circumstances, both local and from central government, which require continuing modification of the school's development plan. Teacher appraisal will have considerable difficulty in succeeding in an atmosphere of political uncertainty and excessive fluidity. If the present

Secretary of State wants appraisal to be effective, and not a scamped paper exercise, he would be wise to slow the headlong rate of change to which schools are currently subjected.

Statements in this section of the document are clearly well intentioned:

> The school's objectives in a particular year should be linked with appraisal, so that, for example, professional development targets arising from appraisal may be related to agreed targets and tasks in the development plan.
>
> (Guidelines §11)

They are dependent, however, on a greater level of stability than schools have had in the 1980s and the opening years of the 1990s.

THE APPRAISAL CYCLE

As everyone expected, the eventual decision was that appraisal would be biennial, but with a formal follow-up in the alternate years. If in mid-cycle the teacher moves to another school, the cycle starts afresh (Guidelines §13). If she moves to a new post in the same school, there is discretion, based largely on a judgment of the extent of the differences in responsibilities.

Substantive promotion to headteacher (Guidelines §14) is regarded as sufficiently different to warrant a fresh start; for acting headteachers the LEA, as 'appraising body', exercises discretion. We hope that it would do so in consultation with the governors and the headteacher herself. We have heard of headteachers being in an acting role for up to two years, and it would seem that in such cases there was a moral and professional right to an appraisal that involved a second appraiser.

THE TIMETABLE FOR THE INTRODUCTION OF APPRAISAL

The wording of this section of the Regulations (§6) even when 'clarified' by the Guidelines (§15) is so complex that the interpretation has defeated many of those with whom we have discussed it. We have constructed a simple chart to demonstrate what a school must do to meet the regulation and at the same time establish a workable rolling programme (Figure 3.1). We make the assumption that job specifications will have been written or revised and targets set for all staff as early as possible after the September 1992 deadline, when the appraisal regulations became effective.

The appraisal timetable

To translate the regulations into a realistic programme that does not put undue pressure on a school, consider the staff in two equal parts, A and B as shown in Figure 3.1.

Date by:	A	B
July 1993	Appraisal interviews will have been held	
July 1994	Follow-up interviews will have been held	Appraisal interviews will have been held
July 1995	Second appraisal interviews will have been held	Follow-up interviews will have been held

© Routledge 1993

Figure 3.1 Timetable for the introduction of appraisal

The Regulations actually specify (§6(2)) that only the first appraisal interview has to be completed by July 1995, and even grant a further year's discretion for any that were not the responsibility of the LEA on 1 September 1991 (§6(4)); but most schools will be anxious to establish an on-going programme that as soon as possible equalises the time costs of appraisal from one year to the next. The first year of the two-year cycle is considerably more expensive of staff time and consequently to get out of phase will lead to administrative headaches.

This is well illustrated by the seemingly reasonable and innocuous requirement that a new member of staff or someone whose role has changed significantly will 'start the cycle afresh'. If, for example, the leaving teacher is halfway through the appraisal cycle – in other words has left at the end of the school year in which he had a full appraisal interview – the incoming teacher does not pick up from where the leaver was, but starts the cycle so that he has the full appraisal interview at the end of *his* first year in the school. An appraiser of four teachers now no longer has her appraisees divided 2:2 but 3:1.

Of greater concern is the situation where the incoming teacher arrives not in September, but in January. Strict adherence to the regulation would have this teacher involved in two classroom observations in the latter part of her first term and a full appraisal interview at the beginning of the next term. Although some observation of progress would obviously be of value, this extensive appraisal at so early a stage might well be counterproductive. Moreover, if that teacher were a middle or senior manager, it would be palpably unfair to expect delivery of managerial targets in so short a time.

Plainly, any well-managed school will use its discretion, and the headteacher will doubtless wish to keep the chair of governors informed when there is a need to apply a commonsense gloss to the regulations.

The way in which a school decides to divide its A and B cycles is a matter of some importance. Clearly this decision must be policy-driven and not be a consequence of whim. A junior school might wish to appraise teachers of Years 3–4 in the A cycle and those of Years 5–6 in the B cycle. Alternatively, it might wish to appraise senior and middle management in one cycle, main grade teachers in the other. The advantages of either policy are plain to see: in the former case, the school is able to look in depth at the relationship between teacher performance and the effectiveness of the school development plan in different age groups; in the latter, at the effectiveness of management from the two perspectives of those who manage and those who are managed.

A secondary school might wish to appraise all staff in half its departments in one year, all in the other half the next. One can see immediate advantages in this since the aggregate of individual appraisals effectively contributes to a departmental review. On the other hand, if heads of department are the appraisers, there is the potentially serious disadvantage that they will be conducting all their full appraisals in the one year, and the far less time-consuming follow-ups in the following year. Decisions on how the A and B cycles are formed have therefore profound implications for the linking of appraisers with appraisees.

WORK TO BE APPRAISED

Appraisal requires an established and up-to-date job description. During our first four years of appraisal training we found the lack of clarity about what constitutes a job description and how to frame one a matter of such concern in many schools that we devote a full chapter of this book to this topic. The Guidelines (§19) point out that the appraiser is entitled to appraise across the full range of professional duties, but at the same time takes the commonsense view (§20) that there is a need to focus on specific areas, including, for many teachers, that of management.

THE SELECTION OF APPRAISERS: SCHOOLTEACHERS

No appraiser should be responsible for more than four appraisees *in most circumstances* (Guidelines §21). Plainly, a primary school of headteacher and nine assistant staff is unlikely to want to have more than two appraisers. Since it is recommended that the appraiser has line management responsibility for the appraisee, the strong likelihood is that these two will be the headteacher and the deputy.

In secondary schools where the head of department is viewed as line manager, the same kind of latitude will have to be allowed. There will also be the problem of small departments – and these will nearly always be highly specialised, such as music and religious education – or medium-sized departments in small schools which cannot muster a viable number for the subject-based appraiser. In these circumstances LEAs and schools will have to devise different strategies to meet the circumstances; but it may not always be easy to meet the requirement (Guidelines §21) that 'the headteacher should appoint as appraiser a person who is in a position, by virtue of . . . experience and professional standing to ensure that the appraisal meets the needs of both the schoolteacher and the school'. Those LEAs which held back from using their appraisal training budget in earlier years have been hard put to it adequately to train enough appraisers even on a basis of one to five or six.

Management responsibility for appraisal needs to be understood as lying within the structure in which the school already operates: to devise appraisal strategies which cut across existing managerial networks will almost invariably lead to excessive complexity and failures of communication. The Dormston School in Sedgley in the West Midlands has for some years been establishing and refining quality circles (QC) (Robson, 1984) as a major element in its managerial structure. The QC is composed of staff from different subject specialisms, with a range of levels of teaching experience, incentive allowances and non-academic competencies. Each circle, usually seven in number, has as its line manager, or counsellor as the school prefers to term it, a member of the senior management team. The group size is admirably suited to discussion of school policy; all staff members, whatever their level of seniority or area of expertise, have the opportunity to contribute to policy making; the two-way flow of information is more easily managed; factions are less likely to occur; and the counsellor takes responsibility within the QC for the professional development of and personal concern for that group of staff.

Plainly, for this school, the rationale for appraisal already exists. That each counsellor may have six appraisees rather than four or five is offset by the fact that a system which has a number of the attributes of the appraisal process is already in place.

There is a concern in many secondary schools that the line management requirement of appraisal will undermine the equality of status between middle managers with curriculum responsibility and those with pastoral responsibility that they have for many years striven to achieve. Certainly the guidelines require only that the appraiser 'should have management responsibility [for the appraisee]'; it does not specify that the management line has to be curricular. It is one of the complexities of the teaching profession, to which we shall return later when we look at the practical ways in which appraisal will be carried out, that, unlike most industrial and commercial concerns, schools do not have simple linear structures. It is essential that a school, in evolving its arrangements for appraisal, does not allow the tail to wag the dog. A school needs to look at its existing managerial structure and gauge how far it is already suited to meet the requirements of appraisal, rather than to attempt to graft on yet another structure.

It is the headteacher's responsibility to select appraisers (Guidelines §22), yet a request for an alternative to the person chosen if the circumstances warrant it should not be refused. A good manager will seek to avoid the need for any such appeals procedure through consultation and negotiation before any final decision is made. Obviously, to present staff with a list of appraisers and invite them to choose would be an abdication of responsibility. Apart from anything else, there would almost certainly be an imbalance of numbers as a result.

A few schools have decided to implement negative choice, whereby all members of staff, in confidence, indicate from the list of appraisers the one or ones they would prefer not to have. Where this has been tried, headteachers have been encouraged by the rarity with which any negative choice is made. When there is a negative choice, although not asked to give their reasons, some teachers have volunteered them.

'Our teaching styles are fundamentally different.'
'We are close friends outside school and I fear this might lead to a less than stringent appraisal.'
'She taught my class last year and may have difficulty in viewing it impartially.'

These and similar reasons demonstrate that, particularly in schools where open behaviour among staff is the norm, the floodgates will not be opened to backbiting and personal hostility. After negative choice has been made, there seems to be no problem over granting each member of staff a suitable appraiser and at the same time balancing numbers. Were negative choice to show that the headteacher had selected and trained an appraiser in whom staff had no confidence, however, it would be wise to heed the message at this stage rather than when dissatisfaction had shown itself in more overt ways.

THE SELECTION OF APPRAISERS: HEADTEACHERS

For headteachers the LEA is required to appoint two appraisers (Regulations §8(1)). For voluntary aided schools there is the requirement (§8(2)) that the LEA and the governing body 'shall endeavour to agree [but] failing such agreement . . . shall each appoint one appraiser'. One of the two must be someone with current or past experience of headship in the same phase as the appraisee (§8(4)); the other, in normal circumstances, an officer or adviser of the LEA. In practice, the latter is usually the local adviser, inspector or staff development officer who will already have a sound knowledge of the school from their pastoral visits and their involvement with headteacher – and possibly deputy headteacher – appraisal.

The choice of headteacher appraiser is proving a minefield in some authorities. Early research (Suffolk LEA, 1985) implied that LEAs might choose to appoint retired headteachers as appraisers, but this has met with little support, if any. Apart from the fact that this would be costly, since a consultancy fee would have to be paid, the rate of change in education is currently so rapid that few retired headteachers would consider themselves competent after two or three years. Furthermore, appraisee headteachers might well have less than entire confidence in some of their colleagues who had removed themselves from the day-to-day management of complex institutions.

On the other hand, with an imposed limit for serving headteachers of three headteacher appraisees (Guidelines §29), one begins to wonder where the volunteers – for volunteers they must be – will come from. First, most LEAs will doubtless exclude from consideration headteachers newly appointed to the authority, and possibly also those with only a year or two to go before retirement. Secondly, there will be self-exclusion from those headteachers who feel that their first responsibility is to the management of their own schools, onerous enough in these turbulent times. It must be remembered that these same headteachers are themselves already responsible for a number of appraisals in their own schools, these the seniormost and therefore the most time consuming. Biennially they will be involved in and concerned about their own full appraisal. Finally, the time required for headteacher appraisal far exceeds that for teacher appraisal. Some of our research findings on this can be found elsewhere in this book.

THE SELECTION OF APPRAISERS: DEPUTY HEADTEACHERS

Deputy headteachers are covered by the arrangements for the appraisal of schoolteachers, with one proviso: the Regulations (§8(6)) permit but do not require the appointment of two appraisers, in normal circumstances their own headteacher as one, and the local adviser almost certainly as the other. The reasons for this proviso are plain to see. In both primary and secondary schools the role of deputy has become one that involves very considerable managerial responsibility. Gone are the days when the deputy's main role was to act for the headteacher in his or her absence and to carry out a number of delegated tasks, most of them administrative rather than managerial. In large schools, both secondary and primary, the range of responsibility for senior manage- ment has become so extensive that collegiality or corporate management has replaced the pyramidal structures that were the norm twenty years ago.

It was partly in recognition of this changing role that the two headteacher associations, the Secondary Headteachers Association (SHA) and the National Association of Head Teachers (NAHT) admitted deputies to membership some years ago; and their urging was instrumental in the inclusion of this proviso. The decision rests with the appraising body, the LEA. The wording of regulation §8(6), 'may determine that two appraisers shall be appointed for a deputy head teacher' contains an ambiguity. Some LEAs have made the blanket decision that no deputies shall be so appraised, on the grounds that this would result in overload; yet it is arguable that the regulation allows of the interpretation that the governors of a school may, probably on the recommendation of the headteacher, request the LEA to appoint a second appraiser for the deputy or deputies in that school. It is extremely unlikely that the LEA would refuse this request in the light of the powers vested in governing bodies under local management of schools. Of the many deputies that we have met on training workshops, almost all have expressed the wish to be so appraised.

The pressure on the time of headteachers has been referred to already, but it is important to look also at the involvement of LEA officers and advisers. As their numbers in most LEAs decline, under financial constraints and where there is an accelerating move to grant-maintained status, so the number of schools for which each is responsible increase. Ten schools each is almost certainly a conservative figure, but that alone entails five headteacher appraisals a year. Given that one of the five were a secondary school with two deputies, there would be a further six deputy appraisals a year in an LEA that had decided to implement Regulation 8(6) fully. Even the most diligent of advisers, ideally arguing that these appraisals are merely part of their normal school visitation programme, see in their mind's eye the ever increasing pile of documentation in the office that makes a mockery of being effective *local* advisers.

THE COMPONENTS OF APPRAISAL: SCHOOLTEACHERS

Appraisal training for each of these components will be dealt with in detail in later chapters of this book. Here we will confine ourselves to highlighting certain implications contained within the documents and specifying those issues that must be resolved, preferably within carefully conceived LEA guidelines, if the school is to work out and implement a viable appraisal strategy.

The initial meeting

There is one element, not strictly listed as a component of appraisal, that certainly does need to be considered in some detail at this stage. It is, say the Guidelines (§33), helpful for the appraisal process to begin with an initial meeting between the appraiser and appraisee. Some schools have argued that, if the awareness raising and information giving with the whole staff have been thorough, this is unnecessary. We maintain that there is always the need to ensure that, whatever may be understood in general, there is between each appraiser and appraisee a clear understanding of the appraisal process as it applies to their particular situation. It is vital, for example, that there is agreement that the job specification, written and agreed as long as two years ago, remains valid and that goals, some of which may have been modified since the initial goalsetting, are accurately recorded. It is also important, particularly in the early days of appraisal or with newly qualified or newly appointed teachers, that the appraisee is reassured that the intentions of appraisal are not judgmental, but concerned with the appraisee's personal and professional development and with school effectiveness.

This is the occasion too for the appraiser to discuss sources of data collection. The regulations make it incumbent on the appraiser to consult the appraisee if there is the intention to 'consult other people to obtain information relevant to the appraisal'. The advice on data collection contained in the Code of Practice (reproduced in full as Appendix 1 of this volume) ought to alleviate any anxieties:

> 18. The appraiser should aim to agree with the appraisee at the initial meeting what information it would be appropriate to collect for the purpose of the appraisal, from what sources and by what methods.

Nevertheless, many teachers remain concerned about this aspect of appraisal.

To counter this concern, one LEA, after discussion with teacher associations, extended the interpretation of the requirement on the appraiser to 'consult' as 'to obtain the consent' of the appraisee. This is certainly helpful in avoiding situations in which an appraiser, having encountered obvious misgivings on the part of the appraisee that a particular member of staff with whom relations may be less than good is to be approached, considers that he has done his duty, according to the regulations, by consulting. Whether or not an LEA has included such a requirement in its general arrangements for appraisal, there is nothing to prevent any school from adding this interpretation. Indeed, the Guidelines (§5) positively encourage appraising bodies 'to give schools scope to put in place arrangements for appraisal' provided of course that they are within the regulations and do not run counter to the LEA's responsibilities.

The general principles (2–10) in the Code of Practice are exemplary; but like all such guidelines they depend on the interpretation, understanding and goodwill of the appraiser and the informant. Ideally, we would recommend that schools adopt an overriding principle of open behaviour in which data were sought in a tripartite meeting. In a well-managed school there will be nothing said that is not already known to the line manager and the appraisee and therefore no reason why it should not be said openly. If it were to be argued that this lengthens the time taken by data collection, we would respond by saying that any misconceptions and suspicions will so undermine managerial efficiency as to add eventually far more to the time than a meeting of three people rather than two could possibly do.

Classroom observation

What goes on in the classroom is fundamental to the effective performance of the school as a whole. Classroom observation is so vital a component of the appraisal process that we devote the next chapter to it in detail. At this stage we would only wish to observe that the amount of time specified in the DES Guidelines is so conservative as to be unrealistic:

§35. Schoolteachers should normally be observed teaching for a total of at least one hour, spread over two or more occasions.

We maintain – and we have yet to have our contention contradicted – that the lesson must be observed in full, with the observer present from the beginning to the end. That in itself makes the possibility of observation on two occasions being covered in sixty minutes unlikely and 'or more' a virtual impossibility. We regularly ask participants in secondary workshops the length of a normal lesson in their schools: the range is enormous, but the majority fall with the bracket of 40–45 minutes. In primary schools, particularly in the early years, the length of a lesson is yet more difficult to define. It is easier to identify for classroom observation a coherent activity or group of activities, what we have heard described as 'a slice of the moving river'. The time for this is certainly not less than that for the secondary lesson and may well be even more.

We have been asked by many headteachers whether there is any point in classroom observation for those members of staff whose management responsibilities are far more onerous and important to the success of the institution than the relatively small amount of teaching they undertake. While some of these senior managers may well wish to have some classroom observation, if for no other reason than to demonstrate to their colleagues that they too are open to suggestions for improvement, it would not seem in the best interest of the school that this was the main thread of their appraisal. §35 fortunately allows some flexibility by its inclusion of the word 'normally'. Deputy headteachers, who in a number of LEAs will be appraised much as their headteachers are appraised, must surely be observed at management tasks. In secondary schools, certainly, and in larger primary schools, there will be others for whom task observation will be equally appropriate.

The appraisal interview

Rightly, the DES Guidelines (§40) indicate that the interview 'should provide an opportunity for genuine dialogue'. A monopoly of the interview by the appraiser will be counterproductive. The appraiser's role, as we illustrate in detail in Chapter 9, is to ensure that the agreed agenda is covered and that skilful questioning and probing gives the appraisee the opportunity to do most of the talking and, through it, heighten her self-awareness.

It is also important to accept that the appraisal interview is reciprocal. There may arise situations in which the appraiser has to recognise that failures on her part to give adequate support to the appraisee has been in part responsible for inadequacies of performance.

The guidelines, in this same paragraph, list seven areas that the interview 'should involve'. If all these were to be included in detail on the agenda of each appraisal interview, it would in our opinion be over-lengthy and decidedly threatening. We make the case in Chapter 9 that the ground to be covered in the interview can only be selective. Good interviewers will readily identify those areas that will yield fruitful discussion and concentrate on those. Were they to take literally even two of the items in §40:

review of the schoolteacher's work, including successes and areas for development identified since the previous appraisal

and:

discussion of the appraisee's role in, and contribution to, the policies and management of the school, and any constraints which the circumstances of the school place on him or her

the interviews would be covering an impossibly wide field. There seems a presumption, too, that the appraiser and appraisee have never taken the opportunity in the period between the setting of goals and the appraisal interview to have any discussion on progress towards those goals. This would not in any institution be considered good management!

The third component of the appraisal interview is the preparation of the appraisal statement. Since this element of the appraisal process has caused teachers more anxiety than any other it is important that we make crystal clear what the regulations and the guidelines say.

First, the statement consists of two elements: the record of the discussion at the appraisal interview, and the targets for action set as a consequence of that discussion (Guidelines §53 and Regulations §10(2)). Copies of the full statement are held by the appraiser and the appraisee, and by the headteacher of the school (Regulation §13 (1a)). The headteacher is required, *on request*, to provide the CEO or his designated representative with a copy. We doubt whether many CEOs will wish to accumulate thousands of these documents annually, particularly in the light of the stringent rules governing their retention. For most, the availability of the statement in the school to the local adviser, if and when it may be needed, will be adequate.

The main anxiety of teachers at the time of the draft regulations concerned the use to which some governors might put their knowledge of appraisal statements should they be available to them. The definitive regulations and guidelines relieve those anxieties entirely, for the assistant teacher at least. No governor sees the full appraisal statement. Only the chair of governors – and no other governor – has a right to, and this on request, 'a copy of the targets for action'. A number of LEAs in drafting their own regulations interpret this as being a single document that consolidates the goals set for all those teachers who have been appraised in that year's cycle, so that individual teacher goals are not identified.

Appraisers would be well advised to share a draft of the appraisal statement with the appraisee before it is finalised. Although the appraisee has the right 'within 20 working days' to enter a note of dissent (Guidelines §52), schools will want this course of action to be a rarity and will naturally prefer negotiation, wherever possible, to this indication of possible discord. The agreed statement is signed by both appraiser and appraisee.

Once the statement has been finalised all associated documentation is destroyed (Guidelines §57). When, after the two-year cycle, the next appraisal statement is finalised, the previous statement is retained by the headteacher for 'at least three months' (Regulations §14(4)), to cover any possibility of appeal that might require reference to it. Most LEAs have made this retention period two years: as the third appraisal statement is completed and agreed, the first is destroyed. Indeed, the guidelines offer to the appraising body – which has to include a decision on this in its regulations – a reasonable interpretation of the phrase 'at least':

> it would normally be sensible to retain statements on file for the equivalent of two complete appraisal cycles.
>
> (Guidelines §57)

We wonder why the regulations and the guidelines are so much at variance over this point: there is a considerable difference between a further three months and two years.

One of the important outcomes of the appraisal interview is the identification of individual training needs. While these are deliberately excluded from the appraisal statement (Guidelines §54), they are noted and forwarded separately. It is essential that the appraiser does not offer hostages to fortune during the interview by making promises that may not be kept. In every school there is an individual – often the headteacher or a senior member of staff – or a team responsible for staff development. This is the initial arena for decision making on training. One individual's needs must be set against those of all who have been appraised – and, incidentally, of those not in that year's appraisal cycle – and also evaluated against the composite needs of the school and the amount of money available for training.

The follow-up meeting

There remains among the components of appraisal only the follow-up meeting, which takes place in the alternate year. While this is not intended in any way as a full appraisal interview, it does have specific purposes which make it more than a casual discussion. It is intended to review progress, discuss whether targets set the year before are still appropriate, look at the value of training undertaken, provide the opportunity for the appraisee to raise any matter of concern and, finally, to consider the appraisee's career development needs (Guidelines §59). The appraiser and appraisee are required to annotate the appraisal statement with any modification to the targets previously set and the reasons for that modification.

THE COMPONENTS OF APPRAISAL: HEADTEACHERS

The components of headteacher appraisal differ from those of other teachers in one respect only: *classroom observation* is replaced by *task and/or classroom observation*. The headteacher of a small primary school may have a full teaching commitment, relieved, if she is lucky and the school budget allows for it, by a decimal point of support staff, releasing her for those management and administration tasks that have to be done in school time. For her, classroom observation is as essential a component of her appraisal as it is of that of her assistant teachers. Headteachers of large and complex comprehensive schools, on the other hand, will these days rarely have a regular teaching commitment, regarding the many unavoidable calls on their scheduled lesson time as unfair on the class and even more unfair on the teachers who are called on to cover. Headteachers in England and Wales have in the past been proud to maintain the appellation of 'headteacher' rather than that of 'principal', regarding themselves as *primus inter pares*. Today's managerial commitments have for most made this an outmoded concept.

The regulations and guidelines are at their weakest in the recognition of the role of the headteacher as manager. There is, for example, no indication of what might properly and advisedly be included within task observation:

> If an appraisal does not involve classroom observation, the regulations require at least one of the appraisers of a headteacher to observe performance of *some other duty*.
>
> (Guidelines §49, our italics)

This vagueness of expression is scarcely helpful to appraisers or appraisee!

The guidelines that specifically concern headteacher appraisal (§43–51) are largely repetitive of those relevant to assistant teachers, with the occasional rewording appropriate to the status of the post. We have encountered on our workshops much concern over the inadequacy of the guidance in these sections, and in particular their failure to recognise that the role of the headteacher has so far been extended by the Education Acts of 1986 and 1988 that 'chief executive' is becoming an increasingly common concept, even if not a title. We have therefore devoted Chapter 12 to constructive and detailed considerations of the components of headteacher appraisal rather than engage here in negative criticism of the relevant guidelines themselves. We would make here only two comments: that we believe that much of what we have to offer in that chapter is equally applicable to the appraisal of those deputy headteachers who have a second, external appraiser; and that, in large primary and secondary schools, there will be other senior managers for whom some of the elements of headteacher appraisal – for example, task observation – will, in the light of the responsibilities of their roles, be no less appropriate.

THE ROLE OF THE GOVERNING BODY

The appraising body, the LEA for all schools other than grant-maintained schools, has overall responsibility for 'all the aspects of appraisal set out in the Regulations' (Guidelines §4). At the same time, schools are allowed a degree of autonomy in the way appraisal is implemented, provided they act within the Regulations. 'All arrangements for appraisal . . . should be drawn up in consultation with teachers' (Guidelines §6). The governing body is charged with the responsibility for ensuring that schools comply with both the DFE and LEA regulations. It follows, therefore, that it must not only have examined scrupulously the school's detailed arrangements for appraisal and satisfied itself that the staff have been fully consulted, but must also monitor the appraisal process to satisfy itself that 'appraisal is operating properly in accordance with school and LEA policy *and that it is properly integrated into the management of the school*' (Guidelines §65, our italics).

This is an area where it is possible for a governing body unwittingly to overstep the bounds of its responsibility. The guidelines make it clear that the source of the governing body's information is to be 'by means of reports from the head [which will avoid] the attribution of targets to individuals [but be] a summary of the targets for action . . . decided at appraisal interviews, and progress in achieving past targets' (§65).

In most schools, where relationships between governing bodies and headteachers are soundly established, the definition of these parameters of responsibility will be readily accepted. There will, however, be some governing bodies, or some governors on a governing body, who will suspect that the blandness and lack of specificity hide problems of, for example, a teacher whose state of health or lack of efficiency is a drag on the progress of the school. How, they may reasonably argue, can they assure themselves that appraisal is 'properly integrated into the management of the school' if they are debarred from information on how the school manages in such a situation?

The answer is that the appraisal process was not designed to deal with issues like this and, were it to be used, overtly or covertly, to this end, the crucial elements of openness and staff trust in the process as one concerned with personal and professional improvement will be sacrificed. There are, of course, other means outside the appraisal process for dealing with inefficiency or ineffectiveness; and the governing body has every right to invoke them. It is to be hoped that in every instance it will act in a humane way, seeking every means available of helping a teacher to overcome deficiencies. Ultimately, however, particularly where absenteeism is making heavy inroads on the school's budget or where the publication of Standard Attainment Tests or public examination results reveal that the school's efficiency is being impaired, the governing body does have the authority to terminate a contract. What it must not do – and might well be challenged before a tribunal were it to appear to have done so – is to use or seek to use data from appraisal as evidence for inefficiency.

Governors and headteacher appraisal

The governing body 'should be informed when information is being collected for headteacher appraisal' (Guidelines §66). The chair of governors should have the opportunity to submit comments to the appraisers 'designed to inform the appraisal interview' (§66). The only reasonable interpretation of these two statements in conjunction is that, while individual governors may not offer comments directly to the appraisers, they may make their views known to the chair, who has that right.

The appraisers have, of course, the right to obtain information from individual governors, but it is evident that the initiative must come from them, that they must have consulted the appraisee beforehand and that information collection must accord with the Code of Practice. It would be improper for any governor to approach either of the appraisers to offer data about the headteacher.

Governor decision making related to appraisal

The summary of targets for action that have arisen from appraisal interviews (§65) is a very real concern for the governing body since the relationship between the targets and the school development plan lies within its remit of responsibility. The governing body, usually through either its finance subcommittee or its staff development committee, has a role over demands for resources that may arise from the appraisal interviews. These may be either for materials and equipment or for inservice training. In either case the governors will be heavily dependent on the headteacher for advice in balancing demands against, inevitably, a scarcity of resources; but the governing body is clearly responsible (§67) for the decisions which are made.

There has been much concern in the teaching profession about the links between appraisal and pay, and this concern has been exacerbated by the introduction of salary regulations which allow for performance-related pay. Heywood (1992) argues vehemently that 'whatever arguments are advanced for performance-related pay for teachers, a biennial system of developmental appraisal is not the instrument to deliver this'.

The Guidelines (§70) make it clear that 'there will be no direct or automatic link between appraisal and . . . additions to salary. But it is legitimate and desirable for headteachers to take into account information from appraisals . . . in advising governors on decisions on . . . pay'. Legitimate it may be, but desirable it most certainly is not. The aims of appraisal as set out in the regulations are avowedly developmental, not judgmental. If there were a secondary, however subordinate, purpose behind the appraisal process, then its purpose will inevitably become suspect. Frank and open discussion is unlikely to obtain, as educationists and teachers have stated repeatedly, if level of salary, promotion and job security of the appraisee were to depend on the outcome of appraisal process. Experts in the industrial field have long since argued this point, with some effect:

> Organisations attempting to develop their staff appraisal and development procedures are strongly advised to plan to keep the three activities of 'performance', 'reward' and 'potential' review not only separate in time but also in paperwork, procedure and responsibility.
>
> (Randall *et al.*, 1984)

The allocation of salaries under performance-related pay depends entirely on how much money is available for teachers' salaries within the annual school budget. The use of appraisal, even 'along with other information' (§70), will force the school to rank performance in order to reward those that it regards as teachers of quality, but only as far as the kitty will stretch. Judgments will be made that have little to do with the teacher performance, and the making of these judgments will do much to undermine morale in the school. If there is to be performance-related pay then it must be on clearly articulated criteria acceptable to the teachers within the school and wholly dissociated from appraisal.

In a case study on performance-related pay, the headteacher of Kenmal Manor writes:

> The way extra money is available is clear to all staff. There are no negotiations behind closed doors. Access to extra funds is *solely by linking pay to performance through the method of appraisal.*
>
> (Tomlinson, 1992, our italics)

It would be interesting to learn how the school's governing body has reconciled this statement with the DFE appraisal regulations.

MONITORING THE APPRAISAL PROCESS

Rightly, the DFE will be seeking information from LEAs 'to confirm that the targets for the introduction of appraisal . . . have been met (Guidelines §71)'. LEAs may commission an evaluation for this purpose but, deprived as they are of resources of funding and manpower, are likely to be able to do this only through questionnaires directed to the governors as the body responsible for the effective running of the school. Governors will therefore be well advised to require a periodic report on appraisal from the headteacher, so that the data for monitoring and evaluation are to hand when they are required.

APPEALS PROCEDURES

We have decided against including here details of the rights of appraisees to appeal against their appraisal statements. We have preferred the more positive approach of demonstrating in Chapter 11 how appraisal statements should be written in terms which are non-judgmental, but which nevertheless are not bland, non-committal documents and of no use to the school or the appraisee. The procedures for appeal, if they were to be needed, can be found extensively in Regulations §11 (1–7).

CORPORATE COLLEGES

The amalgamation of Sixth Form Colleges (SFCs) and Further Education (FE) Colleges in April 1993 as 'corporate colleges' has produced some strangely anomalous situations that, we hope, time will resolve. In September 1992 teaching staff in SFCs were still officially subject to the School Teachers' Pay and Conditions document, and would remain so until the institutions became the new Further Education corporations. It might be thought that, until contracts were devised for them by their new employers, the terms of their former contracts would still apply and they would have been required to enter the appraisal cycle. Yet, because they had ceased to be maintained by the LEA, the LEA was no longer the appraising body under the Education (School Teacher Appraisal) Regulations 1991. Consequently, provisions which were contractual under one government document could not be implemented because of the terms of another government document!

This would be of no more than academic interest, particularly to the student of government, if there were provision for appraisal for those in the FE sector on the same terms as for schoolteachers. After all, a government's concern for staff development for those who teach the 16 to 19 age group in schools should apply equally to those who teach the same age group in FE. Indeed, as part of the 1987–8 pay and conditions settlement for FE lecturers, their unions agreed to cooperate in pilot projects in appraisal with the aim of establishing a basis for implementing appraisal in all FE colleges. These pilots ran in 1989–90 and were evaluated by the National Foundation for Educational Research (NFER).

The NFER report was published in May 1991 and the National Joint Council agreed on a requirement for staff to participate in appraisal in the light of the report's recommendations. Incredibly, the Secretary of State decided not to use the regulatory powers under §49 of the Education (No. 2) Act 1986 – powers which he had used to impose teacher appraisal – but left the process to be pursued locally.

The reason for such a decision, whatever the logic, may well have been this: officially each corporate college is independent and there is nothing to preclude the renegotiation by employers of conditions of employment on a plant-by-plant basis. It was, however, obvious to the new governing bodies that this independence of action had more pitfalls than advantages; and a meeting of representatives of college governors opened negotiations with an existing higher education employers' federation to be also the secretariat for the corporate colleges.

At the time of the divorce from the LEAs, a number of SFCs were already actively engaged in the introduction of teacher appraisal and others were involved in LEA plans for training and implementation. There is no merit in seeking to find out how many were in fact ready to introduce appraisal in September 1992, since there is now no statutory obligation on corporate colleges to introduce appraisal at all.

Why did the government not introduce regulations and guidelines similar to those in place for schools when so much admirable groundwork had been done by the employers, the unions and, above all, the NFER? The inconsistency of treating one sector of education differently from another over the same issue is one of the reasons that schoolteachers feel, rightly or wrongly, that the government has little regard for their efforts and even less for their professionalism.

Yet making appraisal voluntary for the corporate colleges will not necessarily absolve them from the need to put appraisal in place. That he has invoked no statutory regulation will not deter the Secretary of State for Education. He has an alternative: to invoke a statutory right, of a kind already used against some polytechnics and higher education colleges. He may hold back 2 per cent of the college's budget if the institution does not satisfactorily introduce certain efficiency measures, among them undoubtedly appraisal. Since no college will wish to lose any part of its budget, all are likely to comply with this rather more devious approach to securing implementation of an appraisal scheme.

Corporate colleges do, of course, have problems to face as a result of this *laissez faire* approach. LEAs had precise knowledge, on the publication of the regulations, of how long they had to prepare for implementation; indeed, they had had less precise but, in the event, reasonably reliable information for some years on the time scheme. They had had money available for appraisal training from 1987 and a number of LEAs had made such good use of it that their schools were most effectively prepared for the innovation. It is unlikely that the corporate colleges will be allowed as much time.

How far they will be able to synthesise two very different approaches to appraisal remains to be discovered. There was, in the first edition of this book, a full chapter on appraisal in the tertiary sector. In tertiary education, we pointed out, many lecturers spend less time in front of a class than on a wide range of other activities: academic research; course administration, monitoring and evaluation; student records and placement supervision; and, of course, the development of new courses and materials. Staff development reviews have in the past been conducted extensively through self-assessment, and the highly dynamic nature of the institution has made it unlikely that achievement has been related precisely to a clear set of goals to be achieved over a two-year period. Further education institutions are highly departmentalised, and college-wide appraisal may be more difficult to implement than within institutions previously run under schools regulations. If it appears that appraisal will take up a good deal of time – and that is certainly the case in schools – there will be talk about 'time-cost benefits' and a reluctance to spend more time than is absolutely necessary.

CITY TECHNOLOGY COLLEGES

City technology colleges (CTCs), we learn, are independent schools. Technically this may well be so; but so much government money has been poured into them to make up for the general lack of interest on the part of industry and commerce in funding these institutions that ratepayers may well question the *de facto* nature of that independence. Educationists in the state sector may be reassured to learn that, in the words of a DFE spokesperson, 'most, if not all CTCs have addressed the issue of teacher appraisal and are developing their own forms of appraisal'. They will not be so readily reassured when they read (*TES*, 5 November, 1992) that it is a condition of the non-government financial support of Harris CTC that all teachers there will be subject to performance-related pay, the quality of that performance to be determined through appraisal. The government has undertaken that there will be no direct relationship between staff appraisal and pay. But CTCs are, of course, independent schools . . .

Chapter 4

Job descriptions, job specifications and goalsetting

Appraisal has introduced many teachers to a new vocabulary, one which they may associate more with business and commerce than with their profession. It would not be surprising if some teachers were to respond adversely to the terms in the chapter title. Yet there is no need for feelings of concern. Teachers have, for example, always set themselves goals, whether or not they have used that particular expression: in the classroom, learning attainments for their pupils; in management, in relation to those for whom they are responsible; for themselves, in improving their skills.

When appraisal first became an issue for schools and LEAs, there was a tendency to focus on the appraisal interview as the key element of the process. This was understandable, for it was the wholly new and therefore more threatening component for many schools. The pilot studies and the NSG interim report (NDC, 1988) highlighted the fact that an appraisal interview based on fuzzy or taken-for-granted goals would benefit neither the school nor the individual. Just as managers in any enterprise need to know the aims and objectives of an innovative activity before they can evaluate its success, so managers in schools need to agree the goals for and with teaching staff before appraisal can effectively take place.

What was not made clear in the Regulations or the Guidelines is that goals are the starting point, not the end product of the appraisal process. They appear to have been thought of originally almost entirely as an outcome of the appraisal interview, principally in connection with the appraisal statement. There was a growing recognition, as the documents moved from draft stage to final version, that goals needed to be periodically updated, and that it was not enough simply to consider them biennially. The Guidelines for the section entitled *Follow-up: the review meeting* include as one purpose 'to consider whether the targets are still appropriate'(§59). Recognised implicitly (§58) is the fact that goals need to be under constant review and that appraisees may need support if they are to implement them. Somewhat weakly the paragraph concludes that 'systems should be in place to assist the appraisers in this role'. We have too often found that the system is there but the time to discharge this support function is not being made available.

This second edition is being published some six months after the appraisal process has begun and it might be argued that the initial goalsetting is already in place. We would like to think that is so. However, we are aware of LEAs where little or no real training in appraisal has yet taken place; even where that is not the case, in some schools in which we have worked as trainers we have found considerable confusion over how goals are derived from the job specification. There may be, therefore, as school reports so often state, 'room for improvement'! We must also point out that goalsetting needs to be undertaken whenever there is a new member of staff or whenever there is a significant modification to the job specification of an existing member of staff. This occurs more often than people currently realise.

We have to make clear at this stage the distinction between the terms *job description* and *job specification*. The former refers to the school's concept of the post which it is seeking to fill, whether internally or by appointment from outside. The latter refers to the job once it can be related to the postholder. Industry and commerce often use the term *person specification* for the latter.

JOB DESCRIPTION

All readers will doubtless have seen job descriptions for teaching posts, many of them, unfortunately, poorly devised. Some are excessively complex, introducing elements relating to conditions of service or details about the school, the LEA, the neighbourhood, the governing body and so on. It is not that applicants will have no interest in these facts; indeed, most of these details should be available as a routine hand-out to any enquirer. It is rather that the job description should be self-standing, dealing solely with the areas of responsibility for which a candidate is being sought.

Some appear to be primarily concerned with asking for qualities like enthusiasm, imagination, communication skills and the like. It is difficult to conceive of many situations in which an intending applicant confesses to the absence of these qualities. Certainly these qualities will be expected in applicants, but the search for evidence of them will better be found implicitly in the applicant's letter of application.

JOB SPECIFICATION

There was a time when *role definition* was the phrase much used by management in schools to define the apportionment of responsibilities and the delineation of professional relationships (Poster, 1976). Today we are more likely to encounter the term *job specification*. What matters is not the term used but what we understand by it. It is possible that, in preferring *role*, teachers were subconsciously seeking to distance themselves from those who had *jobs*. Teaching was, it might be argued, a profession comparable with that of doctor and lawyer, a comparability that, unfortunately, does not extend to the salaries they are paid.

Job, then, let it be; and let us focus above all on the need for it to be specified. The reasons for this have less to do with appraisal than with good management. A job specification for all members of staff is essential if there is to be clarity about what they are responsible for and to whom they are responsible. Furthermore, they need to know to whom and how to refer when they reach the boundaries of their own decision-making role. The job specification must always reflect what the postholder is actually required and competent to do and not be a pious hope incapable of realisation. The job specification leads to goalsetting, and goalsetting in its turn sets up the criteria whereby the teacher will be appraised. It follows, therefore, that the selection of realistic and realisable goals is vital to the success of the appraisal process.

On the facing page you will find the job specification of Vicky Hoyle, whom you will meet in future training tasks in this book. She is a teacher of history and year head in a secondary school; and we have presented you with the first two of the three elements that make up her job specification, leaving the third for you to add when towards the end of the chapter, on pages 56–7, we provide you with further data.

The job specification of every member of staff must accord with the conditions of employment and, in particular, with the professional duties set out in *School Teachers' Pay and Conditions Document* (DES, 1992) and republished annually with such revisions as are necessary.

The professional duties of a headteacher (§30) cover some 22 areas of responsibility, all of them, of course, couched in terms that make them common to all schools. Some duties will have no relevance to headteacher appraisal. For example, the headteacher's role in the appointment of staff is 'to participate' and is therefore subordinate to the role of the appointing body. One cannot be appraised on an activity such as this. Liaison with staff unions and associations is another such responsibility, one more likely to be observable as a consequence of breakdown than from normal day-to-day activity.

The key professional duty of the headteacher lies in responsibility for the formulation of the school's overall aims and objectives and the policies for implementing them. Of these policies the most important is undoubtedly that for the delivery of a curriculum relevant to the 'experience, interests, aptitudes and stage of development of the pupils' having due regard to the requirements of the National Curriculum and the evaluation of standards of reading and learning.

In order to discharge any policy, the headteacher must, *inter alia:*

• set up an appropriate management structure
• develop sound communication networks within and without the school

Job specification: Vicky Hoyle

Job purpose:

- To establish and maintain relevant and up-to-date teaching practices in her subject of history.
- To create and maintain the highest possible levels of academic achievement and pastoral care for all pupils for whom she has responsibility as year head.

GENERIC RESPONSIBILITIES

Duties as a teacher:

- To teach such classes as have been allocated by the head of department(s) and confirmed by the senior management team, in accordance with the guidelines of the National Curriculum and with due regard for the range of ability within each class.
- Adequately to prepare work for these classes, and to correct, mark and record achievement in accordance with school policy and national requirements.
- To attend and participate in departmental meetings as required by the head of department and to abide by decisions reached therein.

Duties as a year head:

- To coordinate and lead the work of group tutors within the year.
- To promote measures to encourage pupils within the year to become increasingly socially aware and self-reliant.
- To work with group tutors to ensure that academic progress is being monitored, in particular through Records of Achievement, and that the highest standards, relevant to their age, ability and aptitude, are being asked of pupils within the year.
- To be responsible for effective liaison with parents, ensuring that they are kept informed about all significant matters relevant to their children's progress and social behaviour.
- To be an active member of the committee of year heads and to put into effect decisions reached therein.

SPECIFIC RESPONSIBILITIES

© Routledge 1993

- allocate, control and account for financial and material resources
- advise and assist the governing body.

For these general responsibilities all headteachers are accountable, and one of the tasks of the school development review or school inspection is to ensure that they are discharging these responsibilities.

The professional duties of the assistant teacher (§35) are fewer but one alone, cover for teachers 'absent or not available', takes up two-thirds of a page, a quarter of the entire section. We realise from our experience of school management that it is essential that there is absolute clarity over what a teacher may legally be required to do in these circumstances. At the same time this responsibility will not find a place within a job specification, except in a general opening formation: 'is expected to carry out those duties and responsibilities detailed in Part X and, specifically, the following: . . .' What follows is the detail of the job specification.

There is confusion in the minds of some teachers over the difference between the responsibilities outlined in the pay and conditions document and those that appear in the job specification. Occasionally we have heard the view expressed that the former makes the latter unnecessary. Nothing could be further from the case. The very generality and all-inclusive nature of the conditions of service makes it essential to be specific about the headteacher's or the schoolteacher's responsibilities *within the school in which they teach*. The job specification will not, of course, run counter to the professional responsibilities in the document; but without its specificity, the setting of goals by negotiation, a vital component of the appraisal process, would be impossible.

To clarify this in our own minds we looked at just one of the six professional duties of the schoolteacher under the general heading of 'other activities'. We asked ourselves how it might apply, in its present formulation to an early years teacher. 'Providing guidance and advice to pupils on educational and social matters' is not the phraseology that we would expect to see applied to the needs of five- and six-year-olds, even though in general terms the requirement is valid. It continues, however, 'and on their further education and careers' – a most unlikely activity with this age group!

There is, therefore, a need to reinterpret the general expression of professional responsibilities in the light of the age range of the school, any particular conditions that pertain there, and the role within the school of the teacher. In other words, they must be made person specific. Moreover, a job specification, unlike the conditions of service, is a document based on negotiation and renegotiation between individual teachers and the institution in order to bring about the most effective deployment of the teaching force, both for the professional development of the teachers and, needless to say, for the benefit of the pupils.

The job purpose

The job purpose is a statement defining in broad terms that for which the postholder is held accountable. It might well be thought that the purpose of a teaching job is self-evident, implicit in the title of the post – language curriculum coordinator, for example, or staff development coordinator – and in any case clearly understood at the time of the appointment. Yet time can blur the memory, headteachers may come and go, new governors will be appointed. An accurately phrased job purpose is a safeguard for all concerned.

There are two important matters which merit elaboration. It is not pedantic to require that the job purpose points to future outcomes. Generalised statements like 'to organise the department' mean very little and are open to misconstruction. The form of words used must be descriptive of the *end results* for which the job holder is held accountable.

The second point concerns the uniqueness of the job purpose to a particular post. It is not impossible for there to be two teachers for whom the same job purpose is appropriate, but for this to occur their jobs must be wholly interchangeable. In practice very few teachers have job specifications which are not unique to them: while the main teaching role may be the same as that of another teacher, there is nearly always some aspect or extension of the role which is person-specific. Thus, Vicky Hoyle combines the roles of teacher of history and head of year, currently of Year 9. No other member of staff has this job purpose and therefore this job specification.

Generic responsibilities

You will observe that, for Vicky Hoyle, there are two distinct areas for which generic responsibilities are laid down, her duties as a class teacher and her duties as a year head. Every class teacher in the school will have the same formulation of words for the first of these two areas of generic responsibility. For a teacher of special needs or a support teacher working with groups of children who do not have English as their first language, on the other hand, only the second of the two statements would be applicable as a generic responsibility, and one or more statements of specific responsibility would be needed for her specialism.

Vicky is also a year head, one of five in this 11–16 comprehensive school. Because it is school policy that each year head takes his or her cohort of group tutors and pupils through the five-year cycle, all five have, overall, the same generic responsibilities.

There will be generic responsibilities for other posts, such as that of head of department. These will have been drafted by a member of the senior management team and, while it is necessary for them to be reviewed periodically to ensure that they still hold good in every respect, they are reasonably permanent. It is important to note that the phraseology is purposive: 'to coordinate and lead', 'adequately to prepare work' and the like. There is a measure of encouragement to staff behind such language; and, at the same time, without suggesting that there can be objective criteria for 'adequately', it is implied that the school has standards of expectation.

Specific responsibilities

Clearly, these are responsibilities which cannot be generalised, but which nevertheless may be specific to more than one person. Vicky is a member of the history department; and, while her responsibilities there are simply those of a history teacher, she may well have expressed a willingness to help the head of department by taking on a specific role. She might, for example, have agreed 'to act as the head of department's alternate at meetings of the primary/secondary subject liaison group'. Alternatively, she may have a specific interest that lies right outside her subject specialism and her pastoral role: 'to represent the staff on the pupils' charities committee and to report back periodically to her colleagues on fund-raising and other activities'.

Some senior managers may have quite extensive specific responsibilities in that their role in the school management team may give them considerable delegated powers which each holds uniquely. Terms like deputy head curriculum, deputy head pastoral, head of upper school indicate specific roles which will be described mainly through specific responsibilities. Yet even here there ought to be a general description of the expectations that the institution has of the senior management team as a corporate body.

Once the job specification has been drawn up, it will be seen that the responsibilities fall readily under a number of discrete headings. These we find it helpful to 'describe as *key result areas* (KRAs): they are *key*, because each one is crucial to the development of the school and the individual teacher, and they are *result areas* because the consequences of what a teacher does in these areas influence performance outcomes. You can see these KRAs, as they are known, set out in Figure 4.1.

Every assistant teacher in the school will have two key result areas which are immediately identifiable: in teaching and in caring. Additionally, now that schools have become such complex and demanding institutions, most teachers will have a managerial role of some kind, regardless of whether or not it attracts an incentive allowance. For some, the more senior staff, this managerial key result area may be of prime importance to the smooth running of the school; but, however important, it will never wholly supersede the personal teaching and caring role.

Key result areas will alter only as a result of a change in the job specification, either in the generic responsibilities, or were there to be an addition or deletion to specific responsibilities. Were the head of history to leave or to be

```
                        TEACHING

                        CARING

                        MANAGEMENT

                        ADMINISTRATION

              EXTRACURRICULAR ACTIVITIES

                        COMMUNITY

        PERSONAL PROFESSIONAL DEVELOPMENT

                                      © Routledge 1993
```

Figure 4.1 Key result areas

promoted internally, Vicky might view a change from her year head role to that of head of department as a good career move, apply and be appointed. Alternatively, she may feel that, having completed a three-year stint on the charities committee, it would revitalise her if she were to take on a specific responsibility in quite another KRA, that of community, for example.

In some schools, as a purposive management policy, there will be from time to time a deliberate shift of KRAs or of responsibilities within a KRA. One secondary school, for example, with a five faculty curriculum structure, allocated to each member of the senior management team responsibility for liaison with a faculty, but rotated the faculties year by year. In some primary schools the headteacher and the deputy head interchange one key result area from time to time, partly for revitalisation, but particularly to give the deputy the widest possible experience in preparation for a future headship. At middle management level, when a complete job change, with a new job specification, of course, is impossible or undesirable, a job shift involving the internal exchange of a KRA is often a very satisfying alternative.

Normally key result areas will remain unchanged. What will frequently change is their relative importance. This may be a consequence of school policy: the close relationship between the school's development plan and individual goals will be referred to later. Sometimes it is simply a matter of having achieved desired goals in one KRA and of having only maintenance activities to take their place. Consequently, the opportunity now exists to raise for the time being the status of another KRA.

Activities

Important though they are, neither the job specification nor the KRAs can lead directly to the establishment of a teacher's goals. A KRA does no more than delineate an area of responsibility. It does nothing to detail how that responsibility will be discharged. This is the function of *activities*. These are the means of giving substance to the KRAs by setting out what needs to be done to realise them. Some activities are routine: to prepare weekly lesson plans and to evaluate the effectiveness of those lessons. Some point to practices that it is hoped or intended will become routine, but clearly are, in a particular school or curriculum area, not yet so: for example, to improve communication among members of staff over content and methodology in number work. Some are specific to a given stage of an innovation and will change in character as soon as that stage has been attained: for example, to plan and implement for a trial period of two years an equitable system for the allocation under local financial management of resource funding to departments.

There is no upper or lower limit to the number of activities that can or should be devised for any given KRA. The only useful advice is that activities should not be trivialised by multiplicity. It is their quality, not their quantity, which is important. It is, however, essential that they are phrased with absolute clarity and that agreement about their intent exists between appraiser and appraisee. For it is from the KRAs and the related activities that the goals which will form the main basis of the appraisal process will be educed.

GOALSETTING

We have ourselves a very strong preference for the use of the word *goal* rather than *target*. This is not mere idiosyncrasy. Targets in the context of the workplace, whether that be school or factory, tend to imply that which is quantifiable, in terms either of output or of the time taken to achieve the desired end. We regret the growing use of the phrase 'targets for action' in connection with appraisal, in the identification of the components of appraisal in the Guidelines, for example, and in the Regulations in connection with the appraisal records. In this book we intend to hold to the use of words which, while not lacking precision, nevertheless reflect the greater flexibility that is desirable in teacher appraisal.

Figure 4.2 summarises the key considerations in goalsetting. We can only begin to define the goals of any job if we have a clear and unequivocal statement of what that job is in the form of a job specification. From the job specification can be derived the KRAs for that teacher, usually from three to five in number. For Vicky, from the information so far given in her job specification, we can derive three KRAs: teaching, caring and management – these last two within her role as year head. It may be that, when the section *specific responsibilities* is completed, one or more further KRAs are identified.

Goalsetting requires that there be a precise *job specification*. A job specification consists of:

- the job purpose
- generic responsibilities
- specific responsibilities.

Key result areas (KRAs) are a means of grouping responsibilities under a limited number of headings. For most teachers there will be from three to five KRAs.

KRAs must be translated into *activities* in which it is essential to achieve results in order to satisfy the job purpose. They must also be areas important enough to be appraised.

Activities will be either *innovative* or concerned with *maintenance*. The latter are as important as the former.

From the three elements – job specification, KRAs and activities – the appraiser and appraisee will together establish the GOALS of the appraisee.

Goals indicate agreed expectations of achievement or attainment, if possible within an agreed period of time.

Longer-term goals – those that extend beyond the two-year appraisal cycle – will need to be broken down into phases.

The goals of the individual teacher need to be related to the school's overall *development plan*.

© Routledge 1993

Figure 4.2 Goalsetting: a summary

There is one KRA, vital to appraisal, that applies to every teacher: personal and professional development. We are not necessarily talking about seeking promotion or going on courses. There may be teachers whose immediate reaction to this KRA is 'I am quite happy doing what I am doing now. I have no wish to be developed either personally or professionally!' Yet every school is a dynamic organisation, in a state of change and development. By being a teacher in that school you are inevitably influenced by that state: stasis in personal and professional development is an impossibility.

AGREEING GOALS

No appraisal process can possibly be all-embracing. There must be some element of sampling, and it is helpful if the broad outline of the sample is agreed early on. Some goals will be relatively short term, and there is little merit in exhuming them six or 12 months later just for the sake of including them in the appraisal. It is helpful to the appraisee to learn from the appraiser at the goalsetting that the achievement of such a goal may be discussed informally. The creation of a daunting multiplicity of goals, any or all of which may eventually find a place on the appraisal agenda, may easily demoralise an appraisee.

This is not what appraisal is about. We are seeking through consensus to establish goals which will, on the one hand, improve the quality of performance of the individual teacher and, on the other, raise the standard of what the school has collectively to offer to its clients or stakeholders.

Goalsetting is therefore a matter of establishing priorities with those two aims in mind. Some goals will have higher priority because they will best meet the needs of the individual teacher at this point in time; others because they reflect important stages in the schools development plan. In either case they must be seen, not in isolation, but as part of a continuing developmental process. Furthermore, senior management must identify – and share with staff collectively and individually – the relationship between the two sets of goals, and create a time scale for realisation that is practicable.

Figure 4.3 shows the first two stages in the process whereby balance may be achieved between the proposals for action by the school and by the individual teacher. The upper half of the figure equates with the setting of goals, the lower half with the activities designed to achieve these goals. There is a further stage required for the completion of this flowchart which we will be looking at when we consider the appraisal interview.

In goalsetting the individual teacher identifies those areas of the job specification which, for an agreed period, are to be performance priorities. These priorities have been shared with a colleague who has an acceptable level of managerial responsibility within the institution to have the confidence of the appraisee and who, at the same time, is knowledgeable about the school's development plan and the way in which it is being implemented. The level of

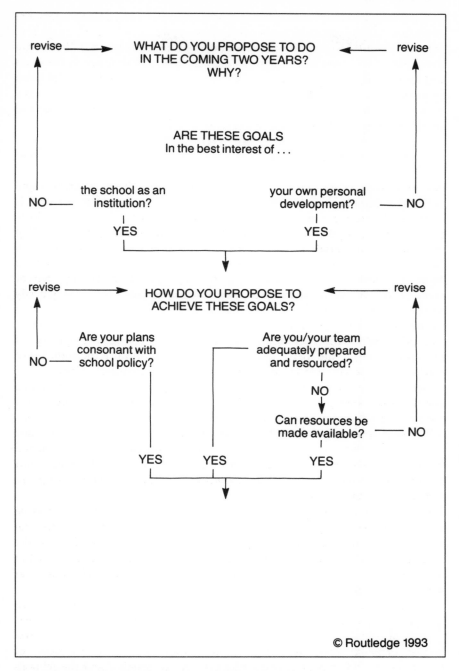

Figure 4.3 Stages I and II of performance appraisal

seniority required to fill such a role will vary from school to school, depending on the institution's management style and structure.

Yet goalsetting is incomplete and ineffectual unless the means of achieving these goals – the proposed activities – are also shared. Even though the goals may be mutually acceptable, two serious hindrances to the realisation of these proposals may be revealed as discussion proceeds. The first is that, while the goals themselves may be acceptable, the means of their achievement may not be in accord with school policy. For example, there may be the intention to proceed unilaterally with a curriculum development within a department or a curriculum area which impinges upon a possible development within another department or area. When this comes to light it may have to be pointed out that to act without full discussion with colleagues is contrary to the school's policy of collegiality, however meritorious the goal that has been proposed.

Secondly, discussion may reveal that there are important resource considerations that may affect the realisation of the goals. These may be human resources, perhaps an expectation of staffing that cannot at this stage of school planning be guaranteed; or material resources, where, to achieve this goal, a decision to divert funds from a no less laudable goal proposed by another member of staff might be required; or a funding resource from the school's INSET budget, where this claim must be weighed against the as yet unknown totality of potential in-service needs.

All this may sound very complex but in reality it is no more than sound managerial sense: the parts of the machine must mesh smoothly if the machine as a whole is to function effectively. Accountability demands that senior management takes a holistic or 'helicopter' view of the enterprise; and goals which, viewed in isolation, appear to be sound may not be timely or appropriate for the institution as a whole.

There is a danger inherent in goalsetting, particularly with keen and enterprising members of staff, that their enthusiasm may lead senior managers to give hostages to fortune: to offer resources or make decisions before the overall pattern of development can be foreseen. This can in part be avoided by having a well-established, updated school development plan; but it also requires a certain amount of constraint in planning so that a balanced progression can be maintained. Goalsetting for appraisal is therefore an exercise that must be seen contextually within the audit of the whole school policy; and modifications to that policy, necessary as aspects of the school's development plan are achieved, as new elements are introduced and as priorities change, will have their bearing on individual goals.

ANTICIPATING CONSTRAINTS

If management has to be wary of promising resources at the time of goalsetting before the totality of resources at its disposal is known, then equally it has to recognise that their absence will impinge upon an individual teacher's ability to attain goals. In goalsetting, therefore, there is a need to apply the 'if . . . then' formula now widely recognised as crucial to planning: *if* one set of resource considerations – the availability of staffing, time, funding – applies *then* the goals as they stand are achievable; *if not* available, *then* there will be certain predictable constraints on achievement.

It is possible to make too much of this. Teachers have made bricks without straw for many years now and in any area of human endeavour occasional and unpredicted – often unpredictable – obstacles are just another challenge to professionals well used to challenges. Nevertheless, it is only fair to appraiser and appraisee that those potential constraints which can be anticipated are noted at the time of goalsetting. It is clearly good management to be able to anticipate problems and to include in goalsetting some contingency planning, rather than to learn at appraisal time that what might have been a minor and removable obstacle has become a serious impediment.

CONTINGENCY PLANNING

This strategy, widely used in management planning, has a key part to play in goalsetting. As Figure 4.4 implies, it is not enough to identify the key activities which will give substance to the goals. It is also wise to attempt identification of the problems that are likely to arise in the process of realising these goals. There are two kinds of problem. There are those which can be anticipated and prevented; and there are those which would require a modification of the plan.

The first kind of problem can be illustrated as follows. An important goal for a curriculum postholder has been agreed: a major curriculum review in the light of the requirements of the National Curriculum. Unfortunately, that teacher is not taking advantage of the reviews taking place concurrently in other curriculum areas, and some excellent opportunities for cross-curricular planning may be missed. Raising this potential problem may suggest to a curriculum postholder the advisability of sharing with other curriculum postholders the review stage by stage and not, as might have been originally proposed, only when the task has been completed. A better, more collaborative way of working is therefore built back into the plan.

The second kind of problem can be illustrated thus. Meeting this same goal by an agreed time may well be dependent on the availability of certain resources: of materials, of information, of time, of training. Without this availability, there would clearly be a negative effect on the achievement of the task, and it would have to be recognised that the goal was incapable of being realised unless those who controlled these resources recognised their responsibility for the success of the enterprise.

Not all potential problems can be readily identified in advance and their harmful consequences negated by improvements to the original plan. Some potential problem may be no more than a hypothesis: if it turns out that we have no success in filling an unexpected staffing vacancy because the required

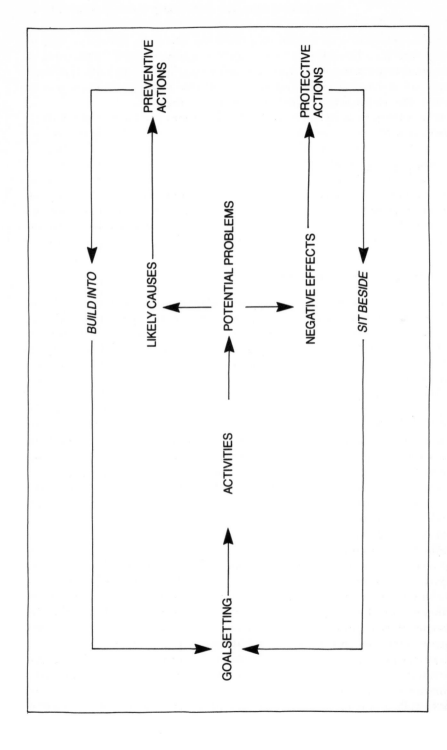

Figure 4.4 Contingency planning

areas of expertise are in short supply, then it might prove to be necessary to modify the goals recently agreed with an existing member of staff since he is the one person capable of filling this vacancy for the time being. This protective action will then sit alongside the plan, ready for implementation should the contingency arise. Examples like these emphasise the close relationship between individual goalsetting decisions and school management considerations.

CONTRACTING

Goalsetting should always end with a written contract. The responsibility for this lies with the appraiser, but that does not mean that the appraisee should not contribute to its drafting. Indeed, in goalsetting interviews we have often heard the appraisee say, when the appraiser has indicated that she will be making notes of the decisions reached, 'Is it all right if I make notes too?' In our view it is not merely all right but highly desirable, since the outcomes of the goalsetting are no less in the ownership of the appraisee and it is important that he has the opportunity to contribute to the drafting. The document must represent a consensus view on what has been decided and include all constraints that have been identified and any contingency actions that have been foreshadowed. If there is no mutually agreed contract, beyond question and dispute, then there is no reliable point of reference about what goals have been agreed.

MONITORING

It would be absurd to go from goalsetting at the beginning of the process to appraisal at the end without any intermediate checkpoints. This is not because people will not work without being 'coerced, controlled and directed' – the Theory X view of motivation posited by McGregor (1960), to which we referred in Chapter 1. Rather it is because probably the highest of all motivational factors is the recognition of achievement by managers and colleagues and the preparedness of all in the institution to help with the removal of obstacles to achievement.

Schools are institutions in which there ought to be much opportunity for regular and sustained human contact, yet the cellular nature of the classrooms in many of our primary and secondary schools has reinforced the traditional autonomy of the profession. Monitoring, however 'light touch', may be thought of as an intrusion on a private domain and to be avoided. Consequently, even though schools have become far more corporate in recent years, many managers in education are still slow sufficiently to praise their teachers, though they may go to great lengths to devise forms of recognition for student achievement. 'He was an excellent head to work for', reflected a teacher we knew well, 'and his staff knew that he valued them highly. Yet he rarely, if ever, was heard to say so. We were not looking for praise, but an occasional indication of his appreciation of our worth would have done much for our morale when for any reason we were in the doldrums.' Whether or not this teacher was aware of it, he was talking about the fourth of the five levels of needs in Maslow's theory of human motivation (1959): *ego* or esteem needs.

In the appraisal process, monitoring should never be left to chance. It needs to be built into the agreed procedures. No one would wish to be so pedantic as to specify that a senior or middle manager is required to monitor, for example, once every fortnight those for whom she is managerially responsible; yet it is important that a review of progress takes place at reasonably regular intervals and is not left to chance meetings. It is plainly not enough to pass someone in the corridor with a breezy 'Everything going all right then?' This approach hardly gives the other much opportunity to say 'No, I need to discuss here and now what is now going wrong with those goals we set at our last meeting and which then seemed so easy to meet.'

In some situations shared concerns can be voiced in departmental and other relatively small meetings, provided time is made available on the agenda; but the provision of opportunities of this kind does not obviate the need for regular one-to-one discussions where the manager can act as facilitator for her colleague so that his appraisal goals can be better attained. The further we get into the role of the appraiser, the more it becomes clear that, among the interpersonal skills that are required, counselling occupies a prime place.

TRAINING FOR GOALSETTING

Earlier in this chapter we gave you the job specification of a secondary teacher, Vicky Hoyle, which lacked the data to enable you to complete the specific responsibilities. That data you will now find on pages 56–7. The same data will also enable you to draw up goals for her for the next two-year period.

For those of you in primary schools there is on pages 58–9, a case study of a curriculum coordinator, Andrea Bull. This provideds you with the data to complete the job specification on page 60 by deciding on the specific responsibilities of this postholder and then to draw up her goals for the appraisal process.

For each case study decide whether this is goalsetting at the beginning of the first appraisal cycle or whether it follows an appraisal interview. The data you have may be more than you need – to agree too many goals can be counterproductive, as we have indicated earlier in this chapter. Draw up your agreed goals in those areas which you feel will be of most benefit to the individual and the school.

We have deliberately introduced extracts from a school development review to enable you to experience the need to achieve a synthesis between personal and institutional goals. We suggest that you refer back to Figure 4.4.

Planning the training task

This can be a self-tutoring exercise. However, you will gain far more out of it if you share it with a colleague and put yourselves in the roles of appraiser and appraisee respectively. We have also used both exercises extensively for appraisal training in whole-staff workshops for secondary schools or consortia of primary schools. Then we work with groups of five to seven, the optimum range to enable everyone to participate.

For the first task, the specific responsibilities, after an allowance of 10 minutes for reading and notetaking, the time needed for a paired activity is about 15 minutes, for a group activity 20–25, with an additional quarter of an hour if feedback discussion in plenary is considered useful.

If the second task, the goalsetting, is undertaken immediately following the first, there is no need of further reading time. If it takes place at a later date, then we suggest a 10-minute refresher. Then, for the pair 20 minutes should suffice; for the group half an hour with, as before, a further 15 minutes of plenary discussion.

We find it advantageous and time-saving to have groups present their findings on flipchart paper which can be displayed in the room. A tutor can then go around and raise discussion points, rather than subject all to lengthy and repetitive reporting-back sessions.

Case study: Vicky Hoyle

Year heads in this secondary school have a B incentive allowance and are each responsible for 155–65 pupils in six tutor groups. Year heads move with their cohort and staff through the whole (Years 7–11) cycle. The line manager for year heads is a member of the senior management team with a D incentive allowance.

Vicky Hoyle is currently responsible for Year 9, having been appointed internally as year head (Year 7) two years ago. Her teaching role is within the history department, where she has recently been asked by her head of department to take on responsibility for the history section of the school library.

A school development review took place three months ago. The report, while generally praising the headteacher and staff for their innovative work and their efforts in times of financial and manpower constraint, indicated certain areas for the school's further consideration:

The school might consider taking a wider view of some of its current developments in order to bring them together into a better strategic focus. One example of this might be to have one working party for both profiling and assessment and record keeping, currently being undertaken by separate working parties.

We attended the Year 9 parents' evening and were impressed by the number of parents attending and the readiness of tutors to give unstintingly of their time and professional knowledge. The documentation on options had been well prepared, but there were instances where the language was 'professional' rather than 'user-friendly'. It was clear that parents preferred the system of personal, handwritten reports to any proposed move to computerised reports. This may be innate conservatism, but their views are not unimportant to the success of school–home relationships. Inevitably some tutors were less well informed

© Routledge 1993

about their students than others, and much of the year head's time was taken up in support of two tutors, one of them relatively new to the group and the school.

The organisation and use of the library leaves much to be desired. It is sad that staffing levels no longer permit the employment of a teacher-librarian. We trust that the school will find ways to overcome this problem: the library is a valuable resource built up over many years.

Departmental report: history department.

We saw some excellent work being undertaken on Key Stages 3 and 4, particularly the former. Within the department there are many good teaching strategies; but the opportunity for sharing good practice should be more frequently found. This would be helpful to the head of department who is concerned that the heavy demands being made on him personally are militating against his responsibilities as a departmental manager. We understand his concern and hope that strategies may be devised within the department so that this load may be more evenly shared.

On some occasions it was felt that the more able pupils were not given tasks that match or challenge their ability; and some volunteered the information that they found the work relatively easy and undemanding.

Task 1:

Devise the *specific* elements of the job specification.

Task 2:

Draw up goals for Vicky for the next two years. She will be appraised in the summer term of 19xx.

© Routledge 1993

Case study: Andrea Bull

Andrea Bull is an experienced primary teacher who returned to the classroom four years ago once her two children were established in primary school. Two years ago she became curriculum coordinator for language when the postholder was appointed deputy head of a primary school in a neighbouring LEA. The school has a number of pupils for whom English is not the first language and ESL (English as a Second Language) is within the remit of the language coordinator. Andrea is class teacher of one of the two Year 6 classes and mentor to the other Year 6 teacher, who is in her first year of teaching.

An LEA school development review took place last term. The report, while generally praising the headteacher and staff for their efforts in times of serious constraints, indicated certain points that required the school's attention. Among the comments recorded the following are relevant to this case study:

> We are concerned over the uneven quality of presentation of written work. While some, particularly in the top years, is of a high standard, there is little evidence of a coherent policy across the school in respect of structure and clarity of expression, the correction of spelling and grammar errors.
>
> We attended the Year 6 parents' evening and were impressed by the number of parents attending and the readiness of teachers to give unstintingly of their time and professional knowledge. The support given to a newly qualified teacher by her colleague was particularly praiseworthy.
>
> The organisation and use of resources leave much to be desired. It is to be deplored that present financial constraints no longer permit the employment of a part-time ancillary helper. We trust that the school will devise strategies to overcome this deficiency.

© Routledge 1993

A slight deterioration in reading standards within Year 4 was evident from the publication of last year's SAT league tables, and the local newspaper was quick to comment. At the first governors' meeting of the year, assurances were sought over the methods of teaching reading used in the school. While immediately conveying to governors the information that 'the school uses a wide range of methods appropriate to the needs of individual children' the headteacher has undertaken to report more specifically at a future governors' meeting on the effectiveness of the school's reading programme. The headteacher and staff, aware that in previous years there had been a steady improvement in reading standards, believe that this may have been a short-term consequence of the loss of the part-time ancillary helper.

Andrea has already indicated that, for the next school year, she wishes to be given a Year 4 class, since she wants to widen her experience of the younger age group. The headteacher has agreed to try to meet Andrea's wishes when she is planning the staffing allocations for next year, but as yet is not in a position to decide.

Task 1:

Devise the *specific* elements of the job specification.

Task 2:

Draw up goals for Andrea for the next two years. She will be appraised in the summer term of 19xx.

© Routledge 1993

JOB SPECIFICATION: Andrea Bull

Job purpose:

- To teach in accordance with the National Curriculum and the principles and practice set out in the school curriculum policy.
- To contribute to the development of a caring school community in which there is equality of opportunity regardless of gender or ethnic origin.
- To promote a moral climate in which there is respect for the property, opinions and beliefs of all.

GENERIC RESPONSIBILITIES

Duties as a teacher:

- To teach the class allocated by the head teacher and to be responsible for creating and maintaining the highest possible levels of academic attainment and personal and social development of the pupils in that class.
- To communicate with parents to ensure that, as far as possible, they are kept fully informed about all significant matters relevant to their children's progress and wellbeing.

Duties as curriculum coordinator:

- To be responsible for updating all class teachers in the curriculum area for which she is designated as coordinator.
- To develop and maintain suitable curriculum materials in that area.
- To promote the sharing by all members of the staff of information and experience of the relevant curriculum content and methodology.
- To explore ways of involving parents and members of the community in contributing to the curriculum.
- To keep the headteacher informed about developments in the content and methodology in the curriculum area for which she is responsible.

SPECIFIC RESPONSIBILITIES

© Routledge 1993

Chapter 5

Classroom observation

If appraisal is to have school improvement as its main concern, then it follows that what teachers spend most of their time engaged in – involving their pupils in the learning process, that is, teaching – must be a central feature of the appraisal process. Classroom observation reveals 'a view of the climate, rapport, interaction and functioning of the classroom available from no other source' (Evertson and Holley, 1981). It is an essential feature of staff development. Not only is it valuable in its own right, as a vehicle for one-to-one in-service education and the sharing of ideas within the school on teaching content and methodology; it also is vital in order to ensure that both the goalsetting and the interview elements of appraisal relate, not to abstractions, but to what is for most teachers the key element of their role.

Teachers have grown used in the past decade to a welter of distractions from the main purpose of the profession. Innovation after innovation has taken them out of the classroom, both physically and in spirit, so that they have become preoccupied with managerial issues, either as part of their role or because these seem likely profoundly to affect their role. Difficult though it may at times be to maintain a hold on this perception, for most teachers, for most of their working day, the preparation and conduct of lessons is their crucial concern.

Yet the teaching profession as a whole remains very uneasy about classroom observation for many reasons, some well founded, some questionable. The appraisal of classroom performance will sit uncomfortably on the shoulders of appraisers and appraisees alike unless and until these reservations are brought into the open.

First, it has to be accepted that we have a long tradition of the autonomy of the classroom. This stems in part from the growth, quite rightly, of the concept that the teacher is a professional and that professions are self-regulating. The work of doctors, it is argued, is not overseen once they have completed their qualifications and their postgraduate experiential training; nor that of solicitors and lawyers when they have completed their pupillage. Yet this comparison is flawed. The medical and legal professions provide opportunities for intra-professional dialogue about their clients at a level which is denied to teachers. Furthermore, their relationship with clients is on a one-to-one basis. The teacher, in contrast, has to engage both with the individual pupil and with that indeterminate unit that we call a class: 'indeterminate' because it has come into being by the sheer chance of age, ability and aptitude in any combination that the school's policy dictates. Until very recently, one might hear the observation, made with a curious mixture of pride and criticism: 'In our profession it is possible, once one has passed one's probation, to go right through to retirement without ever once having one's teaching observed.'

It is a consequence, too, of the physical structure of the majority of our schools. Open-plan school buildings, however one cares to define the concept, provide opportunities for teachers to see what their colleagues are doing, to share experiences, to engage in peer criticism in a non-threatening way and in general to develop a corporate approach to the teaching process. Yet, in spite of the many advances made in school architecture, a majority of teachers are still teaching in classroom cells, effectively insulated from their colleagues, either because so many are teaching in schools which were designed and built long ago or because in some cases they have, in more modern buildings, physically or psychologically recreated the isolation in which they feel more comfortable.

Secondly, there is the argument put forward in some schools that head-teachers – and, in secondary schools, senior and middle management – are 'in and out of classrooms all the time anyway'. While undoubtedly the ready acceptance by pupils and staff alike that classrooms are not restricted domains or no-go areas will facilitate classroom observation for teacher appraisal, it is important that a clear distinction is made between the casual and the structured observation. Both have their uses, but neither is a substitute for the other. As can be seen from Figure 5.1, they have different purposes and will therefore have different outcomes.

Moran (1990) puts it admirably:

> The old methods of walking through classrooms or occasionally shadowing the timetable of a particular teaching group are a poor substitute for the rigour of a structured attempt to improve the learning of pupils and the professional development of staff.

What this practice may well do, however, is to mitigate the effect of 'the stranger in our midst', for both teacher and class, that the presence of the classroom observer implies. This is the third, and certainly most cogent reservation that the teaching profession has about classroom observation. There are, it is true, many open-access and community schools in which the presence in the classroom of adults other than the class teacher goes practically unnoticed by the pupils; but even here the presence of a more senior teacher for a full lesson, possibly taking notes and certainly there in a capacity not readily recognised as 'normal', will make a difference. Some pupils will react by playing to the gallery, others by becoming unusually reticent, to the extent that highly competent

Casual 'drop in' observation

Likely to be non-threatening

Promotes climate of openness and collaboration

Likely that only part of a lesson will be seen. Unlikely that its context will be wholly understood

Provides opportunity for informal and non-threatening offers of support but rarely for in-depth discussion

Under pressure of other demands may become too casual or not happen at all

May be undertaken by any colleague who has time or opportunity

Formal observation

Needs preparation to ensure that teacher does not feel under threat

Specifically concerned with lesson objectives

Provides opportunity to relate lesson to year or departmental goals and to whole school policy on content and methodology

Provides opportunity for reinforcement of strengths, identification of weaknesses and planning for remediation

Required under the appraisal regulations and time must therefore be found for it

Will be undertaken by the appraiser within a line management model

Both casual and formal classroom observation are needed for staff development

© Routledge 1993

Figure 5.1 Classroom observation: casual and formal

teachers may well end up by wondering what on earth was wrong with that lesson that it should have produced such atypical responses.

It is not only the class that may react in this way. Some teachers may feel impelled to 'put on a show' and, in so doing, they are likely to achieve a lesson of far less merit than had they viewed their observation lesson not as a performance on which they were being judged, but as an occasion on which, as far as possible, they would be demonstrating their normal day-to-day skills. There is ample evidence from schools which have been engaged for some years in formal classroom observation as a component of appraisal that teachers and pupils alike soon begin to adapt well to what was formerly an exceptional experience.

Nevertheless, it is important to recognise that there will always be an element of stress for both pupils and teacher in the classroom observation process. The status of the observer and the importance of the occasion will be the main reasons for this. There are those who argue that the unheralded visit will both ensure that the lesson is a natural one and relieve tension. This we very much doubt. There are many occasions during the school week when a lesson may be low-key but still effective; but our observation is that, caught unawares as it will seem to them, teachers will assume that a high profile stance is expected of them and take up a centre-stage position. The situation will then become unreal for the teacher, the class and, indeed, the observer. There is every reason for headteachers and their senior curricular and pastoral staff to visit classrooms as often as their many other duties allow, but it would be erroneous to confuse this casual activity with that of formal classroom observation. If appraisal is to be an experience in which there is trust and mutuality, then the classroom observation element must have a structure which encourages open behaviour, is unambiguous in its intended outcomes and seeks to promote in the teacher the confidence to perform at the highest possible level.

BRIEFING FOR CLASSROOM OBSERVATION

It is essential that there is a briefing session before any formal classroom observation. It should take place at least one day before the lesson which is being observed, in a place and atmosphere in which both observer and teacher can feel at ease. It is likely to take from 15 to 30 minutes and therefore, to play safe, half an hour should be set aside. If the appraisee is providing written lesson notes they need to be in the hands of the observer in advance of the meeting, preferably the day before.

Establishing the context

Every lesson depends for its content and methodology on what has preceded it and what is intended to succeed it: it is part of a teaching/learning continuum. The observer therefore needs to be told by the class teacher where in that

Before the lesson

- Establish the context

- Ascertain the teacher's aims and expectations

- Share the lesson plan

- Identify potential difficulties and constraints

- Agree the observation style

- Agree the focus

- Contract for debriefing

© Routledge 1993

Figure 5.2 Briefing for classroom observation

continuum the lesson stands. Many observers will, as line managers, already have an awareness of the broad context of the lesson, either through lesson preparation notes which they routinely see or from the minutes of departmental or team meetings. That knowledge is, however, too general to make this stage of the briefing process superfluous. Moreover, because the lesson lies within the ownership of the class teacher, discussion enables rapport and confidence to be more readily established.

For early years teachers, for those in schools which operate the integrated day, for teachers of special educational needs and those working in special schools the term 'lesson' must be interpreted with sensitivity. It is no less important that there be mutual understanding of what is expected to take place during the period of time set aside for the observation; but a greater flexibility must be expected and the ability to improvise must be looked for. What the observer will see has been well described as 'a slice of the moving river'. Where there is a wide range of activities taking place, the appraiser and appraisee will need to agree whether it will be more useful for the observer to engage in wide sampling – that is, taking a brief look at as many activities as possible – or narrow sampling – looking more intensively at fewer activities.

Ascertaining aims and expectations

The purpose of this area of the briefing is to ensure that the teacher is being observed in the light of her intended outcomes, not those assumed by the appraiser. Wragg (1987) trenchantly points out that 'the art of constructive observation is to . . . concentrate on helping the teacher'. This is best done by obtaining through discussion, and maintaining through observation, the teacher's perspective on the lesson. Whether the observer might have had different aims and expectations is irrelevant to the task. Alternative approaches in methodology, other ideas about content, are of course worth sharing between colleagues; but to do so at this particular time would be destructive of the teacher's confidence and raises serious questions about the ownership of the lesson.

We have often been asked whether, if the observer considers in this pre-lesson stage that the aims and expectations are manifestly inappropriate for the class being observed, an intervention is permissible. The judgment called for here is that of Solomon: to distinguish in advance between a lesson in which mistakes may be made, but which will still be a valuable learning experience for the teacher, and one which appears to be signalling the distinct possibility of breakdown. Certainly there is no reason why the appraiser should not probe those aspects which give rise to reservations or disquiet. Nor, if there is the likelihood of definite misinformation being transmitted to the class, should the appraiser fail to suggest that some research is called for. The appraiser has no right to take over ownership of the lesson, but equally should not behave like Jove on Olympus, dispassionately watching his puny creature falter and stumble. Nevertheless, in all but the most extreme situations it is for the teacher, not the observer, to decide what needs to be done.

Sharing the lesson plan

Let it be taken for granted that the lesson plan, whether written or not, which a teacher produces for the observation lesson is likely to be more thoroughly prepared and in more detail than usual. There are now relatively few schools in which the rather arid exercise of the preparation of a week's lesson notes is required of teachers by their heads of department or headteachers. There is far more trust abroad than in our early years in the classroom! More positively, individual preparation has been replaced by group planning: not of the detail, since this would be tedious and destructive of individual initiative, but of the broad outline of work for a given period. This has become increasingly the case as the Key Stages of the National Curriculum have been introduced. Sharing of knowledge and resources has become a means of survival; and, as government pressure for ever higher educational standards is applied, this may well become even more widespread, given that rare commodity, time.

Yet neither a line manager who is observing nor the appraisee should ever assume that having a common interest obviates the need for the detailed presentation of the lesson plan for the purpose of effective classroom observation. We believe it to be helpful if the lesson plan is presented in writing. This makes sure that there is a common understanding of the content of the lesson and enables the observer to prepare in advance of the briefing session. However, an excellent sequence in one of the Somerset training videos (see Appendix 2) shows the head of the Infant Department talking through a lesson plan with her appraiser while he takes notes. It may be that experienced and senior teachers will be more comfortable with the informal approach; those whose memories of their teacher training are not so distant are less put out by being asked to present a written outline.

We emphasise that the lesson plan, like the aims and expectations, is in the ownership of the teacher. The observer's main objective is to ensure that there is a full, shared understanding of what it is that the teacher is expecting to happen in the lesson in the fulfilment of her aims and expectations. Good teachers are responsive to stimuli from their pupils, and it should not be in the minds of either party that the plan is a rigid measuring rod against which the success or failure of the lesson will be judged. Appraisal is not about judgment.

You have met Vicky Hoyle in the previous chapter. She has suggested to her appraiser that for the first classroom observation he might like to observe a Year 7 lesson on Roman Britain as an introduction to the Key Stage 3 theme of the Roman Empire. She prepared the lesson outline which appears on the next page. What follows is an abbreviated version of the discussion that took place between Vicky and her appraiser. An outline of a comparable primary lesson appears in the next chapter on training for classroom observation.

Lesson notes: Year 7 History

Preceding lessons:

The Roman invasion; the structure of the Roman army; armour and weaponry; fortified camps; road building.

Present lesson:

The department has obtained an exhibition on loan from the museum with replicas of domestic articles and agricultural implements. We also have maps, photographs and reconstructions.

Introduction: Pictures of a reconstructed Romano-British villa to be compared with a reconstructed Italian villa. Ask children to find reasons for similarities and differences. Suggest possible other differences (clothing, food) because of climate.

   Tell children second instalment of a story about a Briton captive in Rome in the second century AD.

Question sheet activity: Identify artefacts, their purpose and composition.

Written work (to be completed for homework): choice of topics to draw and write about: hypocaust; mosaic pavement; any three of the artefacts.

© Routledge 1993

Discussing the lesson plan: I

Vicky and her appraiser meet in her classroom at the end of the school day, the place at her request. She is unpacking and checking the display as he arrives.

AP: Hello, Vicky. I hope I am not late. I was stopped twice in the corridor on the way here, as usual! That display looks interesting.

VH: Yes, Alec, it is part of the museum's education service. It is much in demand and we had to book it weeks in advance. Jeremy will be using it next week with his Year 7. What pleases me is that the museum encourages children to handle the artefacts.

AP: In my day it was *hands off* everything! Shall we make a start? First, I must say that your lesson outline was very well presented. Even I, a mathematician, could understand exactly what you are planning to do.

   May I start by asking you a few questions? I am not clear why are you doing Roman Britain in Year 7. My daughter is doing it in Year 6 of her primary school. I thought one of the main intentions of the National Curriculum was to avoid overlap?

VH: In theory that's true. In practice different primary schools choose different topics within Key Stage 2. Although for some in the class this lesson does contain an element of revision, it is breaking new ground for others. What I am trying to do is to get them to pool their knowledge to provide me with a jumping off ground for our study of the Roman Empire.

AP: Ah, I take it that the Roman Empire appears in Key Stage 3 then?

VH: Yes. When we did the Roman Army last week we traced on large-scale maps all the places in Europe and North Africa where the army had been. Before we did this, they had no idea of the extent of the Roman Empire.

AP: I know that there are some very specific attainment targets in your subject just as in mine. How does this lesson fit in with them?

VH: There are three attainment targets: knowledge and understanding of history, interpretation, and the use of historical sources. I try to have some element of each of these attainment targets in every new activity. As you know, this is a class of very mixed ability and I would be hoping that every child will, in Attainment Target 1 for example, achieve at Least level 3.

AP: What achievements will you be looking for in level 3?

VH: A child has to be able to explain, for example, why Romano-British villas are different from Italian ones. I would expect a number to reach Level 4 in this lesson and a few to be reaching towards Level 5. I can lend you the attainment levels of these three targets to have a look at before the lesson if you would like. It would be valuable to me to have an outsider give an opinion on the extent to which I am reaching them.

AP: Is that to be the specific focus of this lesson, then?

VH: I would value that. But can you link it with observation on whether the children are working purposefully – I think the jargon term is 'are on task'! – and are aware of the intention of the lesson? In group work particularly it is very difficult to evaluate this yourself as you are constantly being called here, there and everywhere.

AP: Well, that raises an interesting issue. I do not see anywhere in your lesson plan that you are giving time to sharing the purpose with the children. Is this something you take for granted?

VH: No . . . It is not something I have given much thought to, but it certainly sounds like a good idea. Do you think I should start the lesson with an outline of what we intend to achieve?

AP: It's not for me to say: it is your lesson. What do you think?

VH: I think it might well be worth doing, but I must admit I would rather try it out at least once before you were present! On second thoughts, why not? It sounds straightforward enough. We will see what happens tomorrow!

AP: I will be there, without fail, before the lesson begins. Where do you want me during the lesson?

VH: At the back as unobtrusively as possible during the first part of the lesson, then wherever you please. Will you be with one group or will you move around?

AP: Just as you like. Which do you think will be of most benefit to you?

VH: I had not thought, but off the top of my head, moving around might be better this time. I must mention that I encourage children to discuss with each other in informal groups, for example, when they come up to look at the artefacts, so you must expect the noise level to rise. Will you tell me at the debriefing if you think it has got out of hand?

AP: It is perfectly natural for there to be more noise when they are working in this way. You should hear my classes sometimes when we are making mathematical models! Do you have in mind any children in particular who might take the opportunity of group work to misbehave?

VH: There is one, but he is unpredictable. I would rather not name him now, but can we discuss his behaviour at the debriefing if he does play up?

AP: I think I can hazard a guess who it is, but I will come with an open mind! Let us hope that the activity itself will hold his interest. Have you a strategy for dealing with him if it comes to it?

VH: I have, but I hope you will not have the opportunity to see whether or not it is effective!

AP: What do you want me to do during the group work? Do you want me just to observe as I move around?

VH: Oh no, do join in. They will expect you to, because visitors generally do in my classes.

AP: Tell me one thing before we finish. Do you allow children to work together on the question sheets?

VH: Yes, I do, but it does present a problem. How can I tell if one bright pupil is carrying the others, when I have to give the teacher's estimate of attainment level reached?

AP: I can't give you an answer, because it is a problem we are all facing in every subject; but I do think that over a period, and not trying to use a single piece of work, you will be able to make reasonably accurate assessments.

VH: I certainly hope so!

AP: We have developed some strategies in mathematics which you might find useful, but I would not know if they applied to history. Would you like a copy of our paper?

VH: Yes please! I have asked Krishnan to put this on the agenda of a departmental meeting as soon as possible, so it might be very useful to him as well as me.

AP: This story you tell them in the introduction. Is it one by Rosemary Sutcliffe?

VH: (blushing slightly) No, I made it up. There are lots of good stories about Romans that I shall be recommending, but I needed something that fits exactly what I am doing.

AP: Can I have an autographed copy when it is published? It is twenty past. Is there anything else you want to discuss now?

VH: I don't think so. When are we going to meet after the lesson?

AP: Can you manage at the end of school?

VH: Twenty minutes?

AP: Yes, I am quite sure that will be long enough.

© Routledge 1993

Potential difficulties and constraints

You will have noted that the appraiser gave Vicky an opportunity to identify in advance any problems that might arise in the course of the lesson. Hers was a potential disciplinary problem. Nearly every class has the Holy Terror who *may* be cooperative because the observer is present, but is just as likely to use the occasion to be highly disruptive. Vicky, as a year head, will be well used to dealing with disruptive pupils from other teachers' classes, and the appraiser rightly assumes that there is no need to talk this through further. However, if the teacher is new to the profession or the school, she may well look to her more senior colleague to deal with the incident. So may the class. Save in exceptional circumstances, of the kind which would lead to a senior member of staff being summoned to 'firefight', it is essential that the class teacher retains ownership of the situation.

There will be times when the teacher will seize the opportunity to raise more general matters which present difficulties: lack of resources, unsatisfactory accommodation, pupils with special needs that are not being catered for. These should not be dismissed by the appraiser as irrelevant to the lesson observation. For one thing, they are not irrelevant to the teacher, and that is the point of view which matters. For another, a few minutes spent listening may reveal to the observer aspects of school management that he might be in a position to ameliorate or, alternatively, make known to more senior staff who are in a position to act on them.

For teachers who are unused to being observed, this element of the briefing process will prove most useful in reinforcing the concept that class observation is not intended to be judgmental, but is concerned with school improvement as much as with teacher performance. In the early years of appraisal, and for some teachers possibly for quite a long time after, there will be unease, misconception and sometimes downright cynicism about the process. Time spent in dialogue will rarely be time wasted.

Agreeing observation style

Fly on the wall or co-teacher? These are not so much alternatives as extremes of a spectrum within which the teacher and observer will identify the desired observation style. Highly experienced observers – HMI, university researchers, LEA advisers – may have the skill to become 'part of the furniture' within a classroom. For those whom the class will recognise as teachers within their own school but who appear to be wearing, exceptionally, a different hat, this kind of anonymity is not easily achieved. In a teacher-centred lesson, it is more likely that the observer will soon be absorbed into the class: watching, at pupil level as it were, a demonstration science experiment, a video or a film; or listening to a story which leads to questions and answers from the class. In an activity lesson it is not merely that the role of impartial observer would be difficult to maintain; it would lead to ineffective observation. The centre of activity very soon becomes the table where the group is writing, planning and discussing. Only by going round, observing the groups, giving help where it is needed and generally participating in the activity is the observer going to gain any insight into the effectiveness of the learning process that the teacher has set in motion.

If the observer is closely involved in the activities of the class, there will be no time for detailed notes. He needs to cultivate the habit of jotting down 'trigger' words which will act as reminders for the debriefing session which follows. Were the observer, in a lesson in which he adopts the 'fly on the wall' approach, to be seen by the class to be writing copiously throughout – as happens in a secondary school geography lesson on video (see Appendix 2) – he will almost certainly present himself to the pupils as assessor rather than appraiser. Comments like 'What mark did you get for that lesson, Miss?' must therefore be expected.

Whatever the negotiated agreement, whether with the staff as a whole or with individuals as part of the preparation for observation, notetaking must be an open behaviour: the teacher must be given the opportunity to see the notes or any statement written up from the notes, to comment on their accuracy and be given a copy if she so wishes.

Agreeing the focus

An observer who goes into the classroom merely to receive impressions will come out little wiser than when he went in. There is no possibility of covering every aspect of the teacher's performance in one visit and it is therefore necessary for the observer to negotiate with the teacher what in particular is to be observed. These are the *focal areas*.

A teacher may have doubts about the efficacy of her questioning techniques. Here there would be merit in the observer actually recording the wording of a range of questions and the kinds of response that they elicited, so that there could be discussion in the debriefing on the extent to which open and closed questions had been used, and whether or not opportunities for stretching the pupils had been grasped. A teacher engaged in group work might welcome the close observation of the behaviour of a randomly selected group in order that she may learn about their commitment to task, mutual support and attainment of goals. These specific focal areas cannot be multiplied *ad infinitum*. It is unrealistic to expect the observer, however skilled, to focus on more than two or three specific areas in one lesson.

Two of the pilot LEAs (NDC, 1988) drew a valuable distinction between *general focus* and *specific focus* lesson observation. It was then considered likely that the first observation would have a general focus so that the observer might view the learning process through a 'wide-angle lens' and that discussion of that lesson would reveal areas upon which there might profitably be a specific focus during a later observation. While we have found that this is a sound practice with and for relatively inexperienced teachers, mature teachers tend to wish to identify specific focal areas even for the first observation. The appraisee naturally wants the observation time to be well spent, and in identifying her own needs is engaging in a useful self-evaluation.

There will be some teachers, however, whom the appraiser knows to have areas of difficulty – over the use of time, in class control, in the use of resources, for example – and the appraiser will suggest, and if necessary insist, that this is an area of specific focus. While appraisal is not judgmental, it must have a cutting edge: a cosy, bland approach will not lead to school improvement or personal professional development.

Discussing the lesson plan: II

Task:

Go back to the dialogue between Vicky and her appraiser Alec on pages 69–72. Identify the specific focal areas they have agreed on. What strategies will Alec use in observing these?

In their discussion some issues have been raised extrinsic to the observation. Identify these. In discussing them, however briefly, have they deviated from the purpose of the briefing session? If they have, is that deviation justified?

© Routledge 1993

Contracting for debriefing

The teacher needs the assurance that time is being made available for a discussion on the outcomes reasonably near to the lesson observation. The observer needs to ensure that the occasion will be uninterrupted and that he will not be forced by the pressure of other activities into concluding the discussion prematurely. It is very difficult to anticipate just how long will be needed. It is irrelevant whether the lesson has appeared to the observer to be trouble-free or to raise a multitude of issues: the teacher's needs do not necessarily equate with the observer's perceptions.

In planning for debriefing one can only make an educated guess at the desirable duration. The appraiser, in drawing up an informal agenda for the debriefing session, may be well able to determine what will need immediate attention and will fit into the time that has been allowed and what can safely be held over until a further meeting can be arranged. Our experience with schools involved in appraisal trials is that very rarely is the debriefing likely to extend beyond one session of 20 minutes; but that when it does there is good reason for it.

The contract must also include agreement on where the debriefing will take place. We have found primary teachers to be nearly unanimous in the view that it should take place on what they perceive to be home ground: their own classrooms. In secondary schools, presumably because there are more offices available, there is less strength of feeling about the location. Interestingly, teachers seem to regard privacy as less important than feeling at ease. This may be as well. However much one has sought to ensure that there will be no interruption, there will always be the occasion when a face will appear round the door and a voice call out: 'Oh, sorry! I didn't know you were busy!'

DEBRIEFING

It is possible, indeed very likely, that the teacher will seek to discuss the lesson immediately it is over, particularly in a secondary school where there may be a brief intermission between the dismissal of one class and the arrival of the next. There should always be some positive words of encouragement or approbation, but it is better that nothing of substance is said until the debriefing meeting. Confirming the debriefing arrangements is a useful ploy for ensuring that a conversation which cannot be conveniently concluded is not begun.

Self-evaluation

One of the most important functions of classroom observation is to encourage self-awareness on the part of the teacher. It is therefore important that the debriefing begins with the teacher's own views on the merits and demerits of the lesson under review. It might be thought that the teacher will see only the good points of her lesson; but in our experience of classroom observation this is rarely the case. Indeed, there is research evidence to show that self-evaluation is highly effective and that self-perceptions are generally accurate.

Even if this were not so, there would still be a strong argument for opening up a debriefing session by inviting the teacher to give her views. The greater likelihood in those cases where self-evaluation is not accurate is that the teacher is excessively critical of her performance. In this situation the observer

After the lesson

- Confirm time and place for debriefing

- Give opportunity for self-evaluation

- Review aims and expectations

- Identify and analyse lesson strengths

- Identify and analyse lesson weaknesses

- Offer support if needed

© Routledge 1993

Figure 5.3 Debriefing

is in a position to moderate the self-criticism and, incidentally, place himself in the strong position of being the one who can say 'No, really, it was much better than you seem to think'!

Nevertheless, there will be those who, whether or not they have perceived their own weaknesses, are unwilling to disclose them. It is difficult for some teachers to rid themselves of the feeling that self-disclosure is in itself a weakness. We have detected at times an element of sexism: a man finding it difficult to admit to a woman colleague that he is less than perfect, professionally speaking! Situations like this may well call for the use of those influencing skills which we consider in the next chapter.

A self-evaluation proforma may be helpful as a focus for the teacher's consideration of her performance. Some teachers have used one which we have devised (see pages 78–9) as a proforma to be completed. In constructing it we have concentrated on three key areas of performance that relate approximately to the beginning, the middle and the end of the lesson. The questions have been phrased to promote an objective stance: phrasing such as 'Did you feel that . . .?', 'Did you think that . . .?' has been avoided.

Some teachers have simply found the headings useful as prompts to their thinking about the lesson. For most teachers there will be little or no time before the debriefing session to analyse the lesson in any detail, but it helps if they can arrive with some views on their own performance. If both appraiser and appraisee were to complete the proforma it then becomes easy at the beginning of the debriefing for both parties rapidly to identify those areas where they have perceptions in common and those areas where they differ. Time may be saved by passing rapidly over the areas of agreement in order to concentrate on the exploration of the areas of difference.

Some schools have constructed their own self-evaluation proformas as an extension of the session on the criteria for good classroom performance in our workshop programme on classroom observation. The details of that session are to be found in the chapter on training for classroom observation on page 86.

Aims and expectations

It may seem unnecessary for an item dealt with at some length in the briefing now to reappear; but to consider the extent to which aims and expectations have been met is a vital part of the debriefing. It will sometimes happen that the appraiser has seen what on the surface appears to have been an excellent lesson, but closer investigation may reveal that it did not accord with the aims the teacher had set for herself. Teaching is, after all, a purposive activity and it is important that any debriefing reveals whether what was achieved in a lesson measures up to the intended outcomes.

Yet it is vital that neither party regards the aims as a straitjacket. Good teachers take account of the interests, skills and knowledge that their pupils

Classroom observation: self-evaluation

This is to help you to identify the strengths and weaknesses of the lesson that has just been observed as *your* contribution to the debriefing. Under each main heading there are examples of points you may like to consider. Add any of your own if you wish.

How did you ensure that the pupils were readily able to get on with their work?

• Were materials prepared and available?

• Was the room suitably arranged?

• Were your instructions clear and well understood?

How did you encourage good standards of achievement?

• Did you relate well to all the children?

• Did you spend time with individuals/each group?

© Routledge 1993

- Were the tasks appropriate to all levels of ability?

- Was the noise level acceptable and conducive to work?

How did you encourage an awareness of achievement?

- Did you conclude the lesson with a résumé or evaluation of what you had done?

- Was clearing up satisfactorily completed?

- Did the children appear to enjoy the session?

- Did *you* enjoy the session?

What forward thinking have you established for the next lesson?

© Routledge 1993

bring into the classroom. While the central aim of the lesson should not be subverted, diversions on the way that take account of these are desirable and reflect the adaptability of the good teacher.

In most cases the discussion under this head will not take long. A tried technique is to recreate the aims and objectives of the lesson from what actually took place and then compare them with what the teacher had committed herself to.

Strengths and weaknesses

The self-evaluation, if it was undertaken, will have already identified some, at least, of these areas. However, the appraiser may have a valuable contribution to make, having been better placed than the teacher to observe the structure of the lesson, the use of time, the effective use of resources and so on. It is not, however, for the appraiser to talk at length about what he has seen but rather to ask the questions that will tease out the strengths and weaknesses of the lesson. The main concentration must be on strengths. Where weaknesses are identified the role of the observer is to be the enabler whereby these too can be translated into strengths. The appraiser should not take everything on himself, but equally must not enter into undertakings involving other people without their knowledge and approval.

There will inevitably be teachers who are teaching to the best of their ability but still not being very effective. It may be that the teacher needs support from a middle or senior manager, or from a peer with particular skills or empathy. If the content of the lessons is the problem, then in-service training to remedy deficiencies may be needed. If the methodology is at fault, there may be need of sustained help from the head of department or curriculum coordinator. Since a key concern of the appraisal process is staff development, any indications of where remediation is required are of value both to the individual and the school.

In training sessions we have occasionally been asked whether such matters as in-service training are not better left to the appraisal interview itself. Ideally this would be highly desirable. One of the outcomes of the appraisal interviews is that the staff development coordinator or the senior management team – whoever is responsible for INSET – is able to consolidate staff needs and set them against available resources in the budget. In all state schools, grant-maintained, LEA controlled and voluntary controlled, other than the smallest primary schools, decisions on how to allocate invariably inadequate resources are finally made by the governing body or one of its committees. Yet a classroom observation may take place half a term before the appraisal interview, and even longer before all staff training needs can be consolidated and adjudicated on. If the situation is of sufficient seriousness to warrant it, the appraiser should make known to the headteacher his appraisee's training needs so that exceptional measures may be taken or at least sought. It is important to recognise that the appraisal process is continuous and that the appraiser often has to enter into the role of mentor or critical friend in order to support a colleague. Classroom observations and the appraisal interview itself are only highlights in the continuum.

WHO WILL OBSERVE?

In six years of working on appraisal with primary headteachers and their senior staff we have observed a marked change in the response to this question. For some time there was a clear and almost universal expectation that, since the headteacher is responsible for the appraisal process, it follows that the classroom observation, an integral part of that process, is also her responsibility. The recommendation of the pilot schemes (HMSO, 1989) that no appraiser should be responsible for more than four appraisals caused some initial alarm; but for many this was quickly rationalised, except in the largest primary schools, into 'sharing the load with the deputy would be good for both of us' and 'I am sure we might manage six or seven each if we were pushed to it'. Yet even then there were primary headteachers who were urging their colleagues to consider appraisal not in isolation but as a feature in whole school development; and these were asking the vital question 'How can we give sufficient credibility to the role of other managers if we deprive them of an opportunity of observing their colleagues at work in areas for which they are given responsibility?' To create these opportunities within the framework of appraisal is not easy; but to create them outside that framework is even more difficult, indeed, probably impossible to any worthwhile extent in the light of the time costs of appraisal itself.

Some headteachers find this surrender of autonomous power hard to understand and even harder to practise; but there are many educationists (Dennison and Shenton, 1987; Wilkinson and Cave, 1988; Beare et al., 1989) who argue on sound research evidence that there are considerable benefits in the greater managerial flexibility that obtains in the system of loose-coupling first propounded by Wieck (1976).

The very complexity of secondary schools, rather than any greater adherence to less hierarchical concepts of management theory, has led secondary headteachers with whom we have worked to be more immediately aware of the need to establish a devolved policy for classroom observation. Yet, in considering to whom to devolve, interesting issues of policy arise. Some of these are indeed concerned with existing managerial structures and style. There are schools whose appraisal teams have been clearly selected from the most senior staff and one consequence of this has been that major departments may well be represented on the team and minor ones not. This then raises the cognate question of the credibility as observers of classroom performance of those who are not specialists in a given subject.

Two clearly irreconcilable arguments are raised: that at secondary level familiarity with subject content is of crucial importance; and that the classroom observer is concerned with generic teaching abilities and not with content. Common sense suggests that extreme situations are not tenable: for example, that a teacher, however senior, whose knowledge of science extends no further than the content of the O Level examination in general science 20 years ago will have credibility as observer of a Year 11 lesson in combined science today. Yet in other fields of her role as appraiser, in the appraisal interview for example, that person may well be an ideal choice.

Schools will long since have made their selection of their appraisal team but resignations, internal promotions and retirements will provide the opportunity for additions to that team. This will allow for more thought to be given, if need be, so that there can be established, collectively, credibility over the range of level and subject within the school.

As we have indicated in Chapter 3, there is a problem of interpretation between Regulation §9(2) which categorically states that the appraiser 'shall observe the schoolteacher teaching on at least two occasions' and Guideline §35 which refers not to the appraiser but to the appraisee '[who] should normally be observed teaching for a total of at least one hour, spread over two or more occasions'. *Normally*, that word beloved of those who draft documents and want to leave a door open! To what does it apply here: that there is discretion over the minimum time? or discretion over the number of occasions of observation? or both?

This is not a cavil. If there is no discretion that permits the headteacher to substitute a task observation for one of the two classroom observations in certain situations, then, for all those members of staff who have a significant management role, task observation will have to be additional to two classroom observations. We have already pointed out that in very few schools will it be possible to confine the observation of two lessons to the minimum one hour. One and a half hours is far nearer the mark. To this appraisers will, without the ability to exercise that discretion, need to add time for task observation if they are to gain a first-hand impression of a middle or senior manager's ability to manage. We compare a whole range of possible task observations, and their applicability to managers at various levels, in Chapter 7.

HOW TO OBSERVE

Experienced observers of classroom practice hold the view that it is mainly by observing the learning outcomes rather than the teaching process that it becomes possible to assess the extent to which a lesson is effective. Even when the teacher is centre-stage, setting tasks or conducting a plenary discussion, the observer's key role is to study the reactions of individual members of the class. It is unlikely that in any class there will be full attention throughout the lesson from every student; or that there will be full comprehension of every issue. Observers weigh the contributions of students, individually and collectively, in answering, questioning, listening, performing tasks, helping each other in an appropriate manner, and so on.

Nevertheless, there can be no effective outcomes unless there are sound inputs, and the observer needs to be a Janus, looking both ways. We have found that appraisers, who are seldom experienced observers of classroom practice since most of them are too occupied with being practitioners, are asking for help and guidance in establishing criteria and developing a methodology for observation. Despite governmental pressures for standardisation, that standard cannot be prescribed. A teacher may perform outstandingly well with a difficult class, even though the performance levels are significantly inferior to those of another class. The argument for value-added assessment of standards may be derided by government; but, because these children are well known to them, appraisers should bear in mind what might be expected of them and therefore of the teacher. Performance criteria, though they may appear to be valuable in establishing common ground among schools, are counter-productive unless they are moderated by the circumstances that prevail in the class or the school. Of greater practical value are observation schedules, and we have looked at a number of these. We give extracts from a number of these in the next chapter, to enable potential appraisers to decide which style of construct is likely to be of use to them. Two of them we have been able to reproduce in full in Appendix 3, thanks to the generosity of the copyright holders.

Chapter 6

Training for classroom observation

As the previous chapter will have indicated, there are four key elements to training for classroom observation: the establishment of agreed criteria for effective learning; briefing for classroom observation; the observation itself; and debriefing. In our experience, a total of one full day needs to be spent on this training for both appraisers and appraisees. We have often been told, or have ourselves observed, that not enough time and attention have been given to the detail of classroom observation in the early days of appraisal training. In some LEAs there has been an implicit assumption that this comes naturally, needing discussion only, not experiential training.

It is desirable, but not essential, that this training is a whole staff activity. If it is, it might well take place on an in-service day, or on half of two such days. There is need for a team of group leaders – one for every six to eight members of staff – who will have planned the day and themselves trialled the materials that follow.

CRITERIA FOR GOOD CLASSROOM PERFORMANCE

This activity is best promoted through a brainstorming session. It gives rise to useful group discussion and highlights, through the different value sets that become apparent, the importance of consensus within a school.

Although brainstorming is now a widely used technique in in-service training, it is helpful if group leaders remind their group members of the 'rules', included in the rubric on page 86.

The encouragement to all to contribute, without regard to status, is certainly the most important initial benefit of brainstorming. However, the sheer profusion of what is now on the flipchart may lead to confusion if nothing further is done after the generation of ideas. What is more, the opportunity must be given for the reconciliation of any differences of opinion within the group. This is best done in a second-stage activity.

Groups are now invited to create generic categories for the ideas on the flipchart and to recast those ideas under these main headings. One such heading might well be classroom atmosphere; another, teacher–pupil relationships; yet another, classroom organisation. It will often happen that an idea will be seen to be relevant to more than one category. This is in itself valuable in that it demonstrates the holistic nature of criteria.

We have long been of the opinion that there is little value in a reporting back session. In general we have found that there is as much benefit – and a considerable saving of valuable training time – if the final flipcharts are displayed for groups to view in their own time, possibly in a coffee break, before a plenary session. What is far more valuable than a tedious and repetitive reporting back is for the tutor to have spent a little preparation time drawing from the flipchart display some general conclusions and discussion points.

The training module on page 86 offers two variants for the activity. We have found that looking at the task from these differing perspectives promotes useful discussion.

This is an appropriate stage at which to introduce observation schedules, mentioned in the previous chapter. We have seen more and more of these in recent years, and they provide valuable insights into what the appraising body understands by classroom observation and how it expects its teachers to go about the task of observing. In the previous edition of this book we included an extensive checklist of teacher performance criteria devised by the superintendent of Lovington District, New Mexico. Although there is some advantage in the appraiser and appraisee having a shared understanding of what is being looked for, a schedule that covers 10 areas of competence, each with on average half a dozen indicators, may well be counterproductive. To give one example:

The teacher obtains feedback from and communicates with students in a manner which enhances student learning and understanding by:

- [ensuring] that learners recognise the purpose and importance of the lesson;
- clarifying directions and explanations if students do not understand;
- giving reasonable explanations for actions, directions and decisions;
- encouraging appropriate student-to-student as well as student-to-teacher interactions;
- reinforcing and encouraging students' own efforts to be involved;
- communicating regularly with students about their needs and progress;
- providing constructive feedback to students about their behaviour.

(Lovington District, 1988)

It takes a very skilled observer to keep these – and a further 46 – indicators in mind while observing a lesson. We cannot help feeling that this intensive preoccupation with detail may in fact prevent the observer from seeing the lesson as a whole.

A number of British appraisal schemes have produced observation schedules of different kinds. Croydon has prepared a 'teacher talk analysis' based under three headings: organisational; instructional; conceptual/cognitive. The

Classroom performance criteria

For a lesson to be observed with real benefit to the teacher, it is vital that there is agreement on what constitutes good classroom practice.

Appoint a scribe and for 30 minutes brainstorm the question assigned to your group:

EVEN NUMBERED GROUPS: By what criteria do you judge effective teaching?

ODD NUMBERED GROUPS: By what criteria do you judge effective learning?

Keep to the following rules while you brainstorm:

- At this stage all ideas are equally valuable. Do not debate or evaluate them yet.
- Wait until the brainstorming is ended before you ask for any explanations or elucidation.
- Give everyone the opportunity to contribute, including your scribe.
- Do not worry if there is a brief silence. More ideas will probably be forthcoming in a moment or two. The best contributions often come after a lull.
- Reaching the end of a flipchart sheet is not an indication that the brainstorming is complete!

After about 15 minutes, the generation of ideas will have ended. Now is the time for group members to ask for clarification from any contributor. This should take no more than a few minutes, at most.

Next, look at the ideas on the flipchart and identify some common headings under which the contributions can be grouped. Do not worry if some ideas seem to belong to more than one heading. Set out those generalised headings on a fresh flipchart sheet will provide your responses to the question you have been addressing. You have what remains of the 30 minutes for this second activity.

© Routledge 1993

observer puts a tally mark each time, under the heading *organisational*, for example, that the teacher:

- directs child to materials or workspace
- grants child permission
- checks [that] pupil has completed work
- admonishes pupil
- controls pupil
- responds to pupil queries on use of materials.

Observations of this kind may reveal something about teaching skills, but in a very limited way and at a low level. Most appraisers would be hard put to evaluate simply from the sum of the tally marks what 15 against the second item and two against the fourth actually indicated. Were children constantly asking for permission when they should have been using their initiative? or does this indicate a keen interest in the use of resource materials? Does the fact that only two children were admonished indicate that control was poor or admirable?

In the hands of a resourceful – and tactful – observer keeping a tally can be useful, but more effectively as a basis for her own questions:

Did you check that the children had completed their work?
Yes, I asked them at the end. Almost all put their hands up.

Can you remember those who did not?
No. Well some of them.

Can you be sure that all those who put up their hands had in fact finished?
Well, I like to think that they can be trusted.

Can you say for sure that your idea of completion and theirs agree?
No, I don't suppose I can.

How many individual children's work do you think you actually saw in the last five minutes of the lesson?
Six or seven, at a guess.
Actually it was two. . .

This factual evidence is useful to the appraiser because it provides a basis for discussion in the debriefing on any of a range of topics: the need for accurate recording of individual attainment; the importance of giving praise to as many children as possible from a direct observation of their work; the need to share with the children the standards expected of them for completion of the task in hand; and so on. Yet we have to say that the same evidence was available to the skilled observer without the extensive tally sheet. Were we being observed we would feel highly suspicious of an observer activity in which all the time was being spent in recording. There is a danger that too much attention to the parts will blind the appraiser to the merits of the lesson as a whole.

THE SCOTTISH MODEL

The Scottish model offers three classroom observation checklists. The first two follow the same pattern. Against six headings in each case a number of questions are posed. To take one heading as an example:

Pupil Learning

• Was questioning structured?
• What were the teacher expectations?
• What skills were taught?
• What feedback was obtained from children?
• How did the teacher enthuse the pupils?

We find this far simpler than the Croydon model and decidedly less aggressive. The checklist – any checklist – can, of course, be used judgmentally; but the very fact that the observer is asked questions rather than given statements against which to match behaviour is likely to encourage the observer to enter into dialogue rather than to pontificate.

We mentioned three checklists in the Scottish Model: the third is unequivocally judgmental. From a dozen headings we draw three as examples:

Teaching style	Flexible/inflexible
Implementation of the curriculum	Successfully adapts curriculum guidelines/fails to implement outlines, objectives, policies
Questioning technique	Able to stimulate pupil response/ closed inhibiting questioning

Clearly these are not intended as black/white categories, but rather as a linear range on which the appraiser can determine, in the first instance, the teaching style. Yet there is a grave danger of going one step further, deliberately or subconsciously, and assessing teaching style on a five-point scale with *flexible* and *inflexible* at either end. Can we so determine style, without knowing the context? Are there not occasions, particularly when the National Curriculum attainment targets bark at the heels of teachers, when flexibility may be a luxury?

DUDLEY, WEST MIDLANDS

In 1991 Dudley LEA set up a task team on the management of effective learning. The excellent document (Dudley, 1992) which it produced has a wide range of uses, one of which is as an observation schedule for classroom practice.

Five areas were identified as essential for the creation of an effective learning environment, the fourth with three sub-areas:

- atmosphere/ethos;
- the learning environment;
- resources;
- the role of the teacher as:
  - planner
  - deliver and leader
  - facilitator and guide
- the role of the pupil.

Against each area are set from six to nine indicators, deliberately couched in highly positive language.

For each area there is a specific aim, as one might expect of the LEA which has been the leading proponent of the GRASP (Getting Results and Solving Problems) methodology. That for the second sub-area of the role of the teacher, the teacher as deliverer and leader, seems, with its six indicators, to be as useful an example as any of the potential value of this document as an observation schedule for classroom performance:

Aim: To demonstrate personal attributes, technical competencies and subject knowledge that will promote the students' learning in an atmosphere of respect and confidence

Indicators: • The teacher creates an impression of self-confidence and self-control.
   • The teacher shows flexibility and an ability to respond creatively to events.
   • The teacher's instructions, descriptions and explanations are brief and clear.
   • As a result of the teacher's skills as discussion leader, the students demonstrate a high level of participation.
   • The teacher uses effective questioning in order to raise the level of students' thinking.
   • The teacher demonstrates a sound knowledge of the subject matter.

The team acknowledges its indebtedness to the Lancaster/TVEI model of performance indicators by pointing out that the criteria can be arranged in three sets:

- *enabling indicators*, which need to be seen in place before anything can be achieved;
- *process indicators*, which the appraiser can expect to observe during the teaching and learning process;
- *outcome indicators*, which represent the outcomes of the process and can usefully be quantified (for example, examination results, attendance).

Training for the briefing session

In Chapter 5 on page 68 we presented you with the lesson notes of Vicky Hoyle's Year 7 history lesson. We now ask you to turn back to this. If this is not a group activity in a training workshop, work in collaboration with a colleague; or use it as a self-training exercise if you prefer.

The task instructions which follow are common to primary and secondary classroom observation. The task is best done in groups of two or three, but there is no reason why it cannot be a self-training exercise.

For primary teachers the lesson notes immediately follow the background details on page 91. Secondary teachers may wish to use in conjunction with the lesson notes the abbreviated version of the briefing discussion between Vicky and her appraiser which followed (pages 69–72). In that case, the task instructions should be adapted accordingly.

The classroom observation briefing: the appraiser plans

Task:

Refer to Figure 5.2 on page 65 to remind yourself of the seven components of the classroom observation briefing. Put yourself in the role of the appraiser:

- Which of these components do you feel fully informed about from the lesson plan? Will you need to discuss these at all? If so, why?
- What questions will you use to elicit other information you require in order to be well briefed?
- What are the focal areas that you wish to observe?
- How do you intend to act if in your presence a 'problem child' becomes disruptive?

© Routledge 1993

MATERIALS FOR CLASSROOM OBSERVATION TRAINING

There are three sources of material for training in classroom observation: video, case study and direct experience. Although videos of classroom situations have their advocates we have some reservations about this strategy for a number of reasons. First, except for very young children or in situations where there is a high level of pupil activity, pupils are decidedly conscious of the presence of the camera and react accordingly. In the USA this appears not to be the case. There video is widely used in initial and in-service teacher

Training for the briefing session: primary

BACKGROUND

Juniper Street Primary School is a two-form entry school in an urban area. It is well maintained and there are attractive displays in corridors and classrooms, including the one the appraiser is about to visit.

Robert Wilkins is a mature entrant now in his third year of teaching and his second with this class. There are 27 on roll, including six children from ethnic minorities, four Pakistanis and two Afro-Caribbeans. The children are boisterous but, in general, cooperative. There is one exception, a disruptive boy who has been referred for statementing. This is the first of Robert's two classroom observations. Here are his lesson notes.

LESSON NOTES

Year 5 cross-curricular (science, art, language)

This lesson is about observation. We are using lenses and magnifying glasses, partly to help the children observe in more detail, partly to teach them how to use these instruments. I also want them to learn more about colour: in the previous lesson I used a prism and we talked about a rainbow that most had seen the previous morning.

The children are going to use drawing and painting to encourage their powers of observation, and also learn new words to enable them to describe what they see.

1. *Introduction:* care and use of lenses; names of fruit and vegetables.
2. *Oral work:* children to explain what they are looking for.
3. *Activity 1:* looking and comparing in pairs, with the naked eye and with the lens.
4. *Language work (oral):* describing fruit and vegetables.
5. *Language work (vocabulary):* key words on chalkboard.
6. *Activity 2:* drawing and painting the fruit. Writing names underneath.

Next lesson we shall continue by labelling the different parts of the fruit and vegetables and by writing descriptive or imaginative passages about them.

© Routledge 1993

training and by serving teachers wishing to evaluate their own classroom performance. However, we would do well to borrow from other cultures only when our situations are similar; and we have not yet reached the degree of sophistication with television technology that they have across the Atlantic.

Secondly, a choice must be made between the fixed camera and the camera operated by a colleague or a technician. The fixed camera is less obtrusive but has the disadvantages that it invariably focuses on the teacher, that it requires the teacher to be static and that it cannot take cognisance of pupil reaction, except indirectly as we observe the teacher's response to incidents which we have not witnessed but which we may have been able to deduce. The hand-held camera is able to move readily from teacher to learner, but has two main disadvantages: it is far more visible to the class and consequently intervenes in the learning process; and the operator, who may or may not have pedagogic skills, effectively edits the video by what he decides to have in frame at any given time.

Finally, if they are to be of real value in a training experience, videos must be well edited, both technically and from the point of view of the trainer, and produced to a professional standard. Some LEAs, and even some well equipped secondary schools, have excellent audio-visual units well able to do this.

There are also several highly professional productions now on the market (see Appendix 2). In some, classroom observations are already edited down to manageable time. Others run the full length of a lesson and need to be trimmed to suit the time available. Previewing and deciding what to use, and how to skip to the next useful section, may make heavy demands on a trainer.

Written case studies have the merit that they can be structured to bring out the salient points that the trainer desires, in particular those that are felt to be of especial relevance to that school or LEA. All case studies should, it must be said, be drawn from real situations, though obviously there will be some modification of the detail or condensing of several experiences. There is a temptation – which all good trainers must school themselves to resist – to over-dramatise or even sensationalise situations. The closer the case study is to reality the more effective it will be as training material.

For a school conducting its own in-service sessions in training for classroom observation, it is possible to create a 'live' case study. It may be feasible in some secondary schools for a third teacher – an appraiser-in-training – to be present in a lesson as observer, and then attend the debriefing. Both appraiser and appraisee will gain from the observations of a non-participant, while the observer will obviously benefit from having seen what happens in and after the classroom observation of a colleague. This is not a strategy we particularly recommend, but it must be recognised that funding for training future appraisers may not be forthcoming, even though the turnover of middle and senior managers in a typical LEA has ranged between seven and ten per cent in recent years. 'Sitting by Nellie', a traditional industrial training strategy now, fortunately, nearly defunct, may be forced on schools. Nor is it likely even to be a starter in the primary sector.

It may also be argued, with some justification, that those who are prepared to volunteer will be teachers of such confidence that there is not very much to learn from the case study. It is not that one wants bad lessons for case studies – the deficiency model is very destructive of morale – but rather that there must be situations within the lesson that will promote useful learning situations and even some controversy.

One possible and more practicable alternative is that an appraiser and appraisee on a dry-run classroom observation meet after its conclusion to debrief in front of a small group of colleagues, preferably within the same discipline in a secondary school or a similar age range within a primary. The debriefing will not be entirely natural, not merely because of the presence of colleagues but also because appraiser and appraisee will need, from time to time, to explain some detail. The great merit of the home-based case study, however contrived, is that it will reflect the ethos and culture of the school and the context of the learning process in a way in which no devised case study ever can. We have had the experience of being told, after a workshop, that the case study 'was remarkably similar to a situation in our school recently' and, the following week at the end of another workshop, that 'your case study was totally artificial and unreal'! Some you win, some you lose . . .

For those who find case studies useful as training materials, three will conclude this chapter. The first describes Vicky Hoyle's lesson on Roman Britain – her lesson notes are on page 68 – as it actually happened. The second follows directly from the lesson notes on page 91 of Robert Wilkins, Year 5 teacher at Juniper Road Primary School. The third centres on an early years class in another primary school. The background of this school and the lesson plan are to be found alongside the account of the lesson.

TRAINING PROGRAMMES

We have been asked why we did not include specimen training programmes in the first edition. The brief answer to this is that external trainers only produce a programme when they know what the client's needs are: in advance of every new workshop we have engaged in a dialogue with the school, consortium or LEA to discover what stage of understanding of the appraisal process prospective workshop members have already reached as well as the client's desired outcomes and priorities, always bearing in mind the limitations on the time available.

Model programmes, then, are not likely to be helpful. What may be useful is to demonstrate through a specimen programme how we believe programmes should be set out. Some readers may think that to run off duplicated programmes for each member of staff is a waste of resources and time within a school. We would disagree. Workshops should be run to professional standards and the first priority is that those attending them should know what to expect.

First must come a statement of the aims of the workshop. Without defined aims it is not possible to evaluate a workshop, formally or informally: if the trainer does not state clearly what she intends to do, it is impossible for anyone to consider the extent to which she has fulfilled those intentions.

We prefer not to work to a timetable which defines the time to be given to each session. We have a general idea of how long any item will take, but we believe that we must be adaptable, to speed up where it is obvious that the group members have finished an activity or readily grasped what we have been trying to convey, and to give more time when there are still uncertainties or disagreements. Where these come from only a few workshop members, we carry on the discussion in a refreshment break.

The times that are vital and must be adhered to are the beginning and end of the day, and meal breaks. Light refreshment breaks can usually stand a little flexibility, provided no member of the ancillary staff is being inconvenienced.

The structure of each activity should be clearly stated in the programme. It can be very disconcerting to workshop members if they are not sure whether the session begins with a plenary or whether they go straight into groups. When members move from plenary to group it is essential that they know at what time they must conclude their assignment. Time spent waiting for one group to appear is time lost for all. Sometimes the rubric for the activity is brief enough to be included in the programme. If it is not, then it should be part of a handout. The effectiveness of training is diminished if complex verbal instructions are given which could better have been conveyed in writing. Nevertheless, there is much to be said for giving a brief verbal introduction to the activity, which members can then flesh out from the written instructions.

The resource needs for the entire programme must be anticipated and made ready well in advance: flipchart sheets and coloured felt-tip pens in each group room and in the plenary room; overhead projector (OHP) and screen, already tested for focus and visibility by those who will be sitting at the rear and extreme flanks of the plenary audience. OHPs should be set out in order so that there are no delays, and handouts and worksheets next to be used should be ready for distribution, or alternatively batched so that they can be handed to someone as workshop members move from plenary to group-work locations.

If programmes and group lists and locations have not been distributed in advance, they should be placed on the seats for the opening plenary. There should be no more seats than there are workshop members: teachers are not unique in going to any lengths to avoid sitting in the front row! Indeed, avoid rows if possible. Arcs of chairs are better, provided the wings are not so far apart that the trainer gets Wimbledon neck ... Prevent people from rearranging your layout 'to be next to a friend', tactfully if possible, firmly if not. The plenary room is your workplace, to be set out as you judge best.

Figure 6.1 is the first part of a full-day training workshop, dealing with classroom observation. We reiterate that this was negotiated with the consortium headteachers and that the draft programme was checked with those who had commissioned the workshop before we finalised the exercises. The page numbers in the figure refer to the relevant materials in this second edition.

APPRAISAL WORKSHOP PROGRAMME
Consortium Training Day
2 September 199x

Aim for morning session (8.30 a.m. to 12.15 p.m.):
• to train appraisers and appraisees in classroom observation: the criteria, the briefing session, the lesson observation, the debriefing.

Session 1: *Introduction*: Appraising classroom performance
• For whom? How will it be done? By whom? What are the skills? Are there any guidelines on what to look for? Why is it so important?
Plenary followed by questions and discussion.

Session 2: Setting the criteria for good classroom performance.
Group work: Brainstorming session (page 86).

Session 3: Briefing for classroom observation
Introduction: the key components of the briefing session (Figure 5.2, page 65).
Group work: planning the session from the lesson notes: the task (page 90); the primary lesson plan (page 91).
Plenary demonstration of briefing session, followed by discussion.

REFRESHMENT BREAK

Session 4: Observing the lesson
Introduction: what will the appraiser be looking for? How will she plan for the debriefing? What are the key components of the debriefing session? Will self-evaluation be helpful: to the appraisee? to the appraiser?
Group work on case study (pages 97–9).

Session 5: Debriefing (Figure 5.3, page 76)
Demonstration, followed by plenary discussion.

Session 6: Any questions?
Plenary: end of morning programme

© Routledge 1993

Figure 6.1 Specimen programme for classroom observation training day

CONCLUSION

There is a golden rule for all stages of classroom observation: recognise strengths. Give support to weaknesses. Some readers may be critical of our case studies because, while there are weaknesses to be found, the teachers may broadly be described as successful. What about the unsuccessful teachers? Those who are wholly resistant to change? Those whose care for the children in their classes is not particularly evident?

The task which you see above applies equally to whichever of the three observations you now choose.

There are such teachers, we know that well; and as a consequence there will doubtless be some very difficult classroom observations, where the teacher is resentful of the intrusion of the appraiser and makes it all too obvious, to the students as well as his line manager. There will be occasions when a class is quite out of control, and the only thing that the appraiser can do is to take charge, and abandon the observation. Yet there is no point in our offering largely negative, crisis situations, even though there may be something to be learned from them. 'The essence of appraisal should be positive. Appraisal should be about "prizing" and "valuing" what is seen' (Montgomery, 1985). In this chapter and the one which preceded it, we have sought to provide every opportunity within classroom observation for prizing and valuing.

The classroom observation debriefing: the appraiser plans

Task:

In your training workshop group, or with a colleague, or as a self-training exercise:
Look back to items two to five within Figure 5.3, the guide to debriefing. Read carefully the details of the lesson you have selected. (If you are working from a photocopy, you will find a highlighter invaluable.)

• What are the key areas on which, as appraiser, you intend to focus during the 15–20 minutes available for debriefing?
• Which of these do you think will occupy the most time in discussion? What will therefore be your order of priority?
• What kind of questions will you ask to encourage the appraisee towards self-evaluation? Give some examples, one at least in an area where you, or the appraisee, may have some concern over an element in the conduct of the lesson.
• Is there any occasion in this lesson where the observer may have felt it necessary to intervene in any way?

© Routledge 1993

Classroom observation: the secondary lesson

THE LESSON

The museum loan is arranged on separate tables, easily accessible. As the children come into the room, some glance curiously at the appraiser but most are more eager to look at the exhibits. However, Vicky stands by the door and directs them to their seats so that they will get on with the lesson she has planned.

When they are all settled she begins with a few questions about the previous lesson in order to get them thinking in context. Then she goes on quickly to say to them: 'In this lesson I want you to be detectives. That is what archaeologists do when they dig up something old out of the ground that they may never have seen before. They have to work out what it is, what it was used for, and even what kind of people used it. That is exactly what you are going to do.' She goes on to show them maps and pictures of Rome and Britain and draws from them by questioning the differences in the ways of life of the two countries.

continued . . .

Most of the children are responsive and eager to show their knowledge. A few seem to be out of touch. She tries to draw them in by unobtrusively directing easy questions to them.

Vicky draws this activity to a close by picking up some of the main points that the children have made and then goes on to tell them an instalment of a story she has devised about the adventures of a British boy slave in Rome. All are interested in the story, including the ones who did not join in the question and answer session.

She now directs the four groups each to a different exhibition table. Most are well behaved, but a few jostle for a place. Seeing this, she reminds them of their responsibility to take great care of the exhibits. They work in pairs, each pair with a questionnaire. One boy clowns with a ploughshare, and others at the table try to stop him. Vicky goes over to the table and questions the boy about the way the implement is made. He answers intelligently and the work continues.

The noise level grows, but the children move on readily to the next table when they are told. The observer stays with one group of children as they move, while Vicky moves among the other three groups. When the children have done the round of all four tables they are told to settle down quietly to complete their questionnaires. Most finish quickly. Vicky collects the completed questionnaires. 'Now, in the last ten minutes of our lesson, I want you to show me how much you have learnt. Choose one of the three topics I have just written up on the board.'

While they are getting on with this work, she calls five children who have obviously had difficulty with the questionnaire to join her at one of the tables. She talks to them about the artefacts and answers their questions. Shortly before the bell goes she tells them to stop writing and instructs them to complete their topic for homework.

© Routledge 1993

Classroom observation: the primary lesson

THE LESSON

Robert Wilkins is in the classroom waiting with Miss Jones, his appraiser, for the children to come in from morning play. He has ready a wide range of fruits – some cut up into quarters or slices – drawing paper, paints, palettes, water pots. He has just fetched the tray of lenses from the science store.

As they enter the room the children notice the display and start asking excitedly what they are going to do in the lesson. Robert claps his hands for silence and tells the children to sit down quietly or they will not find out. Freddie arrives late and the teacher and the class wait until he is seated and more or less attentive.

'This is a lesson on observation. Who can tell me what that means?' Several hands go up and a good definition is found collectively. 'This morning we are going to observe really closely those fruits on the table. First you will use your eyes and then you will look at them through the lens.' He calls up two children who demonstrate under guidance the use and care of the lens.

'When you have looked carefully I want one of each pair to draw what can be seen with the naked eye and the other to draw a section that can be seen through the magnifier. You will have to be very observant to get all the detail. Miss Jones has come in today to see how well you do it.'

First, he shows the various fruits and checks that the children know the names of them all. Some names he writes on the chalkboard. At one point one of the Asian girls says something in Punjabi which causes her friend to giggle. Robert asks her to share the joke. She hides her face in her hands but eventually tells him 'We don't say it like that, Mr Wilkins.' He asks her for the right pronunciation of the Asian fruit and copies her intonation until he gets it right.

Pairs compare the specimen they have been given with that of their neighbours and the noise level rises. The teacher calls for silence: 'I have not yet told you exactly what I want you to do, have I? I will not go on until you are quite quiet.' The children put down their specimens, face the front and settle down. Robert waits for a few laggards, including Freddie.

continued . . .

'Now what do you think I want you to look for?' Replies come thick and fast: colour, texture, blemishes, seed configurations, irregularity of shape and so on, though not in these words. Robert writes down key words and asks a few further questions. Several children ask if they can eat the fruit. Robert replies, 'I don't think you would like to bite a raw lemon, would you?' There is laughter. 'After the lesson I will let anyone taste one fruit that you have not seen before. But you can touch them. That will help with the drawing.'

Several children take up their pencils. 'No, don't start yet. Spend some time observing. Compare what you see with the eye with what you see through the lens.' They get to work and do as they have been told. The noise level is high, but not unduly so. Robert goes from pair to pair, encouraging them. So does Miss Jones.

Suddenly there is a wail. 'Please, Mr Wilkins, Freddie is not letting me look. Why do I have to have him for a partner?' Freddie just grins and shows no sign of sharing. Robert takes Freddie by the hand to a spare desk and gives him a lens and a half of apple. He stays with him for a few minutes, drawing his attention to the star shape in the middle.

Now he tells the class to put down the lenses. He selects several children to describe what they have seen, prompting them with questions about texture and colour. They now are going to go on to drawing and painting, and Robert reminds them of the colour spectrum and their experiments with mixing colours in the last lesson. He tells them how long they have until the end of the lesson and goes from desk to desk, encouraging them and asking questions.

There is a sudden disturbance as Freddie starts to flick paint at other children. Robert takes away his paints, rebukes him and gives him the crayon colouring he had started the previous lesson. He now stays close by to keep an eye on Freddie and lets the pairs work on their own unless he sees that he is needed.

Three minutes before the end of the lesson, Robert tells everyone to stop, organises the storage of finished and unfinished work and delegates the clearing up to two girls who volunteer. As they leave the room, several children try the more exotic fruits and make faces at the unfamiliar taste.

© Routledge 1993

Classroom observation: the early years lesson

BACKGROUND

Willow Infants School is a two-form entry school in a socially and ethnically mixed area on the city outskirts. The school is well regarded by parents.

We are observing a class of thirty-two first-year infants, all of whom have passed their fifth birthday and have had at least one term of pre-schooling. The teacher, Jill Worthing, has an NNEB-trained assistant, Ellen Brown. In the class is Derek, a severely deaf child with poor speech, and three who have frequent asthma attacks, but funding does not permit any other support for these medical cases, except for an hour a week of hearing therapy for Derek.

LESSON PLAN

The lesson centres on writing and activities requiring hand-eye coordination and control, as a preparation for writing. The children are in groups which rotate at least once a week, but for those in Group 1 writing is taught on an individual basis. Within the group each child has a specific task and, once that task is satisfactorily completed, chooses the next activity, under guidance.

At 10.30 a.m. they will go to a first year assembly before going out to play, but otherwise the session is continuous.

The lesson will begin with the children all together while the teacher shares with them the work they will be doing, and end with them all together again telling or showing what they have done.

The groups are as follows:

- *Group 1:* in the writing corner at a table within easy reach of word banks and materials. They will begin by drawing a picture of the lesson theme and then write the 'story'.
- *Group 2:* with Mrs Brown at the science table where they will observe shell patterns and draw shapes and spirals.
- *Group 3:* at painting easels near to the science table where Mrs Brown can supervise them.
- *Group 4:* on the carpet area with construction toys, their task to make something 'that can fly'. Derek is with this group.
- *Group 5:* with pencils, paper, scissors and large shapes of garden creatures. They are to make cut-outs to fix on a prepared picture of a garden.

In addition there is a table with jigsaw and shape-matching puzzles and a listening table equipped with tape recorders and story tapes.

continued . . .

THE LESSON

At 9 a.m. the observer arrives to see the whole class sitting on a central carpet area. After calling the register the teacher encourages the children to talk about the events of the previous night. The one that most children can talk about is the family Bonfire Night party in the school grounds to which many of the children came with their parents. The children are very excited and all want to talk at once, but the teacher is firm about taking turns. She tells them the story of children marooned on an island without any adults when their plane crashes and who also all talk at once when they try to discuss how they might escape. She explains about the conch (which she calls 'a big sea shell') which whoever wants to speak must be holding. She finds a large woolly ball to serve as the conch. The children accept the discipline imposed by this device.

After 10 minutes she changes the topic and shows them some snails in a box in which there is a bed of grass and earth. She explains how the morning rain makes the snails active, demonstrating with the aid of a small watering can. There are also snails in smaller boxes with magnifying lids which she passes round for the children to look at more closely. Then she settles the children in their groups.

For a while everyone is quiet and busy. The teacher is helping Gary in Group 1 to write 'This is me' under his picture. At this point a quarrel breaks out in the carpet area and the teacher goes to mediate. She prompts the children to explain what they are doing and asks Derek by signs to tell her about his 'flying machine'. He has managed to fit three pieces of Duplo together. She does not understand what he says but the other children explain.

Group 2 have tired of drawing and are eager to paint. With difficulty, Mrs Brown persuades Groups 2 and 3 to change places. Two children go to the listening table and everyone settles down again. The observer notices that the class teacher is put out. She surmises that Mrs Brown has overstepped the mark by allowing the groups to change their activity in this way.

In Group 1 Jennifer has started to write using the word bank independently, and the teacher sees that she needs to add more words. Scott has also gone ahead without help, but it is developmental writing. He tells the teacher what he thinks he has written and the teacher gives him a version to copy.

© Routledge 1993

In Group 5 there are problems in cutting out the shapes. The observer sits with them and helps.

A few minutes later two children from the science table decide to help their friend Derek. He does not want to be helped and flies into a screaming tantrum. The teacher picks him up to comfort him and, when he calms down, tells Mrs Brown to take him into the book corner and show him a zoo picture story book. She names the animals, making sure he watches her lips as she carefully enunciates the words. The class has been disturbed and the teacher spends a few minutes making sure that all are again usefully occupied.

Darren, who has finished making an aeroplane, has gone to the science table and calls out that a snail has escaped. Mrs Brown is still with Derek so the teacher goes to return the snail to the box, to find that the lid is missing. She puts the snail in the large box and then notices that, unobserved at the listening table, a girl has unspooled a length of tape, and is looking at it through the missing magnifying lid. The teacher restores the lid, takes the tape away and sends the girl to tidy the Home Corner.

The teacher continues to work with the children at the writing table for another 10 minutes but by then there is some aimless moving from place to place and she feels that they have reached the end of their attention span. She leaves the writing table, claps her hands to get every child's attention and, when all are absolutely quiet, says 'I am going to listen to the writing group. While I do that I want everyone else to tidy their corners very quietly. When everything is tidy come and sit on the carpet and some of you will be able to show us what you have been making.'

When the clearing up is done to her satisfaction and they are all sitting on the carpet, she passes the woolly ball to one child asking her to show what she has been making and to talk briefly about it. The girl is then told to pass the ball to a boy from another group. There are cries of 'Me! Me!' but she reminds them of the rules. after the fourth talk she looks at the clock and says 'we have to stop now for assembly. Does anybody want to go to the toilet?' Mrs Brown goes with the children to supervise.

As the children file into assembly, the teacher says: 'Mrs Brown, could I have a word with you at lunchtime?'

© Routledge 1993

Chapter 7

Task observation and data collection

The concentration on classroom observation in the two previous chapters and in the regulations and guidelines should not lead us to forget that the observation of tasks is also part of the appraisal process for all. Schools, governing bodies, LEAs and government are at one in wanting to see higher standards of performance by the pupils of our schools. There is less unity of understanding that pupil performance is dependent on many factors in addition to good standards of teaching. Over many of these the school has little or no control: social factors that affect the ability to learn and the behaviour of children; poor school facilities and a lack of adequate resources; insufficient teachers and support staff. Yet there is one factor to which much lip service is paid but which is far too little appreciated: that good management at every level from the classroom to the governing body is a key factor in school improvement. The tasks which lie behind the actual classroom performance as well as those which determine the framing and execution of the policy of the school must be part of the appraisal process. Many of these tasks can be observed and their effectiveness evaluated with the appraisee as part of the process for improving performance.

For the appraisal of the classroom teacher task observation is not a time-consuming activity for either appraiser or appraisee. Indeed, in most cases it will not even involve the appraisee, other than in the possible provision of data.

We have already referred to the excellent Dudley LEA document *The Management of Effective Learning* to be found in full in Appendix 3. The title itself is a clear indication that management is a concern of every teacher. One section, the learning environment, includes an indicator which will illustrate the kind of activity the appraiser will be observing outside the classroom observation, for example:

• wall displays are attractively arranged and are relevant to the current teaching and learning.

It is not, we believe, sufficient for the appraiser to look at the classroom environment only at the time of the observation lesson. As a good line manager she will glance from time to time at the use of exhibition space, at materials for learning that the teacher has created and is displaying, at measures being taken visually to motivate the students; and she will doubtless take the opportunity to comment favourably where these displays are well prepared and of value to the learning process.

The appraiser also needs to ascertain that records are being maintained regularly and in accordance with the school's policy for record keeping. It might be useful to discuss with a teacher the comparison of his assessments and the SATs, particularly since the disparity between the two is still, unfairly in the opinion of many educationists, leading to criticism of the ability of teachers to assess accurately. A sample of students' workbooks should be provided by the class teacher, with a fair coverage of the ability range.

There is a nice distinction between data and task. The records, for example, are the data; maintaining them is the task. For teachers with specific areas of managerial responsibility – curriculum coordinators and heads of department, pastoral heads of house, year or age-defined sections of a school, and of course deputy headteachers and others at the level of senior management – task observation goes well beyond this.

MIDDLE AND SENIOR MANAGERS

All those that we have mentioned above will from time to time run meetings with members of staff for whom they are responsible. The more senior may chair or act as coordinators of working parties or staff committees. Some will plan and run in-service sessions. Others will, as part of their role, be staff representatives on committees and organisations outside the school. Their appraisers may see them in any of these activities in the normal course of events, but sometimes may need to negotiate a specific occasion on which to be present. We argue strongly for negotiation. To drop in on a meeting which happens to be dealing with the details of plans for the preparation of examination papers for a mock GCSE, for example, is not likely to lead to very fruitful observation; or there will be an occasion when the manager knows that an item of discussion will be fraught and the presence of a senior member of staff will only lead to appeals for adjudication over her head.

The meetings to which we have been referring here are those which the appraiser in her capacity as line manager would in the natural course of events attend regularly or from time to time. To observe a meeting at which the appraiser would not normally appear is possible in certain circumstances, but in others might create difficulties.

The presence of an appraiser at a report evening for parents of a year, for example, will not attract attention, even when the line manager is not normally there. She is unlikely to be noticed as parents concern themselves with keeping appointments and with discussing the progress of their children.

For any observation at this level there must, as for classroom observation, be a briefing and debriefing session as part of the task observation. The briefing before the appraiser observes a meeting follows the same pattern as for classroom observation – the equivalent item is shown in parentheses – and should include:

- What has taken place at recent meetings? Are any of the items likely to recur at this meeting? (**Establishing the context**)

- What do you hope to achieve in this meeting? What is your agenda? How much time do you expect to spend on each item? Do you expect to reach conclusions? (**Aims and expectations**)

- Have difficulties arisen at any previous meeting? Have they been resolved or are they likely to affect this meeting? (**Potential difficulties and constraints**)

- During the meeting do you wish to refer to me any points within my managerial responsibilities? Or would you rather that we made it clear at the beginning that I am there only as observer? (**The observation style**)

- What aspect or aspects of your management of meetings do you wish me to concentrate on? (**Agreeing the focus**)

And, at the debriefing:

- How do you think the meeting went? (**Self-evaluation**)

- Did you achieve what you intended to achieve? If not, what prevented you? (**Aims and expectations**)

- What were the strengths of your conduct of the meeting? If there were diversions from your intentions, were they useful or did they detract from the effectiveness of the meeting? (**Strengths and weaknesses**)

© Routledge 1993

Figure 7.1 Task observation: meetings

At more formal meetings, chaired or addressed by the appraisee, the appraiser can easily become just another member of the audience.

Task observation of a manager involved in a staff working party or committee, whether as coordinator or as representative of his subject, year or other area of management responsibility is not likely to cause problems. We would emphasise the need for open behaviour: the unanticipated and unexplained presence of a senior manager at such a meeting might lead to objections from other members. Since many of those present will also be engaged as appraiser or appraisee in task observation, it is sound policy for the staff as a whole to have been given, as part of the appraisal awareness-raising process, full information on how it is conducted, when it might take place, and why it is being undertaken. This general giving of information should not be taken to preclude the good manners of informing those attending any such meeting of the intended presence of the appraiser.

For some meetings a different strategy will be required. A teacher may be one of several members of a school liaison committee with industry and commerce, or with the social services, for example. If the appraiser is not a member of that committee, it is extremely unlikely that any way can be found which would enable her to be present. Indeed, even to start enquiries to this end would flutter pigeons in a number of dovecotes.

There are two possibilities. While an appraiser could not discuss a lesson which she had not seen, it may be possible to 'observe' a task of this kind through discussion before and after the meeting. Alternatively, if the appraisee were willing for one of the other teacher members of the committee to be approached, then the appraiser could be briefed by that person. It has to be said that this vicarious observation is not very satisfactory: it is time-consuming and there are potentialities for breakdown that are far less likely to arise in the direct relationship between appraiser and appraisee. Since task observation can only be undertaken on a sampling basis, appraisers would usually do well to agree safer ground than this.

Shadowing

This is a strategy for task observation that can be very productive, particularly for senior managers. The appraiser of a senior member of a secondary school pastoral team as she conducts her weekly 'surgery' or of the deputy headteacher of a primary school engaged in budget negotiations with individual curriculum coordinators will undoubtedly learn much about the managerial abilities of her member of staff in a relatively short time. Yet there are also very evident dangers. The presence of the appraiser inevitably alters the relationship within the dialogue. There will be those who seek to win the support of the appraiser for their case – indeed, may even appeal to her over the head of the teacher being observed. The appraisee may find himself behaving in an atypical way because of the stress of the situation and do

- Responsibility for classroom, corridor or area displays

- Responsibility for teacher or pupil records

- Membership of staff committee or working party

- Leadership of staff committee or working party

- Planning and/or running INSET session

- Representation on extra-school committee or organisation

- Report evening for parents

- Open evening for parents: careers convention, curriculum demonstration or display, for example

- Sports day, drama or music occasion

- 'Surgery' for parents or pupils

- Advice evening for parents and pupils: choice of secondary school/16+ education/higher education

- One-to-one discussion with staff

- Shadowing by 'walkabout'

- Conducting an assembly

- Observing an appraisal interview

- (Headteachers only) meeting of governing body

© Routledge 1993

Figure 7.2 List of possible task observations

damage to a relationship with parent or staff colleague. It is without question very difficult to persuade those within the confine of a room that you, the appraiser, are 'not there', are the fly on the wall. We urge appraisers, therefore, to use this kind of shadowing with considerable circumspection, and only when the member of staff concerned is genuinely confident of being able to handle all likely outcomes.

There is, of course, another form of shadowing which is less threatening. A profitable strategy, both in likely outcomes and in the use of time, is to accompany the appraisee around the school for half an hour, as she undertakes some prepared – and, doubtless, some unanticipated – management tasks. At the end of that time the appraiser will have observed much, both of the appraisee's management skills and of the context in which she deploys them.

HEADTEACHER TASK OBSERVATION

We evaluated a trial in one LEA of headteacher appraisal in the term before the appraisal process officially started. Of some 20 respondents, nearly half the peer appraisers engaged in shadowing and several spent at least a half day on this activity. There is much to be learnt from shadowing the chief executive, whether of a school or a company, as a number of researchers in the UK and the USA have found out; but the purpose of this task observation is more limited than that of research, and we would urge that the time spent on it bears some relationship to the outcomes. In our view, an hour is sufficient.

There were those appraisers in the trial who argued that shadowing was primarily valuable in that it enabled them to gain an understanding of the context within which they were appraising. Undoubtedly this is important for an effective appraisal, but there are dangers. The school is the context, certainly, but it must be remembered that it is the manager who is being appraised. In the above-mentioned trial, a few appraising headteachers, with the best of intentions, introduced into the appraisal interview recommendations arising from their observation as they walked the school with the headteacher: a display panel here would brighten the corridor; science staff should be encouraged to use the staff room at break and not brew up in the prep room; the coat pegs in the nursery do not encourage children to be self-sufficient. Matters like this might be mentioned, as between colleagues, in an informal talk after shadowing. Even then, one would have to be very sure of one's relationship: these comments might easily be interpreted as 'In my school we do it better'. But the overriding objection is that the appraisal is becoming perilously close to a school review or inspection, and that is not in the remit of the appraiser.

These appraisers have misunderstood the function of shadowing in task observation. Although there will be unexpected and valuable byproducts of the activity, the shadowing must relate primarily to one of the agreed focal areas. Relationships feature strongly among the skills expected of senior managers,

Selecting appropriate task observations

Tasks:
This is an activity best done in pairs and, if this is a training workshop, finally discussed in groups or plenary.

Consider carefully the task observations listed on page 110.

As a pair, agree the level of managerial responsibility of the member of staff to whom you intend to apply this menu of possible task observations: primary school curriculum coordinator, head of early years, deputy headteacher, headteacher; secondary head of department, year head, member of senior management team, deputy headteacher, headteacher. (You may of course choose outside this list if you wish.)
  Agree the amount of time you would expect to give to task observation at this level of seniority.

Stage 1:
The members of the pair work separately, using photocopies of the list. Decide who is A and who is B.

A: consider the list as *appraisee*. Put a cross against those that you judge to be inapplicable to the level of seniority you have agreed on. Then number the remaining task observations in rank order: those that you believe to be the most acceptable to you as appraisee, down to the least acceptable. Put a zero against any that you find totally unacceptable.

B: consider the list as *appraiser*. Put a cross against those that you judge to be inapplicable to the level of seniority you have agreed on. Then number the remaining task observations in rank order: those that you believe will contribute most to the appraisal process, down to those likely to make the least effective contribution. Put a zero against any that you believe will make no worthwhile contribution.

A and B separately: against each of those you have ranked, log an estimate of the time you would allocate to it, up to the point at which your agreed time runs out. Put an asterisk against any below that point which you regret being forced to leave out. Note that there are some task observations which take little or no time, either because the appraiser will be present or because the observation can be made in the normal course of the appraiser's movement around the school.

Stage 2:
Share consideration of the two lists. Discuss significant differences and seek reasons for them.
Finally, if you are working in a training workshop:

Stage 3:
In your groups now investigate whether:
• there are any task observations highly ranked by both appraisers and appraisees
  – when the level of seniority is more or less comparable?
  – regardless of the level of seniority being considered?
• there are any observable areas of general discord between appraisers and appraisees?
In both cases, try to provide reasons.

© Routledge 1993

and shadowing gives the observer the opportunity to see at first hand how the appraisee responds to staff, parents and students, all providing impromptu situations calling for skills in person management. Shadowing is also valuable if the use of time is a focal area. It does not, however, meet all the observational needs of the appraiser. More controlled task observations may serve better there.

Observation of the headteacher running a staff meeting, coordinating a staff working party, hosting a ceremonial occasion – sports day, concert, open day, prize day if this is within the school's culture – is akin to the similar task observations of her managerial staff conducted by the headteacher. The presence of the appraiser at a full staff meeting may be more difficult for the staff to agree, particularly if any contentious matter is likely to arise. Yet the appraiser's presence at a bland, entirely non-controversial occasion may not be a very profitable task observation. To be a guest colleague at a ceremonial occasion is unlikely to present any problems: some headteachers make it a policy to attend a few such occasions each year, if only to show their colleagues that they are not entirely overwhelmed by the tyranny of managing their own schools!

Potentially quite the most valuable observation would be to see the headteacher engaged in the task that would doubtless call for the full deployment of managerial skills: involvement in a meeting of the board of governors. Unfortunately, this is also the most difficult observation for which to obtain agreement. We suspect that few headteachers would be happy to be observed in what becomes at times, often unpredictably, a stress situation calling for interpersonal skills of the highest level. More to the point, we wonder how many governing bodies would accept the presence of a peer headteacher during their deliberations? Even when great care is taken by the LEA to ensure that the appraiser's school is not in competition with that of the appraisee over admissions, governors may still have suspicions that their policies are being appraised, not the management skills of their headteacher.

There are two possibilities that obviate these difficulties, both of which marry task observation with data collection, to which we turn shortly. The first takes advantage of the fact that in many LEAs the local inspector is present at meetings of the board of governors, either as clerk, if the board so wishes, or CEO's representative. Although it is generally understood that the peer appraiser takes the lead in the appraisal interview, it would not be untoward for the inspector to contribute to the discussion from his observation of a governors' meeting. Alternatively, if the two appraisers wished to stick absolutely to the rubric, the peer appraiser could ask the local inspector to brief her on any relevant matters before the appraisal interview.

The second possibility involves the chair of governors. The regulations and guidelines make it quite clear that governors may only make a contribution of data – and that within the conditions of the code of practice – through their chair. There is no reason, however, why the chair of governors should not be the task observer of the headteacher's contribution to a selected governors' meeting, and meet with the peer appraiser to offer those data. One reads in the educational and popular press sensational cases of the breakdown of relationships between chairs of governing bodies and their headteachers. It is healthy to remind ourselves that most headteachers and most chairs of governors – indeed, most governors – have a clear concept that their responsibilities can only be discharged in partnership and the good of the school is their overriding consideration. However, we accept that many teachers, including headteachers, are reluctant to see any non-professional involvement in the appraisal process, and we respect this view.

As so often in this book, we urge that there be always open behaviour at all levels so that appraisees do not feel threatened and inclined to suspect ulterior motives where none can reasonably exist. Headteachers will set an example to all their staff by their attitude to the observation of their own professionalism; and those who appraise headteachers will be demonstrating to all that appraisal is non-judgmental but crucially about personal professional development and school improvement.

DATA COLLECTION

In Chapter 3, in which we dealt with the appraisal regulations and their implications, we made clear that the Code of Practice ought, theoretically at least, to relieve any anxieties about data collection. Yet in reality teachers are likely to remain suspicious, whatever the apparent safeguards, when reference is made to others, even to colleagues, in their absence. We advised that agreement between appraiser and appraisee on those to be approached should be reached at an early stage in the appraisal process; and we recommended that the initial meeting was the ideal time for such a discussion. If there is not a clear understanding between appraiser and appraisee of the purpose of data collection, then there will be, the Code of Practice notwithstanding, unease and even conflict.

Even the phrase is somewhat unfortunate: 'collecting data' seems a strange activity for members of the teaching profession. What does it actually entail?

For a class teacher in a primary school whose line manager is a senior member of staff with shared responsibility for curriculum development, there may well be no need for data collection at all: the teacher's strengths and possible weaknesses in the delivery of the National Curriculum in the full range of subject areas are likely to be well known. Where a school decides that a particular subject area should be explored in depth in that year's appraisal interviews – an excellent strategy for studying the interface between personal professional development and the school's curriculum development plan – then there is a strong case for the involvement of the curriculum coordinator. We suggested in Chapter 3 that, in pursuit of the ideal of open behaviour, there was good reason for the collection of data from such a person as a curriculum coordinator to be conducted in the presence of the appraisee. We would go even further and suggest that in a two-form entry school, for example, a meeting of the curriculum coordinator and the appraisal team with the class teachers of Years 1–3 and a second meeting with those of Years 4–6 would serve to review the development of that area of the curriculum at the same time as the contribution made by these class teachers. The time cost would be low; the threat of the data collection would be much diminished.

Kate's Hill Primary School, Dudley, is a pioneer school in the application of British Standard 5750 to education. One of the senior management team has been appointed to take responsibility for quality control. Although the term 'quality control' may be unfamiliar in schools, the importance of the concept is becoming increasingly recognised; and there will be similar appointments, though with different job specifications, in both primary and secondary schools. Such a senior manager, almost certainly an appraiser in her own right, would be an acknowledged and acceptable source of data about the contribution of individual staff to curriculum development and the achievement of standards of performance.

Secondary school subject teachers are, almost invariably, tutors in whatever pastoral system the school has adopted. They are in dual line management, to a head of department, and to a head of year or house: it would be regrettable if appraisal were to diminish the equality of status between pastoral and curricular leaders that has developed over the last two or three decades. Whether the selected or agreed appraiser is the one or the other is irrelevant. The year head must seek data on the appraisee's contribution to the work of the department team; the head of department must seek data on the appraisee's contribution to the work of the pastoral team. In our experience, this is readily recognised and widely accepted.

In both primary and secondary schools it is unlikely that data collection for class teachers will go beyond what we have described, unless the appraisee particularly cites an area of performance on which she would welcome a colleague's contribution. For middle managers the situation will be similar: where they have multiple responsibilities, they will expect a second senior manager to be consulted by their line manager.

For senior managers, particularly but by no means exclusively in secondary schools, the scope of managerial contact may well be far greater, with governors, parent committees, outside agencies and the like. Here the data collection will quite properly go beyond staff colleagues; and here, therefore, is the greater opportunity for misunderstanding of the purpose and nature of data collection. Appraisers must take especial care when engaged with non-professionals to ensure that the Code of Practice is understood and rigorously adhered to, and that the initial meeting fully explores whatever fears or reservations the appraisee may have. It will not be easy for an appraiser to tell a chair of governors or a parent, however well intentioned the observation, that hearsay evidence is not admissible; but the code is there for all to see and is binding on all in any way involved in appraisal. Wise headteachers will have ensured that discussion on the Code of Practice has taken place on the governing body well before any incident of contravention or misinterpretation can possible occur; and, risking gilding the lily, appraisers should rehearse the key points in the code with any provider of data at the beginning of the discussion.

Nothing is more likely to bring appraisal into disrepute within the teaching profession or to allow the relatively few remaining opponents of the process to say 'I told you so!' than for data collection to be subverted, by chance or design. Viewed positively, data collection is essential if the full range of each teacher's contribution to effective learning and effective management is to be available to the appraisal process. Mishandled, this could well be the Achilles' heel.

Chapter 8

The skills of interviewing

Appraisal demands a high level of interviewing skills: active listening, appropriate questioning, negotiation and, not infrequently, counselling skills. We are well aware that time for appraisal training has been limited and will, now specific funding has ended and other needs have to be met, be even more difficult for schools to make available.

Yet relatively few teachers have had training in these skills and their acquisition is of vital importance to the success of appraisal in our schools. We have therefore always made a point of including in our workshops a half-day session on these skills, knowing full well that we can do no more in this time than raise awareness and give some limited experience of the techniques that will be useful to appraisers and appraisees alike.

It is an absolute priority that there should be trust and respect between the two parties. Without this all the interviewing skills in the world would be worthless.

ACTIVE LISTENING

In their excellent and much reprinted book *Getting to Yes*, Fisher and Ury have this to say about active listening:

> The need for listening is obvious, yet it is difficult to listen well . . . Listening enables you to understand their perceptions, feel their emotions, and hear what they are trying to say. Active listening improves not only what you hear, but also what they say. If you pay attention and interrupt occasionally to say, 'Did I understand correctly that you are saying that . . .?' [they] will realize that they are not just killing time, not just going through a routine. They will also feel the satisfaction of being heard and understood.
>
> (Fisher and Ury, 1981: 35)

Most teachers consider themselves to be naturally good listeners because their relationship with students in both pastoral and teaching and learning situations demands this. Active listening is, however, a skill that can be cultivated and learnt; and there are aspects that are peculiar to the interview situation. It is on these that we will concentrate.

Rapport

It is essential that, even before any interview has begun, the appraiser has created the conditions whereby rapport can most easily be established. Clearly there should be no interruptions: 'Sorry, what were you saying?' kills rapport stone dead.

Other physical conditions for full attention need to be considered. The placing of chairs is important: neither in such a position that eye contact is difficult, nor placed face-to-face so that appraisee and appraiser are eyeballing each other. Chairs should be comfortable, but not to the extent that they cocoon the sitter or make it difficult for either party to maintain attention, as eyelids begin to droop. Any difference between the chairs implies, justifiably or not, a difference in status.

Sheaves of paper are a distraction, even a threat. If they are necessary to the interview, then a small table on which they can be put is helpful. For some people a cup of tea or coffee acts as an icebreaker. For others it may be an embarrassment: being asked a question at the very moment when you are raising the cup to your lips can be most disconcerting!

A few moments at the beginning of the interview dealing with reassuring, non-controversial matters have a part to play in establishing rapport:

> I have heard that staff are well satisfied with the new arrangements for access to resource materials that you have instituted. This must be very pleasing to you.

> Parents have commented favourably on the new appointments system you introduced this year for report discussions. Tutors have commented on how smoothly the evening went.

These are not bromides. Rapport can never be established by asking questions or making statements easily recognised by the appraisee as meaningless or insignificant. What is said at this stage is not expected to give rise to discussion in depth. Yet, despite full preparation, it can happen that a matter expected to be dealt with cursorily in the interview suddenly becomes a matter of great moment. In such a situation in an interview there will have to be a rapid, almost instinctive decision on how to respond: to be prepared to add this item to the agenda proper, recognising that, if it then takes the place of another item, either party or both may feel shortchanged; or to suggest that it be discussed further on another occasion.

The effectiveness of the appraiser can often be measured by the amount of talking he does: in general, the less he talks, the more effective the interview.

Needless to say, there is no standard measurement of what the optimum extent of appraiser participation is; much depends on the degree to which the appraisee needs to be drawn out. It is, however, almost certain that the balance of talking will be towards the appraiser at the beginning, when rapport is being established, and at the end, when summarising most occurs.

There should be no preconception of the way in which the appraisee and appraiser will relate. We often hear it said that two people who work closely together in a school should have no difficulty in relating well in an appraisal interview. There is no guarantee that this will be so and the appraiser needs to be aware that establishing and maintaining rapport is crucial to a successful outcome.

The interview purpose

Clarification of the purpose of the interview is important; however much its purpose may seem crystal clear to the appraiser, reassurance of the appraisee will not be time misspent. With appraisal, as with any interview activity which may appear to the appraisee to have about it an element of threat or discomfort, the early restatement of the purpose is an aid to building rapport.

Many years ago, in a leaflet on interviewing prepared for the Civil Service, we came upon the helpful aphorism: 'An interview is a conversation with a purpose.' One of the tasks of the appraiser is to keep the conversation to its purpose. There are times when considerable judgment is required to know whether what is being said is unconsciously – or even consciously – creating a diversion from the main purpose. That diversion may be important to the appraisee and should not be lightly disregarded. Nevertheless, there are times when it should be identified openly as a distraction from the interview and, if necessary, an undertaking given that time will be found for discussion of that issue on another occasion. Peters and Waterman (1982) in *In Search of Excellence* have the happy imperative: 'Stick to the knitting.'

Verbal and non-verbal signals

There is an ongoing need for the appraiser to indicate to the appraisee that he has heard and understood what has been said to her. This is done in two ways: by verbal and non-verbal signals; and by reflecting data and feelings. The verbal signals are often scarcely words at all, rather murmurs of encourage-ment and agreement; the non-verbal signals are nods and smiles and, above all, a body language that signifies full attention and empathy. It is not being suggested that the appraiser will consciously seek to introduce these signals. They come as part of the normal behaviour of most good listeners. It is, however, helpful to remind appraisers of the powerful effect that these signals have on the confidence of the appraisee. There is research evidence that the appraisee will speak for lengthier spells, be more animated and less repetitive in his responses when these signals are given. Where under experimental conditions those signals are deliberately suppressed, the appraisee will speak more haltingly, be less self-confident, wander from the point or be repetitive.

The appraisee's body language also contributes revealing non-verbal signals. Anxiety is shown by frequent body movements, by the disengagement of eye contact or by 'protective' gestures: folded arms, legs tucked under the chair, leaning forward to show, symbolically, less body surface to the 'aggressor'. The good appraiser will recognise these stress indicators and respond by reinforcing the empathic relationship.

Reflecting data is a more overt technique. This is a specific contribution to the dialogue from the appraiser which says, in effect: 'I believe I have understood you to make this point.' If the appraiser has accurately summarised what the appraisee has been saying this has a twofold effect: first of reassurance, and secondly of encouraging the appraisee either to elaborate further or to move to a new aspect of the matter under discussion. If the appraiser has been mistaken in his understanding, the appraisee has the opportunity to correct the misapprehension. It is unimportant whether the misconception has come from the appraisee's misrepresentation or the appraiser's faulty perception: there is no merit in apportioning blame. An anxious appraisee may well be unnecessarily iterative, and reflecting data is a means of moving the dialogue on to new ground without appearing to be impatient.

Reflecting feelings is no less important. Here the skilled appraiser perceives what lies behind the words: personal anxieties, concerns about what is professionally proper to raise in the interview, self-doubts, something being hidden and so on. It is a matter of judgment on the part of the appraiser as to whether these should be brought to the surface at this stage of the dialogue or even at all. There are no criteria by which one can advise on this. However, if there is a general climate of open behaviour in the institution, it can reasonably be assumed that self-disclosure can and should be encouraged.

There are occasions when the appraiser may feel the need to go a little further than merely reflecting data or feelings. It may be necessary to find out what lies behind an appraisee's words or to draw together what appears to have been implied in a number of different, even seemingly conflicting statements. The skill of interpreting is one of the most difficult for the appraiser, since it is essential for her to avoid making judgments or putting words into the mouth of the appraisee. To keep the interpretation open, that is to give the appraisee the freedom to say 'That is not at all what I was saying', it is necessary to cast the interpretation in the form of a question: 'Is this what you mean?'; or alternatively to preface a statement with the words 'If I understand you correctly . . .'.

QUESTIONING SKILLS

The way in which questions are framed by the appraiser is of considerable importance. They should be purposive and simple. Complex, and particularly multiple questions, can be very disconcerting to the appraisee. They add to the tension that he is already likely to be feeling and consequently set up a need for rapport to be re-established. The appraiser, it must be recognised, may also be stressed in an interview situation. There is a tendency to consider any pause before responding to a question as a void to be filled, usually with a rephrasing of the question, sometimes even by going on to another issue. In training workshops we have from time to time privately asked appraisees the reason for their pause and their attitude to the reformulation or abandonment of the original question. Frequently we have been told: 'I was thinking. This was not a question to which I could give a ready answer' or 'I was much put out when the question was changed. If it is important enough to ask, it is important enough for me to answer. So perhaps it was not important at all?'

Nor is the occasional pause unimportant to the appraiser. She may need a moment's reflection to be sure that the matter under discussion has been as fully dealt with as time allows. Even more to the point, she may need time to phrase the next question accurately and effectively. Formulating the next question while the appraisee is speaking is likely to be indicated by body-language signals of inattention, usually by breaking eye contact.

It is very easy to fall into the trap of asking leading or directive questions: 'Don't you think that. . .' rightly or wrongly suggests to the appraisee that the appraiser is seeking his agreement. Or may it be a trap? Once that kind of suspicion rears its head rapport will be lost and very difficult to regain.

Questions should be focused primarily on the needs of the appraisee. Interviews must never become an opportunity for the appraiser to score points. It is vital that what the appraisee contributes to the dialogue is properly recognised; and, no less important, that what he is as a person is fully valued. Aggressive behaviour on the part of the appraiser will soon create a barrier of mistrust. The appraisee is likely to begin covertly to question the true purpose of the dialogue and to set up further barriers himself.

Yet no dialogue should be allowed to become cosy: this helps neither party. A confrontational question is not of itself a bad behaviour. It only becomes so when rapport is lost and the appraisee no longer sees the value of open behaviour. It should be used with caution. To highlight inconsistencies can be destructive and demoralising or positive and appreciated, depending entirely on the skill with which they are presented.

Questions that probe can either puncture the self-esteem of the appraisee or nudge him towards a greater self-perception. It is of crucial importance for the appraiser not to store up issues and later to confront the appraisee with them: inconsistencies should be identified as they occur and every attempt made to enable the appraisee to perceive them for himself.

The good listener . . .

. . . gives the greater part of any interview to:

DRAWING OUT

This requires:
- full attention
- no undue haste, but an eye on the purpose
- the regular testing of understanding
- the encouragement of self-disclosure
- questions that are:
  - client-centred
  - open
  - clearly phrased
  - purposive.

. . . gives a substantial part of any interview to:

SUPPORTING

This requires:
- the recognition of the client's value
- evidence of care and concern
- an atmosphere of mutual trust

. . . gives some time to:

CONFRONTING

This requires:
- open behaviour
- direct feedback
- the highlighting of inconsistencies
- careful probing

and very occasionally

- unmasking.

. . . gives the least time to:

- advising and informing

© Routledge 1993

Figure 8.1 Listening and questioning skills

Questions designed to unmask must be used with the utmost discretion. By this we mean revealing to the appraisee that he is deluding himself or that there is clear evidence that what he has been saying does not square up with the facts. There are times when it will have to be done; it can be a traumatic experience but it can also be a cathartic one if well handled.

Information should be given at the request of the appraisee: advice very rarely. Whatever goals or modifications to his way of working the appraisee may decide upon as a result of the interview must be in his ownership, if he is to work wholeheartedly to their achievement.

As for advice, even if the appraisee were specifically to ask for it, the appraiser should bear in mind that this may be an easy way to avoid taking a decision, and should consider the possibility of encouraging the appraisee to develop his own ideas rather than become dependent on the views of the more experienced teacher. Indeed, dependence of this kind could be inhibiting to the professional development of the appraisee.

When situations like this arise, the appraiser may turn the question back on the appraisee. This must be done with tact, however; casually phrased it may appear to the appraisee that he is being fobbed off or that the appraiser does not know how to advise him in this situation. Well done, it encourages the appraisee's independent thought and bolsters his self-esteem.

NEGOTIATION

We believe that the function of negotiation in the appraisal process is insufficiently understood and the need for negotiation skills consequently much underrated. The situations in which negotiation is called for occur at every stage of appraisal. Appraiser and appraisee must reach agreement over which class or learning activity is to be observed before classroom observation can take place. In the briefing session there is negotiation over the role of the appraiser, particularly the observation style; and the debriefing may well lead to negotiation over the delivery of professional support needs that have become apparent.

Task observation calls for negotiation over which activity is to be observed, when and in what manner. If the observation is of a meeting or training session not normally attended by the appraiser, then there must also be negotiation with those who will be present. Data collection requires yet more delicate negotiation. It is not merely a matter of reaching agreement on what documentation may properly and with advantage be scrutinised, who may be approached for verbal comment within the terms of the Code of Practice; it is also necessary to determine in advance what use is to be made of the data in the appraiser's preparation for the appraisal interview and in the interview itself.

Negotiation is the dominant strategy in the planning meeting which identifies, among other matters, the possible focal areas for appraisal and in the pre-interview meeting in which the agenda is agreed. Agreement on the appraisal statement, as we point out in detail in Chapter 11, calls for a high level of negotiation skills, as does goal setting with its implications of contracting for monitoring and support.

Fisher and Ury (1981) are at pains to point out that negotiators 'are people first [with] emotions, deeply held values, and different backgrounds and viewpoints'. Positively, they indicate that:

> The process of working out an agreement may produce a psychological commitment to a mutually satisfactory outcome. A working relationship where trust, understanding, respect and friendship are built up over time can make each new negotiation smoother and more efficient. And people's desire to feel good about themselves, and their concern for what others will think of them, can often make them more sensitive to another negotiator's interests.
>
> (Fisher and Ury, 1981: 19)

They warn too of the negative aspects:

> On the other hand, people get angry, depressed, fearful, hostile, frustrated and offended. They have egos that are easily threatened. They see the world from their own personal vantage point, and they frequently confuse their perceptions with reality. Routinely, they fail to interpret what you say in the way you intend and do not mean what you understand them to say. Misunderstanding can reinforce prejudice and lead to reactions that produce counter-reactions in a vicious circle; rational exploration of possible solutions becomes impossible and negotiation fails.
>
> (Fisher and Ury, 1981: 19)

The topic of negotiation skills deserves far fuller treatment than we can offer in this training guide; and we wholeheartedly recommend *Getting to Yes* for further reading. The subheadings of their main chapter on the method of negotiation convey the general stance that we would advocate as highly pertinent to the appraisal process:

- separate the people from the problem
- focus on interests, not positions
- invent options for mutual gain
- insist on objective criteria.

COUNSELLING

We have indicated earlier in this chapter the importance of establishing and maintaining the interview purpose. One of the dangers is that the interview may become, almost by default, a counselling session. This must be guarded against; or, if the need for counselling is overriding, then the appraisal interview may be deferred. It is not possible to have two, quite distinct interview purposes at the same time.

None the less, as with many interview situations that do not have counselling as their prime purpose, aspects and elements of counselling will regularly make their presence felt, and the need for counselling skills cannot be ignored.

> If the main purpose in appraising a person's performance is to contribute to their motivation and development, *appraisal must be linked with counselling*. If appraisal means evaluating an employee's worth, then counselling means communicating that information in such a way that the individual can use it positively.
>
> (De Board, 1983)

This statement, as may be perceived in the phrase 'evaluating an employee's worth' appears in an excellent book on counselling skills in industry and commerce. Despite the different culture there is much there from which managers in schools may usefully learn.

We need, of course, to recognise that few teachers have had formal counselling training; and there is certainly no guarantee that any appraiser will have. Yet all teachers are from time to time cast in the counselling role and find themselves in situations in which they are called upon to deploy counselling skills, sometimes intuitively, and more or less successfully.

De Board refers extensively to the work of Leavitt and Lipman-Brown (1980), who identified two major categories in management style: *direct* and *relational*.

> Direct styles are used by get-it-done, task-oriented people . . . [Those who use] relational styles . . . help, support and back up other people and often get their feelings of achievement by contributing to the success of others.
>
> (De Board, 1983: 50)

Appraisers – one hardly needs to remind oneself that these are also line managers – will not fall exclusively into either category. Moreover, there are occasions when even the most relational of us will find it necessary to be directive. Yet no reader of this book will have failed to recognise our belief that, in those person-oriented situations with which most of the time we engage in schools, relational management is far and away the more effective style, and that direct management should be used sparingly and only in those situations when the clear need for it can be identified.

The style adopted by the manager in her day-to-day dealings with her colleagues will undoubtedly influence, if not determine the style used in appraisal interviewing. For a directive manager to become relational for the purpose of the appraisal interview is more likely to alarm than reassure the appraisee. Fortunately managers in schools have increasingly come to think and operate in terms of teamwork, open behaviour, parity of esteem, collegiality, trust. There will be no occasion for the leopard to change her spots simply for the purpose of the appraisal interview.

Just as in counselling, the positive feelings of the appraiser will engender reciprocal feelings in the appraisee. Yet there are words of warning for the relational manager that the trained counsellor will readily appreciate. Where the relational manager feels that she has a sound understanding, learnt from practical experience, of people's behaviour, she may tend to offer solutions which worked for her. It is irrelevant that they may be offered in a non-directive way. Whether the issues under discussion in the appraisal interview are professional or personal – and most have elements of both – any solution must be wholly in the ownership of the appraisee. This is a cardinal principle to be learnt from good counselling practice.

Kindness and tolerance are attributes to which most managers aspire. Their positive use helps the appraisee to face the facts of a situation and to come to grips with reality. Nobody is helped if the appraiser avoids an issue because it may become confrontational and consequently difficult to handle. A policy of appeasement, we learn from history, leads to disaster. The appraiser who hides the truth from the appraisee does him no service; she merely reinforces his false self-image. Appraisal, like good counselling, must guide the appraisee to see himself as he really is: self-knowledge is a prerequisite for personal and professional development.

Appraisal is a highly personal activity. It will at times unleash in the appraisee emotions that the appraiser may have difficulty in controlling. This we have seen both in role play and in appraisal trials, at all levels of seniority and in all schools of all phases. Not unnaturally, the appraiser may seek to bypass situations likely to lead to the expression of strong feelings. Counselling experience indicates that, while there may be occasions when the appraiser may justifiably seek to avoid a situation she feels she will be unable to handle, to do so is really to the benefit of neither party.

Where there is a climate of openness and trust that head of steam may never materialise. If it does, the appraiser still has it within her power to make a sound managerial decision on whether or not the appraisal interview is a suitable forum for dealing with emotional issues, or whether an alternative opportunity to explore emotive issues should not be found. This might even be, with no loss of face, with another person, particularly if the appraiser is herself a possible source of the emotions.

CONCLUSION

There are five key stages in any interviewing process; and all, to different degrees, make heavy demands on the skills we have described in this chapter. Figure 8.2 summarises much of what we have been recommending. We cannot urge too strongly the need, not merely to establish rapport, but to be constantly alert to the need to reinforce and maintain it.

Establishing and maintaining rapport:
- create the right environment
- keep on course
- give verbal and non-verbal encouragement
- reflect data
- reflect feelings.

Diagnosing the situation:
- identify options
- propose and agree criteria
- decide goals or action plan.

Deciding on future action:
- assess readiness for action
- increase readiness for action.

Evaluating:
- agree criteria for evaluation
- plan follow-up.

Stabilising:
- integrate the change into normal behaviour.

© Routledge 1993

Figure 8.2 The interviewing process and the consequences of agreed action: the five key stages

By 'diagnosing the situation' we mean exploring fully a mutual understanding of what the issue really is, and looking for as many potential solutions or responses as time allows. Brainstorming, a technique to which we have referred more than once, is useful here. There is a common misconception that an interviewing process should be entirely verbal. If there are useful tools that involve writing, they should be used.

Yet which of the proposed solutions is the one most likely to be effective? This can only be established if you also take the time to negotiate criteria for making that decision. Only then can you move to the stage of decision making.

It may be that, in the exploration of the best response, appraiser and appraisee find themselves in agreement that the latter is not ready for change. In the real world it is not always possible to defer a decision while you wait for the perfect climate or for adequate resources. However, time spent in investigating what would make action easier to implement – what will increase readiness for action – is never wasted. At least you will be aware of what your needs are if the means of meeting them become available.

Any decision that leads to activity must be evaluated. We have come to think of evaluation as costly in time and beyond the scope of the ordinary teacher and manager. *Managing Change in Schools* (Newton and Tarrant, 1992) has an excellent chapter on evaluating and monitoring change, both cost-effectively and simply. Indeed, in appraisal evaluation may be no more complex than reviewing what action was agreed on, and what monitoring and supportive actions there were. This is the first step towards establishing agreed criteria for its evaluation and, crucially, deciding on the next action step, whether it be a consequent developmental activity or simply the maintenance of what has been achieved.

Stabilising, finally, is a much neglected stage. Once an activity has become routinely established in the day-to-day running of the classroom or in managerial procedures, then there is need for nothing more than light-touch monitoring, preferably by the appraisee himself, since this ensures that he has taken ownership of the change process.

TRAINING FOR INTERVIEWING SKILLS

One of the most effective forms of training is through triads. When this is experienced within a training workshop it is essential to provide sufficient space to enable workshop members to have their own 'territory' so that discussion in one triad does not impinge upon that in another. It is very difficult for the trainer to ensure that a multitude of groups finish at the same time; and it is therefore helpful if this activity can be followed by a natural break: a tea or coffee interval, for example, or a meal. Beyond that, it requires little planning and only light-touch supervision. Occasionally we have overheard workshop members, on reading the brief for this session (see facing page), saying to a colleague 'I haven't the remotest idea about what issue I can

Working in triads

Each member of the triad in turn takes the role of client, adviser and observer.

As client, think of a professional situation concerning which you would welcome advice. The situation may be one that you are having to address in the near future; or it may be one that you are already engaged in but which appears likely to have further stages of development.

As adviser, your main task is to create an atmosphere in which the client will speak freely, and will seek and value your help in the diagnosis of the situation. In training, establishing rapport usually presents no problem; but you do need to be aware of its importance both at the beginning and throughout the dialogue and to be alert to all opportunities for making the client feel at ease.

As observer, your role at the end of the round is to comment and, particularly, promote discussion on the adviser's role concept, influencing skills and interviewing techniques. These include:

- active listening;
- empathising;
- appropriate questioning;
- defining and clarifying the issue.

It is sometimes necessary for the observer to intervene to indicate that the interview now appears to have gone beyond the state of diagnosing the situation and is entering that of taking action. No other intervention should be needed.

If there is time, the triad should seek to draw some conclusions about the expertise required for any of the skills listed above or for others that they have identified as a result of the exercise.

© Routledge 1993

possibly bring to my triad.' They are almost always seen a few minutes later to be in full spate!

Because this exercise in the use of interviewing skills is not directly concerned with appraisal, though it has much to contribute to the successful relationship between appraiser and appraisee, we prefer to use here the neutral terms used in counselling, *adviser* and *client*.

We make a point as trainers of making ourselves available should there be the need – there very rarely is – but we will not otherwise sit in on a triad. This is for two reasons. The first is that our presence adds an unnecessary dimension to the group and almost certainly detracts from the important learning process for the observer, since we are often looked to for comments which he should be offering. Indeed, it is sometimes not perceived that the observer is required to exercise the same interviewing skills in his debriefing as the adviser in his dialogue with the client.

The second reason is the purely practical one that, were we to move from one group to another, we would find it virtually impossible to time our arrival to coincide with the beginning of the second or third round; and to arrive after the start would be disconcerting to all parties.

It is important that the interview is brought to a conclusion before any decisions are made about what the action steps should be. This is because the adviser is, in a workshop situation, not in a position to take responsibility for the stages which follow. In a school-based situation there is no reason why the discussion should not continue through all its stages.

Many workshop members have described this training activity as one of the most valuable they have experienced; and some headteachers have taken it further by making training in triads possible within a school-based training day programme. Indeed, it does not even need that framework: any three members of staff can form a triad. We have learnt of some teachers who have used the process to explore issues they are faced with in their professional experience, making it an excellent co-counselling tool.

Chapter 9

The appraisal interview

If the appraisal interview is seen as no more than a stage in the process that began with goalsetting and has continued through classroom observation, task observation and self-appraisal, then it should contain no surprises. Nevertheless, it may seem to the appraisee to be a more threatening activity than any that has preceded it. However much it has been emphasised that the whole appraisal process is about individual and institutional improvement and not about assessment, there will always be some who perceive it as judgmental; and this stage, coming as it does as the conclusion of the cycle, may well lend credence to any misgivings that the purpose of appraisal might, after all, be summative. It follows, therefore, that preparation for the appraisal interview must be thorough, and must emphasise that appraiser and appraisee are engaging in a joint activity, each with a responsibility for making sound preparations in order to ensure that the outcomes are as valuable as possible.

PREPARATION BY APPRAISER

The appraiser needs to prepare herself in a number of ways. First, she must go back to the record of the goalsetting discussion which began the process, both to remind herself of what was agreed and to see the goals afresh in the light of what has transpired in the intervening months. She may well discover that goals set two years ago, and even those revised at the follow-up meeting a year ago, need further revision to ensure that they accurately represent what both parties agree to be the present situation. It is, of course, the appraiser's responsibility to note any agreed changes in the goals as they are made. However, managers are busy people. It may slip the mind of a managerial colleague to inform her of a change. She may know of the change but forget to record it.

Similarly, constraints which were identified at the goalsetting may themselves have become more critical, or been modified, or even disappeared entirely, possibly to be replaced by other constraints that had not been foreseen at the time. Again, the appraiser will have been made aware of the state of play at the periodic monitoring meetings which ought to be a regular feature of appraisal; but, human nature being what it is, what was discussed may not have been recorded, may even have been forgotten. By reminding herself of the constraints as they were and as they are now, the appraiser is less likely to be taken unawares in the interview. It is important that the appraiser is prepared to introduce into the appraisal interview a brief review of those constraints. It may be a matter for congratulation of the appraisee that a particular constraint has been overcome; but it is important to recognise that there may also have been considerable time and energy costs on the individual teacher that will show up elsewhere.

The general period of appraisal interviews, best concentrated into a six-week time-span at most, has a way of highlighting interconnections that might otherwise have gone unnoticed: the degree of success in meeting a particular goal in one area of the institution has often a knock-on effect, for good or ill, on another area. Thus a highly successful development of social activities for parents undertaken as a goal by one teacher may have led to an improvement in relationships between parents and staff in general and contributed greatly to more effective communication over curriculum content and methodology. Alternatively, an in-service day ill-conceived and inadequately prepared by one member of staff may have undermined the ability of curriculum leaders in general to generate enthusiasm among staff for their concerns over the implementation of the National Curriculum.

Next, and particularly in the large school, the appraiser needs to assemble information about the appraisee's performance. It is crucial that all data are expressed as fact and not opinion. 'Your head of year thinks that you have not been pulling your weight recently' is the kind of remark that might easily slip out in the appraisal interview. Phrased thus it will almost certainly lead the teacher to whom it is made to conclude that he is indeed being judged, and on hearsay evidence at that. However, the same preparation could well have resulted in the statement 'I understand you have recently had some discussion with your head of year about your strengths and weaknesses as a tutor. Since improvement in this area was, I recall, one of your goals, should we not discuss this further?' This would be an unexceptionable and far more effective use of information received by the appraiser. It would also emphasise the appraisee's responsibility to the head of year for meeting the agreed goal.

It is vital that preparing for the appraisal interview in this way, however large the school or complex its organisation, is not left until the last minute, but is part of the continuous monitoring process. The dictum 'There should be no surprises' applies to the whole range of the appraisal process; and the communication flow within the school should alert any member of staff with managerial responsibility to strengths and weaknesses as they arise. If the appraiser is hearing of these only at the time of the appraisal interview, then there is decidedly something wrong with the system. Nevertheless, there is clearly a need for the appraiser at this time to review her perceptions of those aspects of performance for which she is not directly responsible by talking to those members of staff who are, both to ensure that she is fully updated and to alert them to their vicarious involvement in the interview.

THE AGENDA

Preparation leads naturally into building the agenda for the interview. We feel strongly that anything much beyond an hour for the interview is likely to be counterproductive. This is not an *ex cathedra* opinion, but one borne out by the experience of many whom we have trained as appraisers and who then conducted appraisal trials with volunteer staff before appraisal became statutory. Some acknowledged that preparation which they thought was adequate but which proved not to be was the main reason why they exceeded the time limit they set themselves: they had been too easily side-tracked; taken by surprise by information disclosed by the appraisee of which they were not aware; been oblivious to the intensity of feeling that has been generated by some incident. Yet by far the commonest cause of the overlong interview is the simplest: the desire to leave no stone unturned, no avenue unexplored.

Planning the content

The agenda for the appraisal interview must be selective. The goals which have been set at the beginning of the appraisal process provide the broad ground from which that selection may be made; they are not of themselves the agenda. There will be short-term goals long since delivered and, one hopes, reviewed briefly at the time by appraiser and appraisee. There will be goals that appeared to be of prime importance at the time they were agreed which, for whatever reason, became less so. To spend more than a few moments on these, mainly by way of showing recognition of achievement or of the circumstances that led to change, would not be time well spent.

Planning the agenda

In planning the agenda it is as well to estimate that no main item is likely to take less than 10 minutes and may well take 15 minutes. Bearing in mind that time will also need to be allocated for other key elements of the appraisal interview, three – at most four – goals will be as many as can comfortably be reviewed. How and by whom should they be selected?

If appraisal is to be a process of negotiation and sharing, then part of that choice should lie with the appraisee. Not only does this signal that his own perceptions of the appraisal process are important, it also introduces a concept of interdependence and mutuality upon which long-term confidence is built. It is possible and permissible for the appraisee to include an item in which he feels that he has been less successful than he would have wished or expected, in order to indicate that, given more support or resources, he would have achieved at a higher level.

Some may appear to choose items for the agenda in order to engage in buck-passing or trumpet-blowing. The appraiser may be tempted to consider this an abuse of the 'privilege' of contributing to the agenda, but we believe that it is wise for the appraiser be non-judgmental in such a situation. What may appear to be buck-passing can sometimes be a genuine confusion over accountability roles. Trumpet-blowing may indicate that there has been a failure somewhere to recognise and praise achievement. What often happens in practice, though, is that an item the appraiser is herself desirous of seeing on the agenda is proposed by the appraisee, reinforcing her view that this is an item of mutual concern.

The concept of mutuality referred to above is of vital importance in appraisal. If appraisal is to contribute to school improvement then it must strive to avoid win-lose situations; and there is no better way of doing this than to accept and demonstrate from the outset that the relationship between appraisee and appraiser is not one of subordinate and superordinate but rather of two colleagues seeking mutually acceptable outcomes. In one sense, therefore, in the interview each party may at any given moment be in either role. 'Had you supported me in such a way, I might well have achieved greater success in meeting this goal' is, if accepted as a valid criticism by the appraiser, just such a role reversal.

The agreed agenda

This should be in the hands of the appraisee in good time before the interview: at least 48 hours in normal circumstances. There is no need, in a negotiated agenda, for a catchall item of any other business. This is not the kind of occasion on which any last-minute item is likely to need to be included. Indeed, introduced by either appraiser or appraisee, it would seem to be more of a device to engender suspicion or promote discord and therefore quite alien to the atmosphere in which an appraisal interview is best conducted.

Controlling the agenda

To do this without stifling discussion or riding roughshod over a colleague's opinions is not easy; and there will be many appraisers for whom this is a new experience, certainly in a one-to-one situation. It is better, if it appears that the planned time is likely to be overrun, to pause and agree which item on the agenda cannot be satisfactorily explored in the remaining time and should be left for an occasion outside the appraisal interview itself; alternatively, if there is any feeling that this is an item that must be discussed within the appraisal interview, to agree to meet again to conclude the agenda.

BEFORE THE APPRAISAL INTERVIEW . . .

THE **APPRAISER** NEEDS TO:

REVIEW
- Job specification
- agreed goals
- identified constraints

IDENTIFY
- changed and new goals
- changed and new constraints
- related school developments

ASSEMBLE
- data

SHARE AND PREPARE
- agenda items

THE **APPRAISEE** NEEDS TO:

REVIEW
- job specification
- agreed goals
- personal progress (self-appraisal)

SHARE AND PREPARE
- agenda items

APPRAISER AND **APPRAISEE** NEED TO:

AGREE
- location of interview
- time allocation
- recording

© Routledge 1993

Figure 9.1 Preparation for appraisal

SCHOOL DEVELOPMENTS

Over a period of two years between appraisals, no school stands still. The achievements of any teacher can only be properly understood in relation to the school development plan, which itself needs to be kept under constant review. The experience of the past decade has taught the teaching profession that excessive, imposed change is destructive of morale and leads almost inevitably to indecisive management. There have been times when headteachers have felt that they were running in treacle.

Whether the present decade will allow schools time for consolidation we very much doubt. Even as we write, there are radical changes being made to the structure of our national educational system. Somehow, despite these distractions, the school management has to maintain a sense of direction, convey all modifications, imposed or otherwise, clearly to staff and enable staff to relate what they do and intend to a coherent plan.

Part of any preparation for appraisal must therefore include an understanding both of the context wherein goals were set and of the present context. Teachers will value appraisal the more when they are made aware that changes and constraints not of their making, but imposed on them and the school, are taken account of and brought into the discussion of their goal achievement.

SELF-APPRAISAL

In his teaching the good teacher is constantly going through a process of self-evaluation. Did I achieve my lesson objectives? Did I communicate successfully? Did I pay sufficient attention to the full range of ability within the class? Did I avoid sex stereotyping in my examples? Did I give enough time and the right sort of help to pupils with special needs? Did I get feedback from the class on the outcomes of the lesson? This is not to suggest that he routinely catechises himself with these and other questions. The beginner teacher may and should from time to time; but the experienced teacher has an intuitive feel for the consequences of his teaching and knows where there have been strengths and weaknesses.

Classroom observation, it is widely recognised, is effective not so much for the contribution of the observer as for the heightened self-perceptions of the teacher. This is no less true of the appraisal interview itself. Here, however, we are dealing with a complexity of goals and not simply the aims and objectives of a single lesson; and, because the time-span is greater, there is the need for a more formal framework for self-appraisal. The proforma on pages 136–7 derives, with only minor modifications, from Annex B of the ACAS agreement (1986). That agreement underpinned much of the thinking and work of the pilot appraisal projects.

The questions that appear on the proforma are both retrospective, in that they look back to the previous goalsetting activity, and prospective, in that they begin to identify ways in which goals will be carried forward, revised and renewed in the next review period and, to some extent, the means by which they will be achieved. Important though it is to both appraiser and appraisee that there is a recognisable relationship between the present appraisal interview and future goals, it is essential that the next phase of goalsetting does not dominate the discussion. Goalsetting is a discrete activity and should not intrude unduly on the appraisal of past performance.

The questions merit some detailed comment:

What do you consider to be the main tasks and responsibilities of your current post?

The ways in which appraisees approach this question are, in our experience, many and varied. This does not vitiate the question, for, fortunately, nobody is concerned about comparing or evaluating responses. The main purpose of the question is to enable the appraisee rapidly to identify the areas which will be under review in the appraisal process. In schools where the phrase 'key result areas' has already been absorbed into the accepted language of appraisal, it can be either substituted for or understood by 'main tasks and responsibilities'.

In the period under review, what aspects of your work have given you the greatest satisfaction? And the least satisfaction?

It is important to observe that this question asks about *satisfaction* rather than *success*. This approach emphasises that the central purpose of appraisal is not assessment but personal development. Self-actualisation, as Maslow (1959) terms it, is the highest level motivator in his needs hierarchy.

Did anything prevent you from achieving what you had intended to do? Have these obstacles been removed? If not, how might they be removed?

Here the appraisee has the opportunity to reflect on constraints on his performance. Some of these will undoubtedly have been identified as potential constraints at the goalsetting stage; but others will have surfaced in the period under review. The second question reaffirms the mutuality of the appraisal process by inviting the appraisee to consider the causes of the constraints. There is no attempt in this section to identify whether or not it has lain within the power of the appraisee himself to deal with the obstacles. This can best be considered during the appraisal interview itself. What the questions are likely to do, however, is to stimulate some self-perceptions which will prepare the ground for a profitable appraisal interview.

Are there any changes in the school organisation which might help you to improve your performance?

The relationship between personal performance and school organisation is crucial, but often underestimated by those in managerial roles. While the annual review process or audit increasingly being used in schools gives staff

Self-appraisal: interview preparation proforma

What do you consider to be the main tasks and responsibilities of your current post?

In the period under review, what aspects of your work have given you the greatest satisfaction?

And the least satisfaction?

Did anything prevent you from achieving what you had intended to do?

Have these obstacles been removed? If not, how might they be removed?

© Routledge 1993

Are there any changes in the school organisation which might help you to improve your performance?

What in your view should be your main goals for the next review period?

What help do you need to this end? From whom?

How do you envisage your career developing?

Any other comments?

© Routledge 1993

the opportunity to reflect on the nexus between school organisation and staff performance in general, the appraisal process offers a rare opportunity for considering how personal performance is enhanced or inhibited by school organisation.

What in your view should be your main goals for the next review period? What help do you need to this end? From whom?

The appraisal process is cyclical. The appraisal interview will conclude with the identification of the goals for the next appraisal period. In some cases it will become apparent at an early stage in the interview that a particular goal continues into the next period, though the emphasis – and consequently the activity – may change, perhaps from innovation to consolidation. In other cases it may be judged at the appraisal interview that the goal has been achieved, at least to the extent that it has now become a routine activity. New goals and major developments from existing KRAs are likely to feature in the appraisee's thinking in response to the first question in this section; the importance of support mechanisms is highlighted by the second and third.

How do you envisage your career developing?

There are those who argue that career development reviews should be kept quite distinct from the appraisal process. One secondary headteacher with whom we have worked, who before engaging in appraisal training had built up an extensive and well-structured programme of staff development interviews, took the view that it would be both impractical and time-consuming to maintain two distinct processes and holds that this question is crucial to the appraisal process.

For some members of staff this question in the self-appraisal proforma will be only of passing interest. For others, however, it will act as a powerful trigger to the appraisal of future professional status or even reveal hidden disquiet about present role or status. That the question itself is a valid part of the appraisal process we have no doubt. It is, however, up to the appraiser to decide whether or not the time available in the interview permits the matter to be discussed in the detail it warrants or whether, after an initial airing of it, it might not better be discussed on another occasion. Furthermore, particularly in a secondary school of any size, the question may well arise as to whether the appraiser is the right person with whom this matter can usefully be discussed.

SHARING THE SELF-APPRAISAL

Finally, there is the question of whether or not a copy of the self-appraisal proforma should be made available to the appraiser before the interview. The ACAS document recommends that the decision be left to the appraisee. We can see no circumstance in which it would not be helpful for the document to be made available, provided appraisal is viewed by both parties as a collaborative and not a confrontational activity. There is likely to be much in the document that will contribute to the building up of a mutually acceptable agenda; and there will also be indicators as to which items on the agenda deserve the fullest treatment and the greatest allocation of time. There may also be signals to the appraiser of facts that she should ascertain or areas that she should investigate before the meeting.

Both in training and in trialling the appraisal interview we found a number of people with an initial scepticism and a reluctance to complete the self-appraisal proforma: 'Yet another piece of paper, yet more time to be spent on appraisal' was a common attitude. Those who did complete it soon found it a most valuable document: the simplicity and sensible ordering of the questions clarified their own thoughts, and it was challenging without being threatening. In six years of training through case studies, we can only remember one occasion when a role player was not willing to share it with the appraiser; and in the plenary discussion that refusal was heavily criticised. Furthermore, in no report back from workshop members who have gone on to conduct appraisal trials in their own schools have we heard of a refusal to share.

PREPARING THE INTERVIEW

As with the goalsetting interview, the location depends on both the availability of suitable venues and the wishes of appraiser and appraisee. However, in this case it is more important that the venue is one that can be safeguarded from interruption, by telephone, by visitors, by accidental intrusion, by crises. There will be schools, particularly primary schools, where the appropriate privacy is hard to find. Even in large secondary schools, where offices and similar rooms are more commonly available, there may well be a reluctance on the part of some members of staff to surrender their room, such are the proprietorial attitudes to space in some institutions. Venues for appraisal should therefore not be dealt with on a casual basis, but be planned with the same precision and attention to detail that schools apply to the allocation of rooms for governors' meetings, staff appointment interviews and school examinations. In addition, it would be sensible for this issue to be included on the agenda of a general staff meeting at which either room allocations were being discussed or appraisal procedures were being reviewed.

We have already indicated that an hour is the optimum time for an appraisal interview. This said, however, it is wise to allocate the room for a longer period: a further 10 minutes before and again after the intended hour. This allows for the seating to be arranged appropriately and in advance. A small table is useful, since both appraiser and appraisee almost certainly have papers which they will not want to clutch throughout the meeting.

Time after the allocated hour is also important. Sometimes, even in training situations, there is a good deal of tension in the air, however well the appraisal interview has gone, and the appraiser may need to dissipate this with some general conversation. Indeed, both parties will benefit from a 'cooling down' time, much as sportsmen and women do after a strenuous workout. To expect the appraisee, mind buzzing with all that has been discussed, to go straight from the interview to teach is not advisable, though sometimes it will be inevitable.

Nor is it only in the appraisee's interest that some time is available for unwinding. An appraiser relatively inexperienced in appraisal interviewing will find it helpful to seek the appraisee's perceptions, while the details are fresh in the minds of both, of the way the interview was conducted. Even with experienced interviewers this strategy may be psychologically sound in that it switches the focus of attention from appraisee to appraiser, a move which in itself lessens tension for both of them.

We have often been asked in workshops our views on the possible presence at the interview of a third party, as non-participatory observer. This question has been stimulated by the very positive reception to the role of the observer in the triad training described in the previous chapter. In the appraisal interview itself it is possible that the presence of this third party would radically alter the relationship between appraiser and appraisee. However self-effacing that observer tries to be, however well the role has been clarified, it is still possible that, by the nature of his standing in the school, he will appear to relate more closely to one party than the other: as appraisee's 'friend' perhaps, with undertones of the practices of disciplinary hearings; or as second appraiser. In general, we advise against it. Yet it is only right that we should record that experienced colleagues do not share our reservation. One primary headteacher who had introduced routine appraisal into his school some years before it became a major national innovation included an observer in the interviewing process. He found this to be a means of reducing, not heightening tension: the observer was seen by both parties as a moderating influence on the process.

Another headteacher, for the first trials of appraisal interviews in a secondary school with a well-established procedure of annual staff development reviews, introduced an observer, with staff agreement, with the intention that the appraisal team would profit from an objective monitoring of the process. At the end of this trialling phase, somewhat to his surprise, there was staff unanimity that there was so much merit in the presence of the observer that the practice should be continued beyond the trialling stage.

There is, as both headteachers readily recognised, a considerable time-cost in this practice which they might not be able to sustain without a deleterious effect on other demands on that most valuable of resources. Nobody, it is agreed, should introduce this procedure without full consideration of its long-term implications.

NOTETAKING

In order that an accurate appraisal statement may be compiled after the appraisal interview some recording will generally take place during the interview. Few appraisers will have the confidence to rely on memory alone. There is, not surprisingly, a good deal of unease over the purpose of notetaking, and the most satisfactory way of defusing potential hostility is to ensure that the purpose of notetaking is made clear both to the staff collectively and to individuals at their initial meeting. If there is a section on appraisal procedures in a staff handbook, notetaking should have a place there too. It is important that it be emphasised that these notes do not form part of any dossier but have one function only, to prompt the appraiser's memory. These notes, along with all other data, are by regulation destroyed once their immediate purpose has been fulfilled.

However, it is not merely a matter of whether or not notes are taken, but of how they are taken. The appraiser who writes busily throughout the interview will find it difficult to be responsive to body language signals from the appraisee, may not understand whether pauses signify the end of an answer to her question or a momentary reflection before continuing. Full attention, as we stressed in the previous chapter, is an essential interviewing skill.

Some appraisers already have the skill of 'keywording', that is of making a one-word note that will be a sufficient reminder. Others use the technique of breaking at, say, the end of one item of the agenda before proceeding to the next and briefly reviewing key points with the appraisee. This takes slightly longer, but has the effect of involving the appraisee in the process and therefore minimising the likelihood of disagreement when the draft appraisal statement is discussed. Indeed, it will sometimes happen that clarifying a point in this way actually saves time when appraiser and appraisee meet to agree the statement. More importantly, perhaps, it demonstrates trust and partnership.

The compilation of the appraisal statement is a matter of such importance that we deal with it at length in Chapter 11.

CONCLUSION

We have earlier described appraisal as a cyclical process, one that necessarily begins from goals that have been agreed – or, for new staff, are discussed and agreed soon after appointment – and continues, with 'light-touch' monitoring *en route*, through to the appraisal interview and the setting of goals for the next two-year period. We have also emphasised that there must be a regular review of the alignment between individual goals and school policy as represented in the main by the school development plan. To demonstrate the unity of this process, we conclude this chapter with the completed version of the flowchart, the earlier stages of which appeared as Figure 4.3 on page 49.

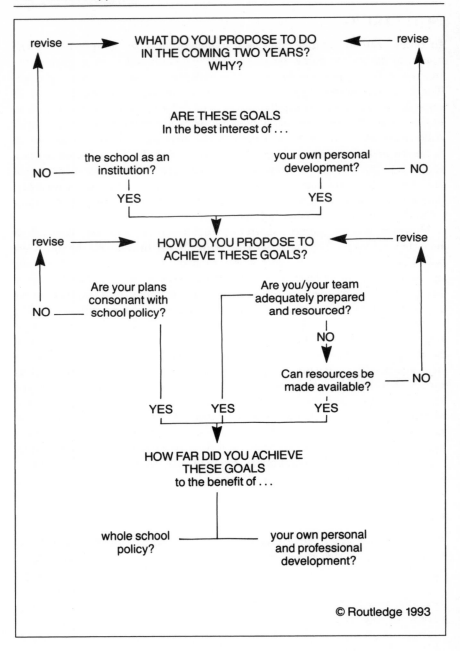

Figure 9.2 The appraisal process: from goalsetting to interview

Chapter 10

Training for appraisal interviewing

In the early days of training for appraisal interviewing, when there was little or no direct school experience to draw upon, we used simulation extensively in our appraisal training workshops. All the case studies that appear in this chapter have been trialled frequently in workshops with clientele varying from LEA appraisal training coordinators, officers and advisers to headteachers, staff teams, school staff development coordinators and interested individuals. The case studies are factually based, though the circumstances have always been modified sufficiently to ensure that there can be no identification of their origins. Each newly devised case study has been assessed by us and teams of LEA tutors with whom we have worked in order to identify and amend any area where the text might be misunderstood or misinterpreted. All have been updated to maintain their contemporaneity. Readers of this book are at liberty to use these case studies as they stand, to adapt them to suit the circumstances of their LEA or school or to model their own simulations on them.

The movement from LEA-based training to school-based training does, however, provide the opportunity for other training strategies. There *is* now in our schools experience of appraisal interviewing. Few headteachers would claim that all their appraisers have sufficient expertise. Indeed, most would deny that they themselves were adequately trained and experienced to be exemplars of good practice. In any case, there will always be a need to update procedures and experience so that the way in which appraisals are conducted by different members of the team, while unlikely ever to be identical, are certainly considered by appraisees to have a measure of consonance.

There will also be new members of staff to consider. Some will be coming from other LEAs or other types of educational institution, possibly able to offer experience of appraisal that will contribute to the quality of that in the school, but in any event needing to understand their new school's policy and practice. Others will be coming into first appointments or be returning to teaching after a break. Our discussion with newly trained teachers, admittedly insufficient in number to qualify us to make sound generalisations, has left us concerned at how little has been done to acquaint them with even the nature of teacher appraisal, let alone give them any understanding of what they will before long experience as appraisees. The responsibility for their training will therefore fall upon their schools. The immediate need will be for goalsetting; but, if they are not to be at best bewildered by, at worst fearful of what they see going on around them, they will need early training in the appraisal interview.

There are several strategies appropriate both to the maintenance function of training and to meeting the needs of newcomers. They require a confident appraiser and appraisee, and we would advise that the training group is small, no more than six, and where possible drawn from those who already have a strong sense of shared identity.

THE REPLAY SESSION

Having conducted a successful appraisal interview, the appraiser and appraisee agree to rerun it, in an abbreviated form, for the group. While it is important to recognise that certain areas will be too personal to the appraisee to cover, it is also important that the presentation is not of an emasculated interview, in which there is no tension, no occasions when probes were necessary, and therefore nothing worthwhile as a training experience for the group.

As with any role play, the presence of an audience may well lead to interactions which will change the nature of the experience from that of the original appraisal interview: a muttered aside in the group, a burst of laughter, anything that heightens the awareness of the 'actors' that they have an audience. Yet, because it is based upon a reality, on communication between two members of staff in a professional relationship, above all on a scenario of shared experience of the school's management policy, the curriculum development plan, the school community of parents, pupils and staff, the replay will be more valid than any manufactured case study.

THE EVALUATION SESSION

Here the appraiser and appraisee discuss openly before a group the impression each has had of the appraisal interview. As this is, in effect, an evaluation of their experience there is therefore need of some preparation for the session. Both appraiser and appraisee should individually review their experience in advance of the training session: they may well find that the observation schedule on pages 154-5 provides useful guidelines, even though it was created and trialled for another purpose. On the whole we think it more effective that they come to the session without having shared their perceptions of the appraisal interview; but that is up to them.

It is important that time is allowed at the end of the replay or the evaluation for the group to give their views. Here one well tried training strategy is for the two to reply 'in role', that is, as each felt at the time of the appraisal interview. It is particularly important that the appraisee, for example, responds to a question like 'Do you feel that she was putting unreasonable pressure on you?' with 'At the time, I . . .' It then becomes possible for the appraiser either to justify her approach or to accept that the criticism was justified. As in all areas of interpersonal behaviour, openness is essential and there is no merit in apportioning blame.

THE POST MORTEM SESSION

This differs from the evaluation in that its main purpose is not to train a group, but to train each other. It may with benefit take place in the presence of an observer, who will act very much as does the observer in triad training (see Chapter 8), that is by not intervening in the duologue, but by asking useful and often probing questions at the end.

The observer may be the appraiser's line manager, in which case the activity will contribute to the greater understanding by senior management of the effectiveness of the appraisal process. It has to be remembered that the regulations make the headteacher of the school responsible to the governing body and, if an LEA school, to the LEA, for a periodic evaluation of appraisal procedures and outcomes. To that end this strategy would provide data. Alternatively, the observer might be any member of staff for whom the experience would be of value, and there is no reason why that should not be a relatively new member of staff.

APPRAISER CASE STUDIES

The first set of case studies are primarily for appraiser training. These studies, one secondary, one primary, take further the situations and the characters that you have already met in Chapter 4 on pages 56–60.

Planning the appraisal interview
- Study all the materials, including those in Chapter 4.
- Decide and prioritise the key issues to be raised in the interview, and from these draw up the agenda which you will negotiate with the appraisee. How much time do you propose to give to each item of the agenda?
- Plan how you will conduct the interview. Identify those areas where you will be addressing the appraisee's strengths and those areas of potential difficulty. What strategies might you devise for either?
- What kind of surroundings will lead to the most fruitful discussion?
- What contingency plans will you have?

© Routledge 1993

Vicky Hoyle: goals

A: MANAGING POLICY

- to collaborate with the head of Year 9 in preparing documentation to inform parents and pupils clearly and fully about options; to share their findings with their line manager before offering the final draft to interested staff for comments; to arrange for the translation into minority languages of the introduction, stressing the importance of parental presence at the options evening.

B: MANAGING LEARNING

- to maintain and, if possible, improve upon the effectiveness of her teaching at all levels, and in particular to contribute to the departmental goal of achieving an annual improvement in GCSE results.
- to attend regularly and to make an effective contribution to departmental and staff meetings.

C: MANAGING PEOPLE

- to represent the year heads on the working party on profiling, assessment and record keeping, and to inform them periodically of progress.

D: MANAGING RESOURCES

- to reestablish the history section of the library by checking stock against the index and, as far as possible, tracing and recovering lost books.

© Routledge 1993

Andrea Bull: goals

A: MANAGING POLICY

- To develop and disseminate to staff broader and more relevant means of language teaching within the school; and, in accordance with the National Curriculum, to devise strategies for the improvement of the teaching of spelling, grammar, punctuation and the use of Standard English.

B: MANAGING LEARNING

- To maintain and, if possible, improve upon her present high standard of classroom work.
- To explore and evaluate methods of approach throughout the school to improve the learning of children whose mother tongue is not English.

C: MANAGING PEOPLE

- To develop among staff, wherever possible, the strategy of collaborative working in language teaching with the peer class teacher that she has herself successfully pioneered.
- In the curriculum committee to continue to collaborate with other curriculum coordinators in the promotion of the school's policies for the improvement of the standards of achievement in learning.

D: MANAGING RESOURCES

- As far as the school's financial resources allow, to add to and improve the quality of reading materials and other resources for learning in the area for which she is responsible as curriculum coordinator.

© Routledge 1993

Vicky Hoyle: self-appraisal proforma

What do you consider to be the main tasks and responsibilities of your current post?

As Head of Year: welfare and academic and social development of pupils of my year; giving support to group tutors; ensuring effective use of tutor time; membership of year heads' management team. To review the options literature in collaboration with present head of Year 9 (completed and discussed with appraiser at follow-up of last appraisal). To represent the year heads on the new working party for profiling, assessment and record keeping (still in progress).

As history teacher: maintaining and enlarging my competency as a subject teacher; re-establishing the history section of the library – mainly indexing and chasing 'lost' books.

In the past academic year, what aspects of your work have given you the greatest satisfaction?

Examination results in GCSE. The students have responded well in combining projects of their own (guided) choice with the requirements of the syllabus.

Learning about management, and especially the conduct of meetings through membership of the year heads' team.

And the least satisfaction?

The lack of a sense of urgency on the part of some members of the working party on assessment, etc. (The last two meetings have been cancelled at the last minute and we have rarely had a full attendance since we started.)

I had not expected that my offer to work on the history section of the library would have involved me in the resources working party.

Did anything prevent you from achieving what you had intended to do?

Lack of time and resources.

Have these obstacles been removed?

NO!

© Routledge 1993

Are there any changes in the school organisation which might help you to improve your performance?

There are more than enough members of staff without pastoral responsibility to provide a supernumerary tutor for each year. Such a person would relieve the problems of staff absence which at present fall to the year head to fill. This prevents us from supporting our group tutors as we should like. (All year heads agree on this.)

What in you view should be the main goals for the next two years?

Equipping my tutor team to cope with the heavy demands in Year 11 of careers and further education advice. Towards the end of that year, establishing contacts with feeder primary schools for my role as Year 7 head the following year with, I hope, substantially the same team. Developing further a corporate spirit among the pupils. Finding time to maintain and improve my own historical knowledge base and teaching skills.

What help do you need to this end? From whom?

I would like the opportunity before the end of this term, if possible, to visit at least one of the 16+ educational establishments.

The introduction of the National Curriculum Key Stages have meant that most of the time at our departmental meetings has been taken up by curricular detail. I would like more departmental discussion where we can mutually update our knowledge and skills.

How do you envisage your career developing?

I have no ambitions beyond my present post at the moment. I want to stay in the classroom; my role as year head gives me all the management I feel I can cope with. Later I may feel differently about this.

Any other comments?

I would like to see over the next few years a greater outreach towards our immediate community: for example, the school doing more for old and handicapped people. This would enhance the concept of 'education as a partnership' referred to in last year's development review.

I would also like to say that, having initially been somewhat sceptical of the value of self-appraisal, I have actually gained a great deal from sitting down and thinking through my answers to the questions.

© Routledge 1993

Andrea Bull: self-appraisal proforma

What do you consider to be the main tasks and responsibilities of your current post?

Teaching my Year 4 class and coordinating work with the teacher of the parallel class.

Developing language work throughout the school.

Promoting liaison with English departments of neighbouring secondary schools.

In the past academic year, what aspects of your work have given you the greatest satisfaction?

Collaborating with section 11 teacher over methods of teaching children with limited command of the English language.

Working with staff to develop language teaching to meet the attainment targets has given me a greater insight into the issues of year-by-year progression and catering for wide ranges of ability.

and the least satisfaction?

Continued lack of resources, particularly insufficient funds for an adequate supply of bilingual reading materials and for new books for class libraries.

Did anything prevent you from achieving what you had intended to do?

Inability to spend more time in the classes of other teachers.

The continuing absence of any ancillary help has meant that existing books and materials are not being maintained in as good a condition as they ought to be.

Have these obstacles been removed?

It is to be hoped that the recent initiative of the deputy head in seeking parental help will have an effect in a number of areas in language, especially in hearing children read and maintaining resources.

© Routledge 1993

Are there any changes in the school organisation which might help you to improve your performance?

I find great difficulty in the music component of the National Curriculum, since I have no instrumental skills whatsoever. Mrs Simkins has taken my class from time to time while I took hers, but I would be happier if this could be made a formal arrangement.

What in you view should be the main goals for the next two years?

Gaining further experience of progression by taking my present class into Year 5.

Continuing to promote improved standards of written work through word processing and display in places accessible to children and also parents.

Reviewing progress of staff in absorbing Key Stages 1 and 2 in language into their everyday work.

Creating a pool of 'trained' parent reading helpers who can be relied upon to support teachers on a regular basis.

What help do you need to this end? From whom?

Instruction from Pauline on improving my word-processing skills, and contributions from all staff on improved display.

Help from deputy head in setting up skills sessions with potential parent reading helpers.

Training or help to gain some knowledge of how to teach adults. The few parents I have been talking to seem very anxious about their own poor educational standards. Can anyone on the staff recommend some useful reading?

How do you envisage your career developing?

I would like to continue to specialise in language work, especially ESL. I would also like more experience of or training in management, with a view to promotion when my children are a little older.

Any other comments?

Having initially been sceptical of the value of self-appraisal, I now realise how much I have gained from sitting down and thinking through my answers to the questions.

© Routledge 1993

ROLE-PLAY

There is great value in role-play as a means of exploring a situation, and gaining first-hand experience of handling it. Self-revelation is difficult enough in a one-to-one situation, and the presence of an audience may stifle fruitful discussion. If, however, the appraisee is metaphorically wearing the mask of an imaginary teacher she is able to speak more freely; and the appraiser too, who is also assuming a different personality, may feel at liberty to practise her interviewing skills and techniques. Having said that, it must be acknowledged that it is particularly important for the observers to cooperate by being as unobtrusive as possible and refraining from comment during the interview.

The case studies which follow can be used in an appraisal workshop, or within a school-based training day, or by a secondary head of department or primary head of section – early years, lower school, upper school – within their own staff meeting time. There are a number of points worthy of the attention of anyone planning this training activity:

• Groups of four to six participants produce the best results. However, in a workshop or school-based INSET day, the total number of members or the availability of sufficient tutors may necessitate larger groups. What is essential, however, is that there is an even number of groups.

• Groups are paired and to the participants in each pair copies of the same case study are distributed. It is important to emphasise that each group has been given exactly the same information. To one group is allocated the *collective* role of appraiser, to the other that of appraisee. The allocation may be by their choice, by the toss of a coin or by the decision of the trainer. Time should not be wasted as group members debate which role to take: there is little difference in the learning experience to be gained. It is important that no early decision is made within either group over which group member will eventually role-play the appraisal interview. The keen Thespian or the experienced appraiser is not necessarily the person who will provide the group with the best learning experience. Furthermore, if the decision is made too soon, the rest of the group is likely to abdicate responsibility.

• For each pair of groups there must be a tutor to act as facilitator. In order to set up a scenario that is open to a wide range of interpretations the information in the hand-out is deliberately kept to a minimum. The function of the tutor is therefore to negotiate any desired information from one group to the other. The first case study at the end of this chapter will serve as an example. No attempt has been made in it to describe the domestic situation of Gerry Manners. It is therefore open to the appraisee group to devise some personal details that suit the character that is evolving and to use the tutor to convey this information to the appraiser group. It will sometimes happen that the tutor is charged with conveying information which proves to be unacceptable to the other group: for example, that certain promises to provide resources were made by the headteacher but not adhered to. The appraiser group has the right in this circumstance to refuse to accept the information as it stands and it is the task of the tutor to mediate until there is agreement. Occasionally mediation gives way to arbitration in the interests of the training exercise. One of the key roles of the tutor is to ensure that the preparation for the appraisal interview does not become competitive.

- Once each group has read and discussed the scenario the members of the appraisee group will urge the appraisers to present them with the agenda for the interview and the production of this then becomes a priority for the appraiser group. At the same time the appraisers will be expecting to see the completed self-appraisal proforma. The discussion within each group as these documents are drafted by the one party and considered by the other will do much to identify and clarify for the workshop members the skills needed to achieve effective outcomes from the interview.
- Each case study will be seen to contain weaknesses as well as strengths, on the part of both the appraisee and other members of staff, not excluding the appraiser. This underlines the point made earlier that in the appraisal interview the appraiser–appraisee roles may at any given moment be reversed, as failures of management, for example, are revealed.
- An hour is a reasonable time allowance for the preparation of the appraisal interview.

The role-play

- Those who have elected – or been selected – to play the roles of appraiser and appraisee need a short time to talk to each other in private. This will serve in part to clear up any minor details, for example to agree the names of members of staff who are likely to be referred to in the interview, and in part to allow them to wind down some of the tension that will inevitably have built up. During this time the tutor will ensure that the scene is set for the interview as planned by the appraiser group, with such furniture as is available. Appraiser and appraisee need to be reminded that, although they will be talking to each other, they need to project their voices sufficiently to enable the observers of the role-play to hear them clearly. The tutor will also refer observers to the observation schedule on pages 154–5 and make sure that all sections of it will be covered. It is advisable that observers concentrate on one, at most two of the sections.
- Although the appraisal interview proper will last an hour or a little more, half an hour is sufficient in a training situation. All those present are well aware that in reality there would be much more factual and first-hand evidence on which to call. It is good practice for the tutor to have arranged beforehand to give a 'two minute warning' signal to the appraiser that will enable her to draw the interview to a conclusion.
- The tutor will also have be observing, mainly in order to be able to guide and

Observation schedule

RAPPORT

- Was rapport easily and competently established by the appraiser?
- How? (Examples)
- Was it well maintained?
- Were there occasions when it was in danger of breaking down?
- Was breakdown averted? How?

QUESTIONS AND ANSWERS

- Did the appraiser in general use open questions? Avoid leading questions? Avoid multiple and overcomplex questions? (Examples of good and bad practice.)
- At what stages were questions asked to narrow down or probe an issue?
- Did the appraisee assist the process in his/her responses?

USE OF TIME

- Estimate the balance between appraiser and appraisee of time spent in talking. Did it vary at different stages of the interview?
- How well was the agenda covered? Was the time spent on different items appropriate? (Ask for a copy of the agenda if you do not have one.)
- Did the appraiser at any stage have to cut short the appraisee?
- Was this done diplomatically?

© Routledge 1993

FACTS AND FEELINGS

- Did the appraiser summarise facts – and, if necessary, feelings – at appropriate stages of the interview?
- How well did the appraiser deal with any defensive or aggressive reactions on the part of the appraisee?
- Was the appraisee given the scope to represent his/her own feelings?
- Were any issues skated over by either party?

DOCUMENTATION

- Were the procedures for notetaking explained and accepted?
- Was the recording in any way obtrusive?
- Did the appraisee make notes?
- Was good use made of the self-appraisal proforma?
- Were the points for the contract satisfactorily reviewed at the end? (It will help if you make your own notes on items for the contract as the interview proceeds.)

© Routledge 1993

prompt, if necessary, the discussion session which follows. Some skilled tutors have the capacity to make rapid notes of the general tenor of each contribution set against a rough time log, and thus be able to show what proportion of the total time was spent on each agenda item. The log also has value in providing evidence of the balance between the verbal contributions of appraiser and appraisee. While there can be no golden rule, one expects the greater part of the interview to be taken up by the responses of the appraisee, so that the overall proportion is about 3:1. However, at different stages of the interview that proportion will vary considerably: at the beginning when the appraiser is concentrating on establishing rapport and at the end when she is summarising, there is likely to be a very different proportion.

Debriefing

It is our experience that most role-plays are extremely competently performed and that most observers make constructive and sympathetic observations – probably on the grounds that 'There but for the grace of God went I'! However, there will be times when the tutor may have the unenviable task of handling the debriefing of a role-play that has gone wrong. In so doing, she must give an object lesson in achieving the greatest possible positive outcome without compromising her integrity.

TRAINING MATERIALS

In all the case studies which follow a first name has been chosen which is not indicative of gender, since the role-player may be of either sex and it is essential that the decision of who will role-play is not predetermined. Yet the text of the case study would be insufferably pedantic if we had striven throughout for a wording which was gender neutral: the avoidance of a 'sexist' personal pronoun – sometimes male, sometimes female, quite arbitrarily – is therefore impossible. It should be explained to workshop members that the sex of the characters is their choice, determined by the eventual selection of role-players.

It is advantageous if tutors intending to use a case study spend a short time, preferably collectively, identifying the strengths and weaknesses of the appraisee, of other members of staff referred to and of the institution. While the role of tutor is that of facilitator, there is much merit in being able to anticipate the issues that are likely to arise.

It is important that the outcomes are as positive as they can be made. There will therefore be occasions when, without being overtly interventionist, the skilful tutor will nudge the simulation in a more profitable direction.

Goals: Lee Smith, head of department, modern languages

A: MANAGING POLICY

- to keep under constant review the school language curricula to ensure that they conform to the National Curriculum and to the latest and most effective concepts in language teaching, and to keep the senior management team informed about developments, either at the time of the periodic departmental review or as the occasion arises

B: MANAGING LEARNING

- to take all possible measures to increase pupil and staff awareness of the importance of learning European languages as the country responds to the challenge of membership of the European Community
- to continue to promote pupil interest in foreign travel as a means of familiarising themselves with both the language and the culture of our European neighbours
- further to explore the use of technology in language teaching, and in particular the potentialities of the use of electronic mail for communicating regularly with the pupils of European schools

C: MANAGING PEOPLE

- to encourage the departmental staff fully to participate in departmental meetings and to take every opportunity for enhancing their own teaching skills, as well as their conformity to the school's policies for correcting and marking pupil work, and for recording and communicating to parents pupil achievement

D: MANAGING RESOURCES

- to maintain and develop the resources of the language department both within the financial allocation provided from the school budget and from such other sources as may be obtained

© Routledge 1993

Lee Smith

Lee Smith has been at the school for fifteen years, as head of department for the past six. He is a highly competent and experienced teacher of modern languages, fluent in French and German and with a good working knowledge of Italian. That he has been learning Urdu has only become known to a few of his fellow teachers because he has been overheard conversing with a group of Asian pupils, to their obvious enjoyment and occasional good-natured amusement. He makes good use of technology in his teaching, is scrupulous in his preparation and marking, and demands the highest standards of his pupils. They may grumble but they produce for him and his team some of the best GCSE results in the school.

He is a firm but unobtrusive disciplinarian. He has taken a number of school parties abroad, always with a thoroughly researched and purposive cultural and linguistic programme. Pupils know that 'you don't go for fun, you go because you want to improve your chances'. And they go. Some of them even acknowledge that they have not only learnt but enjoyed themselves and that 'Smithy isn't too bad, really!'

Lee is now 46, possibly a little disenchanted by failure to achieve promotion, though he shows little sign of real ambition and is even openly critical of those who do. He is inclined to say: 'I came into the profession to teach, not to manage.' He is respected rather than liked, sociable rather than gregarious. His hobbies are sailing and boat-building: he is a competent woodcarver and he has exhibited at local craft fairs.

The Head of Lower School, recently in post, has expressed her disappointment and concern at Lee's apparent lack of interest in his Year 9 tutor group. The school has recently been much involved in fund raising for local charities, and Year 9 has been in the forefront of developing community projects that are enhancing the school's reputation. 9LS has taken little part in these.

Furthermore, when other groups are planning and discussing, or looking at social issues of importance using the study packs recently prepared by the head of Lower School, 9LS is being told to get on with their school work, because 'education is about learning, not sponsored swims'. Lee uses the tutor time routinely to look at pupils' work in any subject, and occasionally to deliver

© Routledge 1993

homilies about the importance of neatness, spelling and punctuation to future good GCSE results.

His students are well aware of what goes on in tutor time in other tutor groups. A few feel that they are being deprived and two bold spirits have been to see the head of Lower School to ask if they can transfer to a 'more interesting tutor group', but so far she has not acceded to any such request. For one thing, she is well aware that most parents of 9LS pupils thoroughly approve of 'the way Mr Smith keeps their noses to the grindstone'.

However, relationships between Lee and the head of Lower School deteriorated recently when she sought to discuss with Lee two cases of serious domestic upset concerning children in 9LS. His response was: 'If the school wants social workers, it should employ them.' She shared her concern with the headteacher, who wondered whether a move next year to a final year tutor group might not be advantageous to all concerned. He floated the suggestion with the head of Upper School, who is, as it happens, a member of Lee's department. He made it clear that there would be considerable difficulties. 'At a personal level I think I could handle it. Unfortunately our management styles are very dissimilar. He runs departmental meetings by giving instructions – I can't remember when we last had a discussion.'

© Routledge 1993

Goals: Gerry Manners, curriculum coordinator for humanities.

In addition to teaching her own class in accordance with the school curricular policy:

A: MANAGING POLICY

• will communicate to the headteacher and deputy head information about curricular changes in humanities subjects brought about by the introduction and consolidation of the National Curriculum

B: MANAGING LEARNING

• while maintaining the required central focus on our national heritage, will encourage the recognition of the part played by ethnic minorities and women, and the importance of global approaches to environmental issues
• will be responsible for ensuring that all class teachers are well informed about the content and methodology of subjects within the broad field of humanities, particularly within the guidelines of the National Curriculum
• will further explore ways of involving parents and members of the community in contributing to the humanities curriculum

C: MANAGING PEOPLE

• will promote through school-based in-service sessions and such other means as may be appropriate the sharing by class teachers of their knowledge and experience of humanities teaching
• will collaborate with other curriculum coordinators as appropriate on projects that emphasise the wholeness of human knowledge
• will enlarge through in-service training her own knowledge and skills in both the subject content and the field of education management as opportunities arise

D: MANAGING RESOURCES

• will develop and maintain suitable curriculum materials and resources within the financial limitations of her element of the school resources budget

© Routledge 1993

Gerry Manners

Gerry Manners is curriculum coordinator for humanities in Willow Lane primary school in a prosperous commuter suburb. She has been teaching for ten years now, for the last five in this school, and is known to be contemplating applications for deputy head posts in the near future.

The primary phase adviser – who happens to be a humanities specialist – has used Gerry on a number of INSET courses and thinks highly of her. The school's headteacher also thinks highly of her contributions to school-based training days.

The written humanities syllabus is a model of its kind and has been used as an exemplar for other coordinators in the school. Its aims and objectives are clear and succinct; the year-by-year sequencing demonstrates a clear understanding of the potential for learning of pupils over the whole primary age range; and the needs of both the gifted and the slow learner have not been overlooked. The approach is pupil- and activity-centred, and each phase of the syllabus is cross-referenced to a materials and resource bank in which local 'living' resources feature prominently. Gerry devotes many hours to updating the syllabus and researching new materials.

Recently the headteacher has become increasingly aware that Gerry's effectiveness as a coordinator does not appear to match up to all this excellent preparation. Except in her own class and that of the newly qualified colleague who teaches the parallel class and for whom she is mentor, most of the actual teaching, though colleagues at the beginning of each school year seem enthusiastic to use her methods, reverts rapidly to 'chalk and talk'. Teachers claim – with some justification – that they find themselves too preoccupied with large classes and the needs of other areas of the curriculum to devote to humanities the extensive planning that a resource-based curriculum demands. They add that what parents want – and indeed what the National Curriculum seems to be requiring – is a good solid basis of factual knowledge in history and geography, 'without frills' as one of them put it. Gerry maintains, citing the phase adviser in support, that the aims of the National Curriculum in these two subjects are being met through an integrated humanities approach.

© Routledge 1993

Chapter 11

The appraisal statement

We have given considerable space in Chapter 3 to the detailed implications of the regulations and guidelines for the compilation and circulation of the appraisal statement. It is worthwhile, we feel, briefly to summarise the key issues before we go on to consider an issue that was not apparent in the early days of appraisal training but which loomed large as appraisers now found themselves faced with the task of writing appraisal statements.

- There are two parts to the appraisal statement: '[a record of] the main points made by the appraiser and the schoolteacher at the interview and the conclusions reached [and] any targets for action which shall be recorded in a separate annex to (but forming part of) the appraisal statement' (Regulations §10(2)).
- The first part derives, *inter alia*, from a 'review of the schoolteacher's work, including successes' (we would prefer the word 'achievements' since 'successes' is value-laden) 'and areas for development identified since the previous appraisal [and] discussion of the appraisee's role in, and contribution to, the policies and management of the school, and any constraints which the circumstances of the school place on him or her' (Guidelines §40).
- Copies of the appraisal statement are held by the appraiser and appraisee, the headteacher and, for LEA schools, *on request*, the CEO or his designated representative. The chair of governors, whether of LEA or grant-maintained schools, is entitled to see the appraisal statement of the headteacher *and of no other member of staff*. The chair, and no other governor, has a right to see, on request, a copy of the targets for action.
- The agreed appraisal statement is signed by appraiser and appraisee; the latter may append a note of dissent if agreement cannot be reached by negotiation.
- All documentation that contributed to the appraisal interview is destroyed soon after agreement is reached; and the appraisal statement is retained for 'at least three months' (Regulations §14 (4)) after the next appraisal, though Guidelines §57 appears to recommend retention for four years, that is, until the next but one appraisal is completed.

THE APPRAISAL STATEMENT: PART I

It was only when a few LEAs and schools, other than those involved in the pilot study in the late 1980s, began to introduce appraisal trials in the period shortly before the start date for appraisal (September 1992) that teachers and trainers alike began to be aware of problems and pitfalls. Teachers are so practised in writing reports that it probably occurred to few of them that there would need to give special consideration to both content and the avoidance of potential disagreements. Negotiation with pupils over the content of school reports is, even in the current climate of collaborative endeavour, a rarity and value judgments in school reports are commonplace. They are prognostic of future successes – or failures – and schoolteachers are much given to exhortation and encouragement. The appraisal statement must follow the appraisal interview in being non-judgmental and, if the appraiser is to avoid the contribution by the appraisee of a note of dissent or, worse still, a request for a second appraisal by another appraiser, it must be negotiated until agreement is reached.

It was in this final pre-appraisal training year that we started to ask workshop members who had been involved as observers in appraisal interview role-play to consider how they would draft the appraisal statement. There was never time in the programme for them actually to do this, and in any case this, the last activity in the workshop, precluded the possibility of our giving any practical response to their consideration. Instead, what happened was that we were asked to provide an example of an appraisal statement; and, though we were reluctant as trainers to provide anything that looked like a model of good practice to be copied or imitated, this we began to do.

In much the same period, we began to work with a group of primary headteachers who had already been fully trained in the appraisal process as it would operate within their schools and who had now volunteered to be the first cohort of peer appraisers for headteacher appraisal. The group agreed to trial the whole process, including the writing of the appraisal statement. We evaluated this trial by means of a time log and a questionnaire. Both revealed concerns over the appraisal statement: the logs showed up to two hours being spent by the appraiser in drafting; the questionnaire responses gave indications of serious unease on the part of both appraiser and appraisee about the content and the structure. Although our evaluation specifically avoided the identification of schools, we were asked by a number of headteachers at our next workshop for this pilot group if we would look at and comment on the appraisal statements that their appraisers had written. We agreed, provided that their appraisers had no objection, since they too would inevitably be identified to us in the process.

From these 'guinea pig' statements and from the admissions of other headteachers engaged in the trial, it transpired that there was little concept of an appropriate framework for the appraisal statement. If these experienced primary headteachers, in all other respects well trained in and well informed about the appraisal process, felt themselves to be in need of guidance over the appraisal statement drafted by a peer headteacher, then plainly they and other headteachers in that LEA would have difficulty in setting up an acceptable common practice within their schools. We asked around during the following half year and found this concern to be common in both primary and secondary state schools, both LEA and grant-maintained. We therefore concluded that this chapter was essential, to headteachers for their own appraisal statements and to provide a framework for appraisal statements within their schools, and to appraisers and appraisees so that they will be well informed and therefore less inclined to be stressed by this element of the appraisal process.

Consistent practice

We have seen a number of LEA schemes for appraisal and in most of them we have found appendices containing appraisal statement proformas. While we admire the thoroughness with which these have been drafted, we doubt whether uniformity of presentation really meets the needs of the users. Indeed, it may actually frustrate good practice. One has to ask oneself, in considering the need for an LEA proforma – or, more accurately, a multiplicity of proformas – who the prime users are. The base location of the appraisal statement is the school, those most immediately concerned with the content of the statement are the appraiser, the appraisee and the headteacher. LEA inspectors have made clear to us that they will have neither the time nor the inclination to exercise their right as the representatives of the CEO to see all appraisal statements. They are likely to limit their reading of a statement to a specific occasion: when it is in the interest of a teacher or the school, and very occasionally the LEA, that they have access to it. This may be when a local inspector has been called in to advise and support, or when a school development review is imminent and it is helpful to have a sight, for example, of the goals towards which a curriculum leader or senior manager has been working. There will *not* be comparability of appraisal statements, neither within the school nor, most emphatically between schools. The LEA interest in the written outcome of the appraisal interview is therefore limited. The school has ownership of the process, subject to conformity with the DFE and LEA regulations and guidelines and, of course, with its own policy statement on appraisal that will have been approved by the governing body. It should therefore have ownership of the product.

There is, we believe, no need for the constraints of space which the proforma imposes, nor for the embarrassment of having more space than the appraiser wishes to fill. In the age of the word-processor the proforma is obsolete. What is needed is clear guidance on the content of the statement. This is a more realistic approach to consistency, as Figure 11.1 demonstrates.

- The appraisal statement is confidential to the appraisee, the appraiser, the headteacher and the CEO's named representative.

PART I

- The record of the appraisal interview is not a narrative of the dialogue. The agenda will usually determine the paragraph headings. The content of the paragraphs will consist of agreed significant points.
- The statement will be non-judgmental. It will record the achievements of the appraisee set against previously agreed goals.
- Where goals have not been achieved, the reasons will be explored in the interview and set out briefly in the statement. The effective appraiser will have identified areas of potential non-achievement in advance in discussions between appraisals and particularly in the follow-up interview. Goals will have been modified or supportive action taken.
- Data collected by the appraiser should not be quoted nor should provider(s) of data be identifiable in the appraisal statement.
- The debriefing will normally have dealt adequately with the outcomes of the specific classroom observations. Where classroom performance is an agenda item, as it should be for all but senior managers, the appraisal interview will cover wider ground, possibly including specific focal areas identified in observation as needing further support.
- The appraisal statement will be drafted by the appraiser, shared with or passed to the appraisee for verification as a true record and, when agreed or amended, signed by both. The wording should be standard within the school and, since the document may be referred to in disciplinary cases (see Regulations §14 and Guidelines §68), this is probably one occasion when, for LEA schools, a standard form of wording is advisable. A suggested format:
  I believe this to be a fair and accurate record of the main points of the appraisal interview held on

  ....
                                              (Appraiser's signature and date)
  I agree that this is a fair and accurate record of the main points of the appraisal interview held on ....
  or I wish to record the following note of dissent.

  ....
                                              (Appraisee's signature and date)
- To this appraisal statement will be added in a twelvemonth the report on the follow-up meeting. This should conform to the general principles outlined above and be signed by both parties, the wording similar to that for the appraisal statement.

© Routledge 1993

Figure 11.1 The appraisal statement: assistant teachers

Contracting for support

The point has been made repeatedly in this book that the appraisal interview is only a part of a continuous appraisal process. Although not to be included in the appraisal statement, it is useful to have a record of agreed actions arising from the interview. It is very easy in the busy life of the school for those short but important review meetings that support the appraisee and update the appraiser to be overlooked and there needs to be agreement on the frequency of these occasions, even to the point of an agreed date for the first one after the appraisal interview. Undertakings by the appraiser to refer to the headteacher of the senior management team requests for resources, support or in-service training need to be noted. Actions by the appraisee that do not amount to goals should be minuted so that later reference to them may be made. A provisional date for the formal follow-up meeting a year later should be decided upon.

Some LEAs have made provision on the obverse of the proforma for the appraisal statement for these and similar details. We believe that this is an administrative error. In the first place, there will rarely be anything here that might be regarded as confidential. Rather, it is an *aide mémoire*, and as such might with advantage be pinned up in an office, and certainly not regarded as having the highly restricted availability of the appraisal statement itself. Secondly, the more the appraisal statement is brought out into the light of day, other than for reasons directly connected with its content, the greater the likelihood that confidentiality will accidentally be breached. Thirdly, it is unlikely that the headteacher and the CEO's representative will be concerned with these minutiae; the more paper there is to read, the less attention is paid to what is important.

THE APPRAISAL STATEMENT: PART II

Here, on a separate annex, the agreed goals for the appraisee for the next two years will be set out. Wherever possible a goal should include a time line. For some goals, those that are immediately identifiable as finite, there should be a completion date. Not all goals will necessarily appear on the agenda of the next appraisal interview, and those with completion dates of less than a year may well feature in the agenda of the follow-up meeting.

Some goals will have more complex time lines. Elements of the goal will be recognised as achievable within the two-year period, but the goal as a whole may extend well beyond that time. It is important, therefore, to be precise about what is expected and agreed to be attained. Such goals, in particular, are likely to interlock with the school's development plan, and there will be external factors which will influence and even determine the time line. We emphasise the need for appraisers to familiarise themselves with the development plan before agreeing goals; and it may be necessary for them to consult senior management at the draft stage to ensure that there is harmony between individual goals and whole school policy.

The goal must be precisely formulated. It helps neither the appraisee nor the appraiser if it is vague. As we have indicated in that part of Chapter 4 that deals with goalsetting, a goal such as 'to improve communication with staff' has no validity. It will end up being no more than a pious hope, since it begs, not merely the question, but a number of questions. What areas of communication in particular? How? By what stage should something tangible have been achieved? and so on. Compare this with the precision and necessary detail of this goal from a headteacher's goalsetting:

* to continue to inform teaching staff about newly established procedures and systems for controlling budgets and finances, and to delegate progressively over the next two years to senior members of staff responsibilities for financial control as part of the school's recently revised development plan and the professional development programme.

While the headteacher has the freedom to interpret 'progressively', for example, in the light of the speed with which members of staff, individually and collectively, have assimilated complex procedures and systems, there is sufficient precision here to make this a goal that is open to monitoring and, in two years' time, to effective and useful appraisal.

The chair of governors has a right under Regulation §13(1)(d) to receive, on request, 'a copy of any annex to the appraisal statement recording targets for action'. It is unlikely that any chair of governors, however well informed, will glean much from the goals of individual members of staff. The wise headteacher will collate them and present them as the means whereby the school development plan is being implemented. In that form, in which no teacher is identified by name or function, the paper may well be presented to governors within a meeting agenda, either when consideration is being given to the development plan or when a report is being made on the progress of the appraisal process.

Exemplars of the appraisal statement

We offer on the following pages two appraisal statements, one for a primary teacher, the other for a secondary teacher. Both Andrea Bull and Vicky Hoyle have featured throughout this book, and the statements derive from the case studies, the classroom observation in the case of Vicky Hoyle, and the appraisal interviews of both. We do not regard these as definitive in form or 'ideal types' but rather as presentations which appraisers might like to discuss and criticise as they seek a format appropriate to their school and their own styles.

For Vicky Hoyle we also give an example of the appraisal statement part II.

Andrea Bull: Appraisal statement Part I

AGENDA:

- class teaching
- work as curriculum coordinator
- standards of written work
- progression in reading
- personal and professional development.

CLASS TEACHING: CLASS 3AB

Andrea's classroom is organised to give easy access to resources and the children are able to work independently. The display at the time of my first visit reflected ongoing work on the family and, on my return visit, on the care of our environment. I have, both before and since the observations, seen attractive displays, all relevant to work in hand or recently completed, over a wide range of curricular topics. The work of children of all abilities is displayed.

In spite of the lack of funds there is a wide range of reading resources reflecting the multi-ethnic nature of the class. These are much used, and kept in a good state of repair, by the children themselves, and, so I was told, also by parents. Some 'storyboard' books, intended for ESL children, have been used with the whole class, enhancing the status of the children from minority ethnic groups.

There is a variety of teaching strategies. The children work often in small groups, socially mixed and compatible. Each group has a leader responsible for orderly behaviour and for asking for help when it is needed. The leadership changes from time to time. The children are able to explain clearly what they were doing. Andrea is unobtrusive but clearly in control, and gives help where needed. The atmosphere of the class is happy and cooperative and they are keen to share their work with visitors.

Andrea asked me to make my specific observation focus the children's attention spans. Possibly because of her longer experience with older primary children, some of the activities make demands that a few in this class initially found difficult to cope with. Andrea is well aware of which children might be flagging and gives help and encouragement. We agreed that to break down tasks into sub-tasks might enhance self-esteem, particularly

© Routledge 1993

among slow learners. We have discussed this issue several times since the observation lesson and Andrea feels increasingly confident.

CURRICULUM COORDINATOR

Andrea has collected a wide variety of inexpensive language resources over the past 18 months and makes sure they are available to other teachers. She recently organised a half day's INSET for the whole staff on language teaching, including ESL work, where she made good use of the section 11 teacher.

WRITTEN WORK

In response to the Development Review report, Andrea has revised the school's guidelines for presentation of written work and work in all classes is beginning to reflect the influence of these new guidelines.

READING

A variety of methods has always been used throughout the school and Andrea can see no good grounds for changing the reading policy. Real books have their place alongside phonics and whatever other methods meet the needs of the individual child. This policy is well understood and supported by all members of staff and has recently been reinforced, having been an item on the agenda of a full staff meeting.

PERSONAL AND PROFESSIONAL DEVELOPMENT

Andrea would like more experience and training in management, with a view to eventual promotion. She wishes to continue to specialise in language work.

In my opinion this is a fair and accurate record of the main points of the appraisal interview held on..

Signed..(appraiser) Date:...................

I agree that this is a fair and accurate record of the main points of the appraisal interview held on ....

Signed... (appraisee) Date:...................

© Routledge 1993

Vicky Hoyle: Appraisal statement Part I

AGENDA

- work as Year Tutor
- history teaching
- improved presentation of pupils' written work
- library
- personal and professional development.

YEAR TUTOR

In particular we considered Vicky's work with group tutors. She has led discussions with all tutors on the agreed tutorial programme, to encourage its implementation. She has provided INSET for less experienced tutors, both by working alongside and by giving the opportunity of watching more experienced tutors at work. The time for this has been limited by the need to fill in for staff absences, and senior management is asked to consider appointing as from next term supernumerary group tutors for Lower School where pupils have the greatest need of support.

HISTORY TEACHING

Vicky is now following the National Curriculum and in the view of her head of department is making a significant contribution to the history team. She has been observed with a Year 10 and a Year 7 class, the former by the head of department, the latter by me. In all her classes a friendly atmosphere is to be seen, yet there is firm control. The pupils are on task and aware of the purpose of the lesson. Younger pupils have a wide range of tasks appropriate to the variety of levels of potential attainment. Those in and approaching their GCSE year showed great enthusiasm for most aspects of the syllabus but may need firm guidance towards the less attractive areas of the syllabus.

WRITTEN WORK

Vicky has developed a variety of techniques appropriate to the age and stage of the pupils and is consistent in her use of them.

© Routledge 1993

LIBRARY

Vicky willingly took on the tasks of indexing, chasing lost books and accessioning for the history section of the library. She did not expect that this would involve her in the wider scope of the IT resources working party, and has taken part in its frequent meetings, albeit with reluctance. There seems to have been a failure of communication and understanding by others of her job specification, which, she wishes me to state, has not been extended to include this further commitment. She has undertaken to clarify her role in the working party with the member of the senior management team concerned.

PERSONAL AND PROFESSIONAL DEVELOPMENT

Vicky seeks wider knowledge of tutorial methods, in particular of the 'help scheme' she has been working on. To this end she would like to visit a nearby school where she and I both understand good work to be taking place. She does not have career advancement in mind at the moment.

In my opinion this is a fair and accurate record of the main points of the appraisal interview held on..

Signed...(appraiser) Date:...................

I agree that this is a fair and accurate record of the main points of the appraisal interview held on ....

Signed... (appraisee) Date:...................

© Routledge 1993

Vicky Hoyle: Appraisal statement, Part II (Goals)

School year: 199x to 199y

As Year Tutor:

- to maintain the help and support she has been giving to group tutors
- further to develop her oversight of pupil and parent relationships with the school appropriate to the year for which she is currently responsible
- to widen her knowledge of tutorial methods and share her information with Lower School group tutors
- to develop a suitable role and plan an induction programme for a possible supernumerary tutor.

As history teacher:

- to maintain her present high standards of teaching at all levels
- to continue her contribution as a member of the history team
- in collaboration with the head of department, to develop the department's use of resources by means of exhibitions and displays.

Written work:

- to share her methodology when the senior management team's review of the strategies for improving written work is undertaken.

Resources:

- following her discussion with the chair of the IT resources working party, to continue her membership of it, but with a role specific to the interests of the history department.

This is an accurate record of the goals agreed following the appraisal interview held on ....

Signed..(appraiser) Date:..................

I agree that this is an accurate record of the goals agreed following the appraisal interview held on......................................

Signed...(appraisee) Date:..................

© Routledge 1993

Chapter 12

Appraising headteachers and deputies

Until the late 1980s few LEAs had given their headteachers any indication of the criteria under which they were accountable. Morgan *et al.* (1983) had in their research into secondary headteacher selection, the POST project as it became known, found 'only one of 85 LEAs [which] provided a written description of its view of the full range of secondary heads' duties'. They found no instance of selectors using even the most elementary job analysis to identify the requirements for a particular post. Two years later the same team, now completing a follow-up study on the role of the secondary headteacher, concluded that 'a satisfactory definition of headship must include how heads approach the job as well as the tasks they perform' (Hall *et al.* 1985).

It may be argued that we have come a long way since then. No headteacher is without a job specification. All are aware of their goals and the requirement that, through appraisal, they will regularly examine the extent to which they have attained those goals, both through self-appraisal and in the appraisal interview and its follow-up. Yet we cannot help wondering after some of our workshops whether there is sufficient recognition, both by the appraisees themselves and by those peers and LEA inspectors who will appraise them, of the radical shift in the role of school leadership over the past decade.

If it is important for the appraisal of assistant teachers that they have a clear concept of goals agreed with their managers and consonant with whole school policy, then it is even more important that headteachers have similar clarity. Headteacher goals are the prime means whereby that whole school policy is implemented, and are the crux of the school's success. Yet can any headteacher today be the sole implementer of policy?

CORPORATE MANAGEMENT

The weight of administrative and managerial responsibility has led many headteachers, particularly of secondary schools and large primary schools, on the road towards corporate or collegial management. The senior management team is no longer, as it was once in many schools, a convenient shorthand form for the headteacher and the deputies, with possibly several other senior members of staff, but without any clear definition of the team's function. It is now coming to mean a team of senior staff, sometimes selected not merely for seniority but also for their specific functions which contribute to the effective performance of a team (Belbin, 1981). They not only share with the headteacher the decision-making but also severally assume responsibility for particular areas of management. Readers will not need to be reminded that the ultimate responsibility rests with the headteacher; but, the more the school is charged with complex and innovatory task networks, the more delegation with authority to act becomes the necessary mode. Implementing and monitoring the National Curriculum, for example, may become part of the job specification of the deputy head, working with curriculum coordinators or heads of department and in accordance with guidelines planned by the senior management team chaired by the headteacher. Budgetary control may in a secondary school become the province of a non-teaching member of staff, a bursar, responsible for advising the senior management team on policy options and implementing those which the team determines upon. With the headteacher, the bursar may well be a member of the governors' finance committee, which will have delegated powers from the governing body.

This radical shift in the role of the headteacher was foreseen long since. In the mid-1970s, Meredydd Hughes, himself a former headteacher of distinction and shortly to become professor of education at Birmingham University, contributed a chapter entitled 'The professional-as-administrator: the case of the secondary school head' to a symposium edited by Peters (1976). In it he sought, on the evidence of an extensive research project, first to differentiate between two models of headship, the head as chief executive and the head as leading professional, and secondly to reconcile and unify the two models. He concluded that it was now patently obvious that 'the specialised work of maintaining the organisation in operation' (Barnard, 1938) could no longer be reserved to the headteacher as chief executive, but must be shared if headteachers were to survive. Even more to the point, if one accepts the contention by Hughes 'that the chief executive is concerned both with what happens within the organisation *and with the relation of the organisation to the wider system of which it is part*' [our italics], the increasing contact between individual members of the senior staff of schools and officers and inspectors of the LEA of itself leads to a corporate concept of the chief executive role.

In his attempt to reconcile the chief executive role with the leading professional role, Hughes draws a distinction between the traditional and innovative aspects of a headteacher's professionalism, and concludes 'an innovating emphasis is more easily reconciled with the head's managerial responsibilities'. Today few educationists would talk about the 'traditional', but rather would differentiate between the maintenance and innovative functions of leadership. The message here is surely that, if all the members of the collegial team are successfully to combine the chief executive and the leading professional roles, they must each have within their job specifications goals which are concerned with maintenance and with innovation.

If it is accepted that headteachers' successful management of their schools will be heavily dependent on the achievements, at all levels, of their staff, it would seem to follow that their appraisal ought to focus on the processes of management rather than the quantifiable outcomes. Much energy is currently being expended on setting up batteries of performance indicators whereby one school can be measured against another. Accountability is, of course, the vogue word for the new decade; but it may well be that the expenditure of energy and ingenuity in seeking measurements of 'throughputs' and 'outputs' will in the long run prove to be counterproductive to sound educational management. The appraisal of headteachers and their deputies must primarily to be concerned with the extent to which, on the one hand, they have facilitated, inspired, planned, evaluated and stabilised within the school; and, on the other hand, sought and achieved for the school a public image as a caring centre of learning. It is not easy to find measuring rods which will quantify achievements in these domains.

In one respect the role of headteachers is unique: however much they may share or devolve responsibility, each is the member of staff wholly accountable to the governing body for what goes on in the school. Their appraisal must therefore look inward, to the success of the leadership of the school, and outward to the success of relations with governors, LEAs, parents, pupils and the wider public and to the implementation of local and national policy.

THE APPRAISAL INTERVIEW

There are important differences in appraisal at the level of top management, and in particular that of headteachers, that materially affect the way in which the appraisal interview is planned, prepared for and conducted and in which, finally, the appraisal statement is drawn up. In the first place, since every headteacher, even of the smallest primary school, is a manager, management must be the significant feature in the appraisal interview. Yet management cannot properly be appraised without being in some way observed any more than classroom performance can properly be appraised unless the appraiser has seen the teacher teach; and so the same rigour must be applied to the appraisal of management as to classroom observation.

Some aspects of management can of course be observed casually. Just as a classroom display with an out-of-date exhibition of pupils' work, badly mounted and gathering dust, sounds a clear note of concern over the class teacher's performance in those important peripherals, regardless of whether or not she may give an outstanding 'demonstration' lesson, so the entrance to a school which is not welcoming and informative speaks ill of a headteacher's attitude to the world beyond the gates. There are many such casual observations that an appraiser may make that take up no time, neither hers nor that of any member of staff:

- How are visitors received? If the school serves a multi-ethnic population, are there greetings and directions in ethnic languages and scripts?
- Do students move about corridors purposively? Do they demonstrate good manners to a visitor? If addressed, do they answer sensibly and helpfully?
- When pupils are in playgrounds, what is the general nature of their activities? Is there anti-social behaviour? Are there any areas of physical danger? What supervision is there and how is it exercised?
- What is the atmosphere in the staff room? Whether staff are discussing work, pupils or their leisure activities, is there a general attitude of friendliness and cooperation? Are they welcoming to a visiting colleague? Are there cliques?
- Are notices, in the staff room and elsewhere, well displayed? Are obsolete notices still in evidence?

This list of indirect observations could be much extended. Inspectors and governors who visit schools frequently have their own pet areas of observation. One (male) ex-HMI of our acquaintance always made a beeline for the boys' toilets, claiming that it told him more about the school than anything else.

Some headteachers may react to these apparently trivial observations by saying: what have they to do with my management of the school? These are all matters that I delegate to others. Our response is that the effectiveness of delegation is certainly a matter of considerable relevance to the headteacher's management expertise. The appraiser is, however, not going around to jot down Brownie points and black marks. Only in the appraisal interview is it possible to explore what lies behind the observations: how far what has been seen is a consequence of good management and how far major shortcomings are a reflection of deficiencies in management which might be translated into useful goals for the future.

What has been seen casually is as much part of data collection as any formal interview session with staff member, parent or governor, and is important to the headteacher's peer appraiser. It must be remembered that, unlike the intra-school appraisal of assistant teachers about whom much is already known to the appraiser, here the appraiser has a need both to capture the atmosphere of the school and to create for herself a backcloth for the appraisal interview. Only if the appraisal interview is well structured and relates to specific and aptly defined goals can the appraisal statement possibly be an effective document. It is clear from our evaluations, endorsed in workshops, in discussions and in one-to-one interviews with peer appraisers, that time must be given to this familiarisation activity.

The appraisal process does not, we have emphasised repeatedly, start with the appraisal interview. For the headteacher – and for the deputy headteacher where the practice is for the deputy of another school to be the second appraiser – the process begins with the first visit to the colleague's school. Much has been made of the need to support an appraisee in the period between the goals set at the appraisal interview and the selection of those for the agenda of the next appraisal interview two years later. Little has been said about the need, whenever appraisal involves someone from outside the school as it does here, and particularly whenever a new appraiser is appointed, for time to be allocated in which the appraiser gains the confidence of the appraisee and the essential background of the context in which management skills are exercised. The argument for the continuity of the appraiser-appraisee bond as long as possible is overwhelming.

ALL HEADTEACHERS AS PEER APPRAISERS?

It is probably this more than any other single factor which has led some LEAs to decide that, in effect, all their headteachers will be appraisers. This is a bold step, but it is one which has four signal advantages:

- It challenges the concept that there is a hierarchy of headteachers in the authority, based upon long service or some other criteria, and therefore, inevitably, an élite which can appraise and the rest who can but wait their turn.
- If every headteacher is a peer appraiser, then the considerable time load involved in headteacher appraisal is reduced by a factor of three.
- No distinction need be made between training for peer appraisers and for headteacher appraisees, appropriately so since it is virtually impossible to differentiate between their respective needs.
- The continuing relationship between peer appraiser and appraisee is likely to develop the concept of *critical friend*; as the inspectorial-and-supportive function of the LEA advisory service is handed over to an external team with the sole remit to inspect, the peer appraiser may well fill the vacuum.

There are some obvious concerns:

- *Surely there will be some headteachers who will not have the confidence of their peers, for whatever reason?*
There may well be, is the response, but we prefer to take an optimistic stance and to have contingency plans for individual cases of breakdown.
- *Will newly appointed headteachers, until they have undergone a training programme, have sufficient knowledge of their new LEA's appraisal procedures to be appraisers?*
Since they will have to begin the appraisal cycle afresh on assuming their new post (Guidelines §13) it is vital that training takes place soon after

appointment; and that training will equip them to appraise as well as to be appraised.

• *Will there not be those whose retirement date is imminent making it impossible for them to see a colleague through the whole of an appraisal cycle?*

This is so, and here too there will be need of contingency planning. However, the expertise and wisdom of such headteachers should not be too quickly discarded. Some may even be able and willing to carry on their peer appraisal role for a while, as they may within the regulations.

Interestingly, the principle behind this construct for peer appraisal has much in common with the 'each one teach one' principle established by Paulo Freire for the eradication of illiteracy in the underdeveloped countries. The purpose may be quite different, but the concept of believing in the mutuality of the teaching and learning processes in any activity is the same.

Matching appraiser and appraisee

There are two ways of doing this: by pairing and by a 'net' in which A appraises B, B appraises C, and so on, as we have explained in an earlier chapter. Most LEAs adopting the one-to-one formula have chosen the latter. There is a danger of cosiness in paired appraisal; or, if not of that, of others thinking that the appraisal has lacked rigour. The size of the net can be controlled: six to eight seems the ideal number. There can be a geographical spread, if this is desired, though, for primary schools certainly, some LEAs may prefer to capitalise on the existing links within consortia or clusters. A headteacher willing to act as 'net coordinator' can set up the net, allowing the members negative choice; and she may be a useful point of reference if problems arise.

CREATING THE AGENDA FOR HEADTEACHER APPRAISAL

It will be surprising if the agenda contained more than two or three items. One reason for this is that goals at this level are complex, covering a number of areas of management. This we can best demonstrate by analysing the headteacher's goal that we commended to you as an exemplar earlier in the previous chapter:

> to continue to inform teaching staff about newly established procedures and systems for controlling budgets and finances, and to delegate progressively over the next two years to senior members of staff responsibilities for financial control as part of the school's recently revised development plan and the professional development programme.

Here we have a proliferation of management issues and appraiser and appraisee have to answer the question: do we explore in depth the extent to which this goal has been achieved and risk not having the time for even a second item on the agenda? Or is there some way in which we can explore aspects of this goal, not by selecting at random but by making an informed choice? Fortunately there is.

THE SCHOOL MANAGEMENT COMPETENCES PROJECT (SMCP)

In Chapter 10 you may have observed that we applied the goals of Vicky Hoyle and Andrea Bull to four main heads: managing policy, managing learning, managing people and managing resources. These are the key functions of the SMCP.

In 1991 Wolverhampton Polytechnic, now the University of Wolverhampton, was selected to structure, trial and pilot a project in nine West Midland LEAs to create national benchmarks for management competency. They did not have to start from scratch. The Training, Enterprise and Education Directorate (TEED) had already explored the ground but, as that body's title implies, not with specific reference to standards of management in schools.

The main findings of the project have now been made publicly available (University of Wolverhampton, 1993) and the details are too extensive to be set out in detail here. The standards framework consists of six elements, the first three of which we believe provide a taxonomy useful in goalsetting, the selection of task observations and, above all, in contributing to the selection of those goals which will most effectively form the agenda of the appraisal interview. The first three elements are: the key purpose, or mission statement; the four key functions, to which we refer above; units of competence, which are subdivisions of the functions, 10 in all. Beyond this there are further subdivisions, called elements, performance criteria and range indicators. These, while appropriate to a finely tuned exploration and evaluation of the management of an educational institution, are beyond the basic needs of the appraisal process.

The 10 units are simple subdivisions of the key functions as can be seen in Figure 12.1 on page 180.

Even by using only the key functions, it is now possible to analyse the management issues. The main thrust of the goal, the effective management of the delegated budget, unquestionably equates with key function D, managing resources and with D2, if one wants to refine it further. The concern to relate this aspect of school management with overall school development equates with 'A: Managing policy' and specifically with A1. All other aspects of the goal – staff training and development, communication, delegation, but 'progressively' and therefore, by implication, monitoring – are contained within 'C: Managing people' and reflect three of the four units, C2, C3 and C4.

This analysis helps appraiser and appraisee to decide what best to appraise.

A: Managing policy	A1: Review, develop and present school objectives and policies
	A2: Develop supportive relationships with pupils, staff, parents, governors and the community
B: Managing learning	B1: Review, develop and implement means for supporting pupils' learning
	B2: Monitor and evaluate learning programmes
C: Managing people	C1: Recruit and select teaching and non-teaching staff
	C2: Develop teams, individuals and self to enhance performance
	C3: Plan, allocate and evaluate work carried out by teams, individuals and self
	C4: Create, maintain and enhance working relationships
D: Managing resources	D1: Secure effective resource allocation
	D2: Monitor and control the use of resources

© University of Wolverhampton School Management Competences Project

Figure 12.1 School management competences

This goal is obviously an important area of the managerial activity of this headteacher and therefore must be included, but to examine every one of the units detailed would certainly take up an excessive amount of the appraisal interview. Managing resources (D) might be considered less a concern of appraisal and more a concern of the school development review. What stands out is this headteacher's concern, as a matter of policy, to involve members of staff in this innovation, at the simplest level by ensuring that they are informed, at a higher level by giving to selected staff responsibilities for the execution of the innovation, at the highest by including them in the decision-making process. This suggests that a suitable task observation might be of the conduct by the headteacher of a staff – or joint staff and governing body – finance committee; that data collection might include a talk with one teacher at each of the three levels indicated above; and that the agenda item uses this goal to explore the philosophy and practice of interpersonal relationships between senior management and the main body of the staff.

Clearly, one headteacher goal, at least, on the appraisal interview agenda is likely to be multifacet. The choice by appraiser and appraisee of the other one or two agenda items – bearing in mind that 'personal and professional development' should also appear as a matter of course on every appraisal agenda – ought now to be of single-issue items and, by design, in management areas other than those covered by the item we have analysed.

THE HEADTEACHER APPRAISAL STATEMENT

In the light of what we have written, it is possible to modify Figure 11.1 in the previous chapter so that it reflects the differences in the conditions that determine the presentation of the headteacher appraisal statement, as shown in Figure 12.2 on page 182.

The regulations state clearly that 'the appraiser and appraisee should record, on all copies of the appraisal statement, the fact that the [follow-up] meeting has taken place, any modifications to professional targets which have been decided and the reasons for those modifications' (Guidelines §59, final paragraph). For headteacher appraisal this means that the chair of governor's copy of the appraisal statement will have to be reclaimed, unless it has been placed for safe-keeping in the hands of the appraiser, and brought up to date.

APPRAISING DEPUTY HEADTEACHERS

Nowhere are the DFE Regulations and Guidelines so deficient as in their concern for the appraisal of deputies. §22 of the Guidelines, on the selection of appraisers for 'school teachers (including deputy heads)' states that 'headteachers should not refuse requests from staff for an alternative appraiser if there are particular circumstances that suggest that this might be appropriate'. One can imagine that, for assistant members of staff, most headteachers will

- The appraisal statement is confidential to the appraisee, the two appraisers, in LEA schools the CEO or his representative (who may well already be one of the appraisers) and the chair of governors.

Part I

- The record of the appraisal interview is not a narrative of the dialogue. The agenda will rarely determine the paragraph headings; these are more likely to be the management issues that can be extrapolated from the discussion.

- The statement will be non-judgmental. It will record the achievements of the appraisee in the management of the school, as perceived through the in-depth study of the goals that formed the agenda.

- Where goals have not been achieved, or, more commonly, where some managerial aspects that relate to goals have been less successfully dealt with than others, the reasons will be explored and set out briefly in the statement. *The effective peer appraiser and his co-appraiser will have identified in advance, in discussions and particularly in the follow-up interview, areas of potential low achievement. Goals will have been modified if this is possible – it rarely is for headteachers – and, more usefully, supportive action will have been taken.*

- Data collected by the appraisers should not be quoted verbatim nor should providers of data be identifiable in the appraisal statement.

- Task observations will more often be ancillary to the appraisal interview than of direct relevance. They are intended to assist the peer appraiser to develop the necessary background for the interview and are most unlikely to be referred to directly in the appraisal statement.

- The appraisal statement will have been drafted by one or both of the appraisers, shared with or passed to the appraisee for verification as a true record and, when agreed, signed by all three. The appraisee has the right to sign a note of dissent.

- To this appraisal statement will be added, one year later, the report of the follow-up meeting. This should conform to the general principles outlined above and should be signed by all three parties.

© Routledge 1993

Figure 12.2 The appraisal statement: headteachers

sympathetically hear a case for an appraiser other than the one assigned, and negotiate a change with the least damage to that appraiser's self-esteem. After all, headteachers will be well aware that appraisees may appeal later against their appraisal statements, through procedures which will make far more waves than a skilfully managed internal rearrangement.

What of deputy heads? Their line managers are their headteachers, the very people to whom they must appeal if they believe there are 'particular circumstances'. These, the paragraph concludes, are likely to be exceptional, for all assistant teachers. This is irrelevant, we believe. If there were only one case, it would be wrong that the decision on whether or not to grant an alternative appraiser were made by the person in whom a deputy had, as demonstrated by the fact of the appeal, no confidence.

We believe that there should be machinery whereby the deputy could seek to be appraised by the headteacher of another school. The Guidelines offer no guidance as to whether this would or would not be acceptable. Certainly such an alternative could not possibly be the deputy's line manager; the merit of the suggestion lies in the fact that (s)he has experience as a line manager of those of equal status.

It may be because of this confused situation that many deputies, advised by their local, regional and national union committees, are seeking the implemen-tation of Guidelines §30, whereby there may be appointed 'two appraisers where this is considered appropriate by the appraising body'. Yet even that conciliatory arrangement, allowed under regulation §8(6), is immediately followed by the statement that 'the headteacher will normally be one of the appraisers'.

This is a safeguard, we accept; yet where the appraising body has decided that two appraisers will indeed be 'considered appropriate' for all deputies, the added burden for the LEA inspectorate, already involved in the appraisal of all headteachers, will be considerable, for there are more deputies in an LEA's schools than headteachers.

LEA inspectors are not involved to the same extent as the peer appraisers of headteachers or the headteachers of deputies. They will be involved in the preliminary meeting, in agreeing the agenda, in the appraisal interview itself, in some cases in the writing up of the draft appraisal statement and in the meeting to agree the statement and future goals. They will also be involved in the follow-up meeting. Time logs of trial appraisals suggest that each appraisal of a headteacher or a deputy will occupy the inspector for 6–10 hours over the two-year cycle. As the number of LEA inspectors diminishes, the load on each one left will increase. There will come a time when the involvement of the LEA in the appraisal of a school's seniormost staff will be untenable.

Implicit in the appraisal of deputies on the same terms as headteachers, by two appraisers, ought to be their right to have their management skills appraised in similar fashion. The components of appraisal for headteachers includes 'task and/or classroom observation' (Guidelines §43), and most headteachers, except for those in the smallest primary schools where they carry a full teaching load, seem to have opted entirely for task observation. It would be surprising if they did not: their teaching skills may well be taken for granted; their management skills are at the heart of their appraisal interviews.

Yet there is no mention of any such alternative for deputies, or, in large secondary schools, other members of the senior management team. If the Regulations and Guidelines are not modified, then, as we have pointed out in Chapter 3, any task observation for these key personnel in school management will have to be additional to two classroom observations. This is not good time management! There would seem to be a regrettable ignorance on the part of the DFE of the managerial load currently being borne by the seniormost teachers in our schools.

SELF-APPRAISAL

The self-appraisal proforma in Chapter 9 is not really applicable to preparation for the appraisal interview by a headteacher or a deputy. If it were to be completed before the appraisal agenda had been agreed, it might well be a lengthy and not wholly helpful document. Indeed a full self-audit of this kind would be more applicable to preparation for the whole school review or inspection.

Given that the goals for the appraisal interview are agreed, then what the headteacher or other senior manager will find useful is to gain some perspective on the achievement of these goals. Figure 12.3 provides a means of relating these goals to a number of benchmarks. Once again these can be categorised under the SMCP key roles.

THE FOLLOW-UP AND FORMAL REVIEW

As with other members of staff, this is an important element of the appraisal process. Follow-up is less easy to bring about informally when neither appraiser is within the school. There is the likelihood that occasions will be agreed for discussion and that meetings will be called, urgent business for either the appraisee or peer appraiser arise, and there will be an increasing drift in these planned sessions. Equally, the appraisee may feel the need to discuss some matter well before an agreed date. This is where the concept of the critical friend is of such value: the appraiser as someone just a phone call away!

For many headteachers the role is a lonely one, though less lonely if it is shared with deputies and other senior staff. Yet there will always be situations that cannot be shared within the school for reasons of confidentiality and particularly when there are vested interests in high places. The long history of the headteacher as 'captain of the ship' willing to let it go down with all hands rather than send out a Mayday is over. The more exacting the demands of the teaching profession become, the more ways of breaking down traditional isolationism must be sought.

The formal review is easier to establish as a procedure. Its timing is known – a year after the appraisal interview – and an approximation of the time it will take. There will be no task observation, no data collection; the main purpose is to have a staged review of the progress made towards achieving goals, to modify them if necessary, to seek means of support when this may be wanted. Quite properly, it is recorded as an addendum to the previous appraisal statement; but its main purpose should be seen as supportive of a colleague in the onerous task of managing a school.

To prepare yourself properly for your appraisal interview it is wise to relate the goals on which you are being appraised to a number of qualitative indicators. Not all of them will be applicable to each of the goals on the agenda, and it is just possible that one or more may not be applicable to any of your chosen goals. You may find it valuable to share any written responses with your appraisers, but the activity will be no less useful if it is conducted at a purely personal level.

A: MANAGING POLICY

- How far have you through these goals reviewed and maintained existing school policy?
- Have you felt the need to modify or extend that policy? How far are you along the road to achieving this?
- Have you in any way sought and achieved the support of staff, parents, pupils and the wider community towards the implementation of that policy?
- How far has any of your goals maintained or developed relationships with other schools/colleges? local business and industry?

What circumstances have helped you? What hindered you?

B: MANAGING LEARNING

- To what extent have any of your goals been *directly* concerned with the management of pupil learning: as teacher and/or with responsibility for the development of learning programmes? To what extent have you achieved this goal?

What circumstances have helped you? What hindered you?

© Routledge 1993

Figure 12.3 A self-appraisal prompt list

C: MANAGING PEOPLE

• To what extent have these goals helped to build staff teams? to include staff, teaching and non-teaching, in the decision-making process? to devolve responsibilities without losing control?
• Through these goals has a greater awareness of the school's mission or key purpose been achieved among governors? parents? pupils? the wider community?
• How far has the quality of your staff improved, either through staff changes or through in-service education?

What circumstances have helped you? What hindered you?

D: MANAGING RESOURCES

• Have you achieved your goal of budgetary management?
• How far has the appearance of the school – its fabric, environment and general air of welcome – improved as a consequence of your management?

What circumstances have helped you? What hindered you?

AND FINALLY . . .

• Consider your personal development in this post. What satisfactions have you derived from the period under review? What have been the main frustrations?
• What goals would you consider appropriate for the next review period?

© Routledge 1993

Chapter 13

Grant-maintained schools and the regulations

In the light of the Conservative government's expressed desire to see a great number of schools become grant-maintained within the lifetime of the 1992 Parliament – and thus make them an integral part of the educational system which no change of government would be able to undo – it is not surprising that specific references to these schools are built into the Regulations and Guidelines. First, and most importantly if there was not to be a chaotic stop-start in the introduction of appraisal, there had to be continuity as a school achieved grant-maintained status. §16 of the Guidelines therefore makes it clear that, when a school becomes grant-maintained, all teachers who have started the appraisal cycle will continue it without a break.

This guideline appears to disregard the likely facts of translation from one type of school to another. For all teachers in a school which becomes grant-maintained there must be an updating of job specifications and identification of goals. Some teachers, indeed, may have entirely new managerial responsibilities as the school reorganises to meet its new obligations. We have heard a number of different reasons for this reorganisation: the appointment of a bursar has radically altered the role of the member of the senior management team responsible for financial control; the opportunity has arisen to add to the staff or increase the salaries and add to the responsibilities of some existing members of staff as a consequence of the additional funding that became available with grant-maintained status; the new status has provided greater flexibility, freedom from what were seen as bureaucratic control by the LEA, the opportunity for a rethink, radical or otherwise, of the management structure. In some schools all or many of these reasons have applied at the same time. What this means for appraisal is spelt out in Guidelines §13, applicable to all schools and not specifically to grant-maintained schools:

> If a teacher moves to a new post within the same school, there is discretion as to whether to start the appraisal cycle again or carry on the existing cycle. *Much will depend on how similar the responsibilities of the new post are to those of the old post* . . . (Our italics).

It would be surprising in these circumstances if many grant-maintained schools did not wish to make a clean sweep and a fresh start.

Furthermore, for schools that have become grant-maintained since September 1992, the appraising body will have changed; and it will have been necessary for the headteacher to re-present the school's appraisal policy for the approval of the new governing body, which now has unilateral responsibility for that policy, provided it does not conflict with the DFE regulations. It may be that there are elements of the LEA policy which the headteacher or the governing body felt to be inappropriate, given the school's new status.

Those schools which had grant-maintained status before September 1992 will have devised their appraisal policy in the light of that status. For them there are no complicating factors. The schools that will be particularly between the devil and the deep blue sea are those which have applied for grant-maintained status after September 1992 and which will have had to begin the appraisal process under one dispensation, and then have to make a rapid change to the other.

Having regard to the widely accepted and positive contribution of teacher appraisal to staff development, it would be regrettable if a grant-maintained school governing body decided to avail itself of the clause which allows their teachers exemption from commencing the appraisal cycle until *1 September 1995* (Regulation §6(4)). Furthermore, among those thus exempted would undoubtedly be some who were trained appraisers. We suspect that they would have little credibility among their colleagues if they were not themselves being appraised.

Fortunately the clause ends by stating that 'schools which become grant-maintained may introduce their school teachers in advance of the deadline if they wish'. Indeed, since the governing body of the grant-maintained school makes the appraisal policy for the school, who could or would stop it from so doing?

APPRAISAL OF HEADTEACHERS

This is the element of the appraisal process which the change to grant-maintained status will most affect. Regulation §8(3) requires the governing body of a grant-maintained school to appoint two appraisers for the headteacher. Grant-maintained schools are not exempted from the requirement in Regulation §8(4) that one of the headteacher's two appraisers will be a peer headteacher, one who is or has been employed as a headteacher in the same phase: primary, middle, secondary or special. Within LEAs these headteachers can be found and trained, as we have indicated in the previous chapter.

Selecting the peer appraiser

In grant-maintained schools the peer appraiser may not be so readily found. In areas where there is a high concentration of grant-maintained schools, Bromley and Hillingdon for example, there is inevitably a degree of competition among the schools, as evidenced by the number of multiple applications that were made by parents before sanity prevailed and some means of rationalising them was established. To say that such schools are 'in competition' is not to imply that they may not also be in collaboration; but it does suggest that they may not find it appropriate to agree to any form of mutual appraisal. LEAs have, as we have discovered from our survey, in the main found ways of avoiding the potential pitfalls of peer appraisal. For example, they group schools for headteacher appraisal that do not draw their pupils from the same geographical areas. The grouping is usually in the form of the appraisal 'net' A that we have described elsewhere.

This, we have learned, is the system that has been adopted by one group of grant-maintained schools in a northern county where there is no element of competition because of the geographical scatter of the schools. Grant-maintained schools in metropolitan boroughs have explored the possibility of 'cross-border' appraisal, though it has to be remembered that there is by legal interpretation of the education acts no restriction on cross-border applications to grant-maintained or LEA schools by parents, and in certain cases a potential competitive element may still be a consideration. There remains the possibility, of course, of taking advantage of the phrase *or has been . . .* and appointing a retired headteacher, who will not be constrained by the maximum of three appraisals, since she is not a serving headteacher (Guidelines §29). While this may sound an attractive solution in some areas, governing bodies should be cautious over agreeing to such an appointment, since for some years to come it is unlikely that there will be available anyone with personal experience of the management at this level of grant-maintained schools. We believe that such experience is no less important than the requirement to have had experience of the same phase, even though it is not specified explicitly in the Regulations. It is already becoming obvious, even in the early days of the transition to grant-maintained status, that there are significant differences between the managerial conduct of these schools and that of LEA schools.

Selecting the second appraiser

If the selection of the peer appraiser presents some difficulties, then what of the second appraiser? Within the LEA that is the local adviser, inspector, school development officer or other representative of the CEO: we have discovered as yet no exception to this practice. There is no parallel to this functionary in the grant-maintained sector.

All that the Regulations specify is that there shall be two appraisers. They offer no guidance as to where the second may be found. Some grant-maintained schools, where relationships with the former LEA have not been irrevocably soured, might wish to consider contracting with a member of their *quondam* advisory service. There is more evidence, however, of links being established for the purpose of inspection and support with the advisory service of a neighbouring LEA. Great Barr Grant-maintained School in Birmingham, for example, commissioned the Warwickshire advisory service for this purpose (*TES*, 19 June 1992). It is of course vital that a clear distinction is made between inspection and appraisal; but LEA advisers have for many years found no difficulty in being a member of a team conducting a school development review at one time, and at another being the person to whom members of the school staff will readily turn for advice and support, in other words, for personal and professional development.

Provided that both the adviser/inspector and the appraisee headteacher accept that this duality of role is not an obstacle, this may, for some grant-maintained schools, provide the headteacher's second appraiser. There is evident value in having someone who is already well acquainted with the school and the way it is managed. While headteachers, whether of grant-maintained or LEA schools, 'should not be able to choose their appraisers', they do (Guidelines §28) have the right to request alternative appraisers and their requests 'should not be refused where the circumstances suggest that they might be appropriate'. No headteacher is likely to have imposed an appraiser to whom it is impossible to relate. It has to be admitted, however, that the governing body of the grant-maintained school, the final arbiter, appears to be very much more powerful than that of the LEA school were there disagreement.

Governors as appraisers

We know of other grant-maintained schools where the role of second appraiser has been taken on by the chair of governors. In the grant-maintained school, where governors have total responsibility for the management of the institution, a case can be argued for the involvement of the chosen lay leader in a process which looks at the effectiveness of the appointed professional leader. Yet, as we shall demonstrate, there are also powerful arguments to the contrary.

The first is based on sheer practicalities. For those governing bodies who might wish to appoint a governor as appraiser, there is yet another hurdle to leap. Since the chair of governors alone has the right to see the headteacher's appraisal statement (Guidelines §53), we concluded that no governor other than the chair could be the appraiser. That might in itself be no serious problem, since the chair is likely to be the governing body's first choice. However, since standing orders usually require that the chair is elected or re-elected annually at the first meeting of governors in the school year, continuity as appraiser, even through a single two-year cycle, would become dependent on an extraneous circumstance. We believe that, for an activity as important to both the headteacher and the governing body as the appraisal of the 'chief executive', a four-year period of service as appraiser, two full appraisal cycles, is the desirable minimum.

In any school, whether grant-maintained or LEA, primary or secondary, the amount of time required by both appraisers to plan and prepare for the headteacher appraisal is considerable, as our evaluation of an LEA trial, referred to in previous chapters, indicates. We believe that this amount of time will decrease as appraisal enters its second and subsequent cycles and appraisers are increasingly familiar with the school and its management; but frequent changes of appraiser might well vitiate this development.

Following a workshop which we ran for the Grant Maintained Schools Centre at which questions were raised over the interpretation of the regulations covering the position of governors as appraisers, we asked the Deputy Director to seek clarification from the DFE. The reply confirmed that any governor, not only the chair, might be appointed as appraiser, provided that the second appraiser met the conditions of Regulations §8(4), '[a person] whom the appraising body consider has had *experience relevant to current conditions in the school at which the appraisee head is employed*' (our italics). This reiteration of the precise wording of that paragraph and section raises another issue which we will set aside for the moment.

We were concerned, as was the Grant Maintained Schools Centre, that the DFE letter had not satisfactorily addressed the issue that had been raised: that there was, so it seemed, within the regulations a clear prohibition, that no governor other than the chair might see the headteacher's appraisal statement; yet the DFE accepts that any governor, once appointed as appraiser, might be a party to its compilation. We are reminded of the conversation at the Mad Hatter's tea party:

> 'You should say what you mean,' the March Hare went on. 'I do,' Alice hastily replied; 'at least – at least I mean what I say – that's the same thing, you know.' 'Not the same thing a bit!' said the Hatter.

We decided to seek the advice of the National Association of Head Teachers. In a most explicit response, from which we have permission to quote extensively, the NAHT finds that 'as far as the letter of [the] regulations is concerned, there is nothing to prevent [the appointment as second appraiser of a governor other than the chair]' but continues:

> It is as you follow through the implications of a governor acting as appraiser that the problems arise . . . (S)he would have knowledge in his/her role as an appraiser to which (s)he was not entitled as a governor. Would this be a problem? Appraisal outcomes and targets for action will not be discussed by the governing body, as they are confidential . . . It would be the responsibility of the appraiser-governor to decline to take part in any discussions at meetings of the governing body if (s)he or other governors felt it would compromise the confidentiality due to the appraisal process.

Outside meetings of the governing body, of course, the appraiser would be bound by the same rules of confidentiality as any other appraiser.

In general terms, then, there is nothing in the regulations to prevent a governor acting as a headteacher's second appraiser but in practical terms the confidentiality issue might put the governor in an untenable position as time went on.

The confidentiality issue could still arise for the chair of governors: as chair (s)he is entitled only to the appraisal statement, whereas as appraiser (s)he would be a party to the appraisal interview and the possibly highly personal discussions that will have formed part of the appraisal process. While it is not illegal for the chair to be the appraiser, the relationship between appraisee and appraiser may not be compatible with that between head and chair.

GOVERNORS AND DISCIPLINARY PROCEDURES

There is, however, another issue to which chairs of governing bodies might like to give consideration before deciding whether or not to involve themselves directly in the appraisal of the headteacher. This concerns disciplinary procedures. The Guidelines make it clear that 'appraisal should be clearly separated from disciplinary procedures' (§68). However the same paragraph draws attention to Regulation §14(1):

Relevant information from appraisal records may be taken into account . . . in advising those responsible for taking decisions on the promotion, *dismissal* or *discipline* of school teachers . . . (Our italics).

This paragraph is clearly intended for LEA schools, both on internal evidence – there is reference to CEOs – and because there exists no machinery for offering advice to the governing body of a grant-maintained school, since it is supremely responsible for its own decision making. Nevertheless, implicitly it conveys to the governing bodies of grant-maintained schools that there are circumstances relevant to disciplinary procedures in which the appraisal statement may be used.

The complexities and potential hazards to which this gives rise are exemplified in Guidelines §69. We reproduce the first sentence in full:

[Chairs*] of governors sitting on any sub-committee of the governing body which considers an appeal from a member of staff against a dismissal or disciplinary decision are advised to take care not to prejudice their impartiality as a result of having seen, and taken action, on any appraisal statement which is drawn on in the proceedings.

(* We wish to dissociate ourselves from the DFE's use of the sexist term 'chairmen' throughout the appraisal regulations and guidelines.)

To have seen the statement, the paragraph continues – and we must point out that the chair has no right to see any appraisal statement other than that of the headteacher – would not of itself debar the chair from serving on the sub-committee, provided she had taken no action on the appraisal statement. However, it is obvious that to have played a part in the compilation of the appraisal statement goes well beyond this exemption.

We would like to think that relationships between governing bodies and headteachers would always be such that disciplinary procedures would never need to be invoked. Yet it is salutary to recall the long-running saga in 1992 of Stratford Grant-maintained School when certain members of the governing body sought the dismissal of the headteacher on grounds which do not concern us here, save for the comment that they were proven wholly untenable. That sad chapter in educational history took place before appraisal was inaugurated. Had it taken place a year later, and had any member of the governing body been in any way involved in the headteacher's appraisal, there would have been legal implications that would have kept lawyers occupied for months!

The peer appraiser

We wish briefly to take up the issue which we set on one side earlier: that the second appraiser must have experience relevant to current conditions in the school at which the appraisee head is employed. We think that potential second appraisers who are or have been headteachers of the same phase and also have had experience of conditions in a grant-maintained school will be few and far between. We suspect that, in drafting Regulation §8(4), the DFE did not give sufficient consideration to the situation of these schools.

Yet in the problem lie also the seeds of its solution. The headteacher of a particularly eminent school, now grant-maintained, expresses a view held by many of his colleagues, that appraisal – and therefore especially headteacher appraisal – is a professional matter. He strongly supports, not merely for his own case, but as a matter of principle, the concept of round robin or mutual appraisal that we cited earlier. Far from being liable to cosiness, as some might suspect, we believe that their professional approach will enable them the more rapidly to conduct effective appraisals: for one thing, they will all have had experience of appraisal within their own like-minded schools.

This headteacher would go further. He would encourage his governing body to invite the principal or a senior member of staff of a corporate college, or alternatively the headteacher of a primary school, to be the second appraiser. For the appraisal of deputies, he would like the same principal of mutuality, whereby the deputy of another grant-maintained school in the neighbourhood was his co-appraiser for his deputies, and for this to be reciprocated.

It is clear that this thinking goes well beyond the desire for professionalism in appraisal, important though that is. It implies collaboration, shared learning, a desire to break down barriers between phases: all headteachers, in LEA as well as grant-maintained schools, would do well to give consideration not so much to the process, since that will not necessarily suit their conditions, but the educative principles behind the process.

Data collection

The members of the governing body of a grant-maintained school are to be informed when data is being collected for headteacher appraisal (Guidelines §66). Any comments they may have to make must be transmitted through the chair, whether or not the chair is one of the appraisers. It seems a wise requirement, since it enables the data to be put into some kind of reasonable order. It also ensures that any comments which do not accord with the code of practice are filtered out as unacceptable.

APPRAISAL OF DEPUTY HEADTEACHERS

It is obvious that deputy headteachers of grant-maintained schools have the same right as their colleagues in LEA schools to request, under Regulation §8(6), a second appraiser. Indeed, it is arguable that the managerial responsibilities that they are likely to exercise in these schools may be such that the presence of a second appraiser is not merely desirable from the point of view of the deputy, but advantageous to the appraisal process as a whole. Where a headteacher and the deputies operate on a collegial basis as a senior management team, often with complex, overlapping responsibilities, it will not be easy for the headteacher to dissociate her own management role from that of the deputies in the appraisal process. Certainly the headteacher would expect to be the prime mover in the dialogue of the appraisal interview; but in the data collection, for example, she might be too close to the action to see the detail with clarity.

It is worth considering the possibility of the use for the appraisal of deputies of one of the headteacher's two appraisers. Since the main consideration of that appraisal will undoubtedly be the effectiveness of the deputy's role in the management structure of the school, the data collected will contribute also to the headteacher's appraisal. This is not merely a matter of saving time, that valuable commodity. It will also considerably extend the appraiser's knowledge base of the school and thus increase the value of the contribution to school, personal and professional improvement made through the appraisals.

MONITORING AND EVALUATION

The DFE has made it clear (Guidelines §71) that it intends to seek, at a later unspecified date – we hazard the guess that it will be towards the end of 1995 – information to confirm that the appraisal process has been introduced in accordance with the regulations and that it follows the principles as well as the practice outlined in the Guidelines. Governing bodies of grant-maintained schools therefore have a particular responsibility – since there is no superior level of administration to remind them – to maintain a progress record of the school's introduction of the appraisal process so that they have all the data available for the completion of a questionnaire or the compilation of a report whenever it may be required by the DFE.

Chapter 14

Appraisal in Scotland and Northern Ireland

As in England and Wales, consultation on the introduction of appraisal in Scotland got off to an acrimonious start. Michael Forsyth, the then Education Minister, spoke on television in April 1989 of plans to improve the quality of teachers – not the quality of teaching, be it noted:

> We are going to identify the teachers who are underachieving and help them to do better . . . For too long have we had a system controlled by the bureaucrats and the politicians.
>
> (Quoted in Kerley, 1989)

The last phrase is a little difficult to understand, since Mr Forsyth is himself a politician. However, the invective becomes clearer when we interpolate 'local authority, Labour' before 'politicians'. 'Bureaucrat' we all recognise as a term of opprobrium, whoever may make use of it.

This aside, to make the main thrust of his argument for appraisal the identification of underachieving teachers is sadly to miss the point of the process. It is reminiscent of the earlier DES statement which we quoted in Chapter 2, save that he held back from being 'ready to use procedures for dismissal'.

The General Teaching Council (GTC) has consistently taken a firm stance on appraisal. As in England and Wales, it must have as its main purpose the professional development of all teaching staff, not the 'identification of underachieving teachers', an implicitly judgmental phrase. Fortunately, the GTC was able to observe for itself that, whatever the Minister might say in public, the Scottish Education Department (SED) consultation document 'Professional Development into the 1990s' placed appraisal unequivocally in the context of staff development.

The main criticism of the SED document at that time was that it assumed staff development to be a 'management tool'. This concept, that it was somehow to be deployed by rectors, principals and headteachers as a device for the management of staff, more appositely warrants the use of the term 'bureaucratic', not as invective but in accordance with the definition first used by Weber (1947) and adopted and adapted by other writers on management ever since.

To understand why this phrase so riled Scottish teachers, it is helpful to recall some of the characteristics of bureaucracy as Weber defined them:

- Fixed, official, jurisdictional areas and positions governed by laws, rules and regulations
- Regular activities distributed in a rational, fixed way as official tasks and duties
- A firmly ordered system of supervision and subordination.

(Wilkinson and Cave, 1987)

In the light of this classic definition, the SED statement appeared to teachers to indicate a desire to perpetuate top-down models of management with strictly defined line management within which assistant staff made their regulated and supervised contributions in those areas of activity allocated to them.

Yet the GTC appears to have overreacted. It claimed that 'the purpose of appraisal must be related to the development of the individual' ignoring, as Kerley (1989) points out 'the organisational dimension and thus [placing] the process out of context.' The symbiotic relationship between the goals of the individual and the aims of the institution has been stressed throughout this book, and is now firmly embedded in the appraisal process in England and Wales. There is little doubt that this concept of mutuality, once the thunder of political statements died down, will have gained ground in Scotland.

The Minister, seemingly unaware of the unanimous view expressed by representatives of the DES, teachers' unions and LEAs in England and Wales (ACAS, 1986), was dismissive of self-appraisal. The Scottish Secondary Teachers' Association was on record as having seen self-appraisal as the start of a process in which appraisees were as able as appraisers to have a view on their performance and the right to express that view openly and candidly. Fortunately the SED was soon to be seen, Minister or no Minister, to support this view.

THE CRIEFF NATIONAL SEMINAR

In November 1989, five months after the deadline for the consultation document, the SED held a three-day seminar on appraisal. The SED proposal had met with some hostility, or, as the SED more urbanely put it, 'a mixed reaction' in particular to its view of the appraisal of teacher performance as 'a management tool to raise the quality of teaching' (TSES, 1989a). Since the Strathclyde Region, far and away the most populous and influential of the Scottish local authorities, and the powerful teachers' association, the Educational Institution of Scotland (EIS), were both highly vocal in their opposition, the SED claim of 'general acceptance' was undoubtedly somewhat far-fetched.

The SED reported that 28 of the 48 pilot staff development projects had been completed by mid-1989 and had reported their findings. In most of these schools there had been a positive response, with better staff motivation and improved effectiveness. Those schools in which departmental and school reviews were already in place, and where staff were involved in whole-school activities and school review procedures, had welcomed the initiative from the beginning. Other schools where these characteristics were absent or less apparent had been initially cautious or even suspicious, but even here there was a noticeable increase in the willingness to participate.

Readers will observe a highly significant difference from the pilot schemes initiated by the DES. In England – Wales was not included in the pilot scheme – six LEAs, selected as demographically representative, were invited to take part in the pilot study and they then invited a range of schools, themselves representative of the primary and secondary phases. Each LEA appointed a team of coordinators, almost all with some experience of appraisal schemes either as headteachers or administrators. The scheme was overseen by a powerful superstructure, the National Steering Group, and supported by a coordinating body, the National Development Centre for School Management Training based at Bristol University.

In Scotland individual schools were given the opportunity to volunteer but, as far as we can ascertain, there were no criteria for acceptance. We can discover no evidence that the SED sought the reasons why so high a proportion of the pilot schools, over 40 per cent, failed to complete; or, if it did, the department does not appear to have made these reasons public. We can posit a number of reasons for the high rate of drop-out, among them the lack of opportunity for pilot schools to share their developing experience of appraisal in a series of conferences as had happened in England.

The SED stressed in one of the nine papers presented to the Crieff seminar the essential case for appraisal:

> Without it managers are deprived of much of the information they require to produce effective programmes of staff development. With it, staff, institutions and authorities can benefit from regular reviews of policies and practices and from training and developmental programmes designed in the light of these reviews.
>
> To be effective, such appraisal procedures have to apply to all members of staff from principals and headteachers to lecturers and teachers. Self-evaluation should play an important part. However, if procedures are to be systematic and standardised, management must also be involved in the processes of appraisal.
>
> (*TSES*, 1989a)

In background notes to the proposed national guidelines the SED identified four key benefits from appraisal, which were ranked in order of importance as seen by the Department:

- better motivation and communication between staff and management
- review and improvement of professional performance
- the highlighting of staff needs
- career review.

On the contentious matter of the 'underachieving teacher' the background notes now offered a more conciliatory approach:

> For some, appraisal will help to identify standards, either of overall performance or of performance in critical aspects of the work, which fall below acceptable levels. Appraisal should not replace existing management arrangements for dealing with and counselling unsatisfactory staff. All it can do is provide one method of initiating such procedures.
>
> (*TSES*, 1989a)

The Crieff seminar relieved many of the anxieties previously expressed by the GTC, the Regions and teachers' associations. The then chair of the GTC made it clear that the Minister's extreme view of appraisal expressed earlier that year was dead and buried:

> The elimination of incompetent teachers was not high on anyone's agenda.
>
> (*TSES*, 1989b)

NATIONAL GUIDELINES FOR SCOTLAND

The SED announced its plans for appraisal in schools and further education colleges towards the end of 1990. Appraisal was to be phased in over a four-year period beginning, as in England and Wales, in 1992-3, with half the teaching force to be 'within the appraisal arrangements by the beginning of the 1994-5 session' (TSES, 1991), one year more than in England and Wales.

A significant concession appears to have been wrung from the SED by the powerful combination of the Regions and the teachers' association: appraisal would not be imposed by regulation provided that education authorities and schools produced schemes in line with the SED guidelines then being distributed.

The introductory paragraphs of these guidelines made it clear that appraisal must be integral with school management. Here, for the first time, was a firm commitment that the school was the true locus of the appraisal process. For teachers it was to provide a regular and systematic procedure for career development review and the provision of advice and support. Implicit in this statement was the rejection of the concept that underachieving teachers could be singled out as having these needs; advice and support is a right for all teachers, even the most proficient.

Then the SED set the cat among the pigeons. While not replacing existing procedures either for promotion or for dealing with unsatisfactory performance, appraisal would 'make a contribution to these procedures *through the provision of relevant information*' (our italics). Schools were actually charged in the guidelines with making formal arrangements within their appraisal schemes indicating how 'relevant information from appraisal procedures will be fed into the other processes'. Suddenly it seemed that the issue of the use of appraisal to identify the underachieving teacher – now the teacher whose performance is 'unsatisfactory' – was far from dead; it was subtly obscured by being linked with the use of appraisal for promotion.

The SED guidelines may well have stated openly what has been disguised in England and Wales behind repeated statements maintaining that there will be no *direct* links between appraisal and pay and promotion. The existence of any such links, overt or covert, will signal the end of that open behaviour between management and staff without which the appraisal process will be vitiated. What is more the arrangements for the confidentiality and restricted circulation of the appraisal statement would be negated by the requirement to provide 'relevant information', whatever that may mean.

By late 1991 all education authorities had submitted their schemes, though only three of the Regions had reached prior agreement with the teachers' associations. The Minister accepted the schemes, though less than graciously:

> In a number of aspects . . . I expect [education authorities] to move closer to the guidelines before the end of the phasing-in period. We will monitor progress as implementation proceeds. Meantime I do not intend to make regulations.
>
> (*Scotsman*, 1991)

It is worthy of note that the Minister had earlier been at loggerheads with the EIS which had threatened to boycott the entire appraisal policy. Teacher union strength in Scotland is such that the Minister backed down from this confrontation. Not surprisingly, the main concerns were over the potential use of appraisal as a means of disciplining teachers individually and the teaching force collectively, and as a means of introducing performance-related pay.

Two further demands had surfaced, expressed forcibly by the general secretary of the EIS:

> [We] will continue to resist schemes which contain compulsory appraisal or which place undue stress on line management rather than on a collegiate approach in which arrangements are seen to be 'owned' by school staffs.
>
> (*Scotsman*, 1991)

Those education authorities which had cleared their schemes with the teacher unions before presentation to the SED had all included exemption from compulsory appraisal in some form or another. Tayside's scheme allowed teachers to opt in. Grampian, while not explicitly conceding voluntary status to appraisal, allowed any teachers unwilling to be appraised by the immediate superior allotted to them to name an acceptable alternative. This aspect of voluntarism seemed to satisfy their teachers, though, as we shall see in the case study which follows, individual schools were to include in their schemes a radical alternative to line management.

CASE STUDY: BANCHORY ACADEMY

Early in 1989 the Rector of the academy, Stewart Wilson, accepted membership of a Regional group charged with investigating the steps which would need to be taken to introduce an acceptable scheme of appraisal. Within a month a starter paper on a draft model was in circulation and widespread discussion began. It was clear to the Rector that some preliminary staff training was necessary, even before any commitment to introduce appraisal in his establishment. Accordingly, in October 1989, a large group of staff attended a two-day workshop on appraisal and, the following month, a smaller group received a three-day training in interviewing and counselling skills. In December 1989 the academy bid for a budget to introduce a scheme of formal appraisal and was granted £12,000 for a pilot study in 1990–91.

It was evident that there had to be preliminary awareness raising for staff as a whole, even before the pilot study itself began. In April all staff who had not attended the earlier appraisal workshop were given the opportunity of an induction day, and all but two took advantage of the offer. The following month saw a two-day residential 'training the appraisers' workshop and this, with those trained previously, gave the academy a core of over 20 trained appraisers. Most were, not unexpectedly, senior staff of the level of Principal Teacher and above; but, interestingly, four 'rank-and-file' teachers had been included.

Implementation

Plans were now made for the session 1990–91 and a small steering group was constituted. Again, it is worthy of note that, the Rector apart, only half of its membership came from the senior ranks of assistant staff. It was decided that, if the scheme was to have credibility with appraisees, the appraisers must themselves be appraised. Staff changes had reduced the appraiser team to eighteen all of whom took part, appraising and being appraised. The Rector was appraised by two peer headteachers and the others chose from within their own number.

The steering group met later that term to review the scheme in the light of that experience and a position paper was issued to all staff. Although earlier the academy staff seem to have been somewhat dubious about the nature and extent of the documentation, it now became clear that three written products of the process were needed:

- a summary of the discussion between appraiser and appraisee (the equivalent of Part I of the appraisal statement in England and Wales)
- agreed priorities (goals)
- training needs.

Regional teacher union representatives were kept fully informed of the pilot scheme and at a meeting at the end of the year it was agreed that the initiative be known henceforth as the 'Staff Development and Career Review' and 'reviewer' and 'reviewee' would replace the terms 'appraiser' and 'appraisee'. This may seem a pettifogging change to many a reader, but it needs to be understood in the context of the acute suspicion of the political motives of those in high places promoting the introduction of appraisal, not least those of the Minister, as the earlier pages of this chapter will have indicated.

In January 1991 the finalised position paper was issued to all staff and all who had not yet been through the review process, as it was now called, were invited to take part. Twenty-four additional staff members now volunteered, each choosing a reviewer from the list of trained reviewers. Within that academic year all but 10 staff had taken part in a full self-review followed by a one-to-one interview of a kind determined through the pilot scheme, excluding a handful of senior staff who were already committed to a prior scheme in which the Rector was their annual reviewer.

The Staff Development Committee

Introducing an initiative is only part of the innovatory process. It is essential also to establish a body which will deal with maintenance issues. The Staff Development Committee followed the same practice as the Steering Group: half its members were what in Scotland is delightfully known as 'unpromoted teachers'! The committee has the dual role of continuing the initiative and planning appropriate in-service training to meet the needs of staff as identified through the review process. To achieve this objective, it produces an annual programme of staff development activities based on declared needs. In May 1992 a Staff Development coordinator was appointed, since there was an obvious need for a single member of staff to service this committee and to be responsible for the implementation of training decisions.

Budget

The money allocated for the pilot budget was spent on training courses and staff cover to allow the one-to-one review to take place. It is not possible to make comparisons with the costing of the DES plot scheme since that funding was not devolved to schools. It is our impression, however, that the academy was – rightly – generously funded and that a continuation of funding at this level is unlikely, even when account is taken of the reduced need for expenditure on training workshops and courses for the review process. Some continuing training needs there certainly were. The academy saw the need, with staff changes and for other reasons, to increase the number of reviewers; and second-phase training was introduced for some experienced reviewers. However, with £4 million a year for two years set aside for the Scottish scheme compared with £10 million a year for the period 1990–92 for preparation for appraisal in England and Wales, Scotland is advantaged over England by 4:1 in comparative terms. As a spokesperson for the NAS/UWT plaintively remarked: 'Scotland is getting the goodies and England and Wales are not' (*TES*, 1991).

It will come as no surprise to readers to learn that, as a consequence of the obvious success of this pilot scheme, Stewart Wilson was seconded from his headship for a two-year period charged with the task of introducing appraisal into schools within the Grampian Region.

NORTHERN IRELAND

Wisely, the Department of Education of Northern Ireland (DENI) held its fire, as it has done with many initiatives that have emanated from the mainland. DENI is independent of the DFE, largely because of the particular circumstances prevailing in Northern Ireland. There are five Education and Library Boards (ELBs), all serving populations equivalent to a relatively small LEA on the mainland, but, except for Belfast and South Eastern, covering geographical areas far larger than any in England and Wales. Selection is still an integral part of the Northern Ireland educational system and half the secondary schools and three-quarters of the grammar schools are maintained or voluntary, the equivalent of what we would call 'church schools' on the mainland. Although numbers in the Catholic Teaching Orders have waned dramatically in recent years, the principalship of most of these schools is held by a Brother or Sister. There are many single-sex schools; mixed schools are mainly to be found in rural areas where numbers would not make single sex schools viable. Even so, there is a substantial number of schools with rolls of less than 300 or 400, which might be thought uneconomical were it not for the distances which pupils might otherwise have to travel. Many primary schools outside Belfast itself are small: the average size in the non-metropolitan boards is 150–200 and, in the west of the Western Education and Library Board's area, for example, many will be as small as the traditional village school on the mainland a century ago.

With well over 800 primary schools and 200 secondary schools in Northern Ireland, and of such variety of control, the introduction of appraisal in Northern Ireland is far from easy. The training of those who will appraise, as will be seen, appears to require a cascade model, which teachers and officers alike have resolutely opposed in England and Wales. In most other respects

John Leonard of DENI, charged with making recommendations for a Northern Ireland pilot scheme, drew extensively on mainland experience.

THE PILOT SCHEME

During the academic year 1991–2, 24 schools covering the full range of size, phase, funding status and location were selected by the ELBs for a pilot study to take place during the following academic year. These schools were divided into three geographical groups each serviced by one of three appraisal pilot coordinators, whose responsibilities were twofold: in cooperation with staff from the ELBs in their area to train the principals and staff in the pilot schools; and, at the conclusion of the pilot collectively to evaluate the pilot scheme. When appraisal is fully in place, each employing authority will need a small appraisal management team with its own appraisal coordinator and trainers. The involvement of ELB staff in the pilot scheme sows the seeds for this development. A Joint Working Party has been responsible for central planning: devising the pilot scheme and considering training and resource needs.

Training

The recommendations (Leonard, 1991) observed that pilot work in Great Britain 'showed a great variety in amount, method and content of training' and drew the conclusion that, for Northern Ireland, there was a need 'for general awareness raising [and] to provide adequate training for appraisees as well as appraisers'. The report also stressed 'the need to plan training to take place as near to the actual experience of the review procedure as possible'. This has been borne out by our experience. We have found that the most effective training has followed the pattern of: training workshop, period for trialling back in the schools, review day. The addition of the review day has added to the cost, but it has also thrown up a host of issues arising from the trialling period most of which could not have been anticipated and all of which added to the general ability of headteachers and others to handle appraisal without undue stress.

The use of the phrase 'review procedure' above shows that Northern Ireland is following the Scottish terminology, though not to the extent of using *reviewer* and *reviewee*. There will be those who may say that the name is irrelevant, but there is no doubt that much teacher antagonism and anxiety about the exact nature and purpose of appraisal would have been dissipated had the more 'user-friendly' term been found acceptable to the Secretary of State.

Awareness raising has played an important part in establishing a favourable climate, and will be no less necessary in the dissemination period after the pilot scheme. One full day of training for appraisees – that is for all staff during an in-service day – was also strongly recommended, to 'introduce teachers to the methods of self-appraisal, classroom observation, interviews and target setting'. For appraisers in the pilot there was additional training, 'to develop the practical, interpersonal and classroom observation skills [and] the opportunity to practise interview and observational skills and receive feedback on this practice'. At least one day of in-service training was to be given for this. We doubt whether a training programme covering a set of aims as wide as this could be successfully run in a single day, without some sacrifice to the elements of experiential learning.

THE PILOT PROCEDURES

The DENI proposals followed the pattern of line management in the regulations for England and Wales, and intended by the guidelines for Scotland, though this intention appears to have been largely negated by the strongly expressed views of teacher unions there. It was recommended that teachers should not be allowed to choose their appraisers. Regrettably, no provision seems to have been made for teachers to appeal against their chosen appraiser, as in the DFE regulations, though this necessary proviso may well be included in the regulations that will result from the pilot scheme. The recommendation that appraiser be permitted to appraise six appraisees may be appropriate for a pilot, where a tight control of procedures is desirable; but if carried into the main scheme the time cost on the individual will surely be too great.

For the selection of appraisers for headteachers the recommendations offered four options: two much like that operating in England and Wales; the other two making it possible for a governor to be one of the appraisers. We have made clear in Chapter 13 the potential pitfalls of such a procedure, as well as the desire of headteachers to be appraised by professionals. Northern Ireland headteachers felt likewise, since the Working Party decided that a headteacher's appraisers should be one member of a panel of consultant headteachers and an ELB officer.

The components of the appraisal process are identical with those in England and Wales, with the sensible recommendation that the appraisal activity for any individual should be contained within a period of eight weeks. Job specifications are seen as essential and self-appraisal, though it cannot be compulsory, is recommended as 'a key part of the process'. As for classroom observation, the report sensibly recommends the more realistic total of 1.5 hours for the two observations. Task observation for headteachers is undertaken by the peer headteacher, drawn from a panel selected by the ELB, but with the proviso that each 'consultant appraiser' conducts no more than three appraisals. The appraisal interview has the same objectives as those on the mainland, and the appraisal statement follows the same pattern.

In Northern Ireland ELBs are less resistant than LEAs and Scottish Regions to central documentation from DENI. For this reason the pilot was able to argue that 'centrally produced appraisal documentation can help to structure the process at school level, and schools can develop a sense of ownership by refining the documents to suit their own circumstances'. In addition to pro-formas for the three main stages of the process, self-appraisal, classroom observation and the interview statement – the second may prove to be not so easily adaptable to use for teachers of all levels of responsibility in both primary and secondary schools of all sizes – publicity and awareness-raising leaflets and booklets, and handbooks of advice on management and implementation of the scheme were provided.

THE FUTURE OF PERFORMANCE REVIEW IN NORTHERN IRELAND

A decision has already been taken to 'implement an agreed scheme of teacher performance review commencing in 1994' under regulations already in place under Article 151 of the Education Reform (Northern Ireland) Order 1989. This means that, following the completion and evaluation of the pilot studies, the final shape of the scheme can be realised in the academic year 1993–4. A management team consisting of representatives of DENI, the ELBs and other employers has been set up serviced by the Teachers (Pay and Conditions of Service) Division of the Department of Education.

Certain principles are already established, all of which bear, not unnaturally, a marked resemblance to the mainland schemes. What is clear is that, unlike the pilot projects in England, where procedures were determined 'on the hoof', and even more unlike those in Scotland, where there appeared to be no control by the SED over the selection of pilot schools, in Northern Ireland the piloting was done as a controlled experiment, well researched and well supported by a team of coordinators, working both centrally and in the schools. It is always unwise to make forecasts, but it appears to us very probable that the finalised procedures will be arrived at more harmoniously than on the other side of the waters.

Chapter 15

Quality control and appraisal

The Great Debate, with its concern over educational standards, marked the beginning of public and professional interest in appraisal in the United Kingdom. Since 1976 there has been much argument about the purpose of appraisal and the way in which it would be introduced. It is reasonable to suppose that the dust has now settled, only to be stirred up if governmental pressures to introduce concepts such as performance-related pay are linked directly or indirectly to the outcomes of the appraisal process. There is, within all the current regulations and guidelines, a firm commitment to appraisal for teacher improvement and staff development and it would require a complete *volte face* were extraneous consequences to be tacked on to or infiltrated into the process. One has to be realistic and recognise that such changes of direction have not been unknown in other areas of education in recent years.

Thorough measures by LEAs to raise awareness among their teaching force of the detailed processes of appraisal and their implication have done much to relieve anxieties. We wish that we were as confident that there had been adequate appraiser training in all LEAs before the deadline of 1 September 1992. We have heard glib talk of 'a running-in period' and of 'learning by doing'; this is disturbing because, while experience will always lead to improvement, teacher confidence in the appraisal process will be shaken if appraisal is not seen to operate at a professional level from the outset.

Furthermore, there are no short cuts, as we hope we have demonstrated repeatedly in this book. Classroom observation, data collection, task observation, the appraisal interview, and, above all, the day-to-day support for teachers by teachers, call for allocations of time the cost of which cannot possibly be found within the niggardly additional sums that have been made available. As evidence of this the appraisal coordinator of one LEA, doubtless speaking for many colleagues, has told us:

> We have allocated time from GEST funding on the basis of one day for the work of heads as appraisers of a colleague and two hours per member of staff.

It is not the fault of this LEA that a time allowance of this kind is totally insufficient: we know few LEAs that are able to offer more. Yet all our experience tells us that twice this time is barely sufficient. As usual, the teaching profession is being asked to make bricks without straw; and will doubtlessly be blamed if the bricks crumble and the edifice topples.

The vehement critics of appraisal within the profession have not gone away. As recently as April 1992 at the NUT conference 'a succession of speakers from the floor denounced appraisal as a means to sack staff' and 'one delegate described the government's plans for appraisal of teachers' classroom performance as a Trojan Horse which critics suspect will be used as an excuse to sack staff'. One delegate sought to drive a wedge between headteachers and teachers by claiming:

> There is a new mood out there amongst some of the more bullish headteachers. Appraisal will be used by unscrupulous heads, desperate governors and local authorities keen to lose jobs. It will be used to engineer a climate of despair and demoralisation. The schemes are superficial and underfunded, cheap, shoddy and ineffective.
>
> (*The Guardian*, 1992)

It is easy to dismiss claims like this as demagogy, but there was, and still is, much concern among teachers that beneath rhetoric of this kind lie potentialities for uncomfortable truths.

There is no merit in trying to respond to these concerns and antagonisms by counter-argument. Appraisal has to prove itself in the field, by demonstrating that it has a major contribution to make to effective learning and management. It will do this best if we recognise that it is not an isolated process, but one which is integrated with all the elements that make for quality control.

THE SCHOOL DEVELOPMENT PLAN

There was a time when school development depended more on inspiration than on planning. The day of the charismatic headteacher is over, if indeed there ever was such a day. Such a person ranks with the myth of the hero innovator. Today a school development plan is recognised as the crucial element in school management and needs to be in the ownership not of an individual leader-figure, but of the whole staff. The plan begins with the mission statement, the school's *raison d'être*. This is then given flesh in the form of a catalogue of the key activities which the school desires to introduce, implement, modify or maintain (the objectives); how they are to be achieved (the strategies); and what the impact will be on the improved learning and wellbeing of the school's students (the outcomes).

Ideally, the school development plan should be implemented over a three-year cycle, updated annually through an internal audit, one element of which is the appraisal process. The collection of data for the audit may occur at any time of the school year, arising out of staff meetings, parents' evenings, governors' meetings and visitations, working parties, government statements and the like. The development plan should prescribe when in the school year the audit will take place and collate the data for that occasion.

The objectives, strategies and desired outcomes for the immediate year should be regarded as constituting a clearly articulated and definitive plan for implementation. Minor adjustments in the light of experience or advice will of course take place during the school year, but it is important that school management is able to distinguish between adjustments which are easily assimilated and significant change which is not. Deviations from the plan should only be made either in response to imposed change or when, after careful consideration, it is obvious that the plan is not meeting the desired outcomes. It may be, in such a situation, that it is no longer possible to attain the desired objectives; but it is much more likely that the strategies are impracticable or incorrect.

The second year of the development plan should be a continuation of the previous year, but recognising that it is open to modification in the light of any formal evaluation or internal audit of the preceding year. As it becomes the substantive year – as the rolling programme promotes it from second year to first – its objectives, strategies and desired outcomes should be verified.

It is obviously more difficult to plan ahead with any degree of certainty for the third year. Consequently this stage of the rolling programme is more tenuous, to be thought of as a framework consistent with that of the two previous years, but to be modified in the light of experience and improved judgment.

THE CURRICULUM DEVELOPMENT PLAN

This is a vital element of the school development plan, since it is concerned with the school's main purpose, the key domain of teaching and learning. It is more subject to governmental external control than much of the school development plan because of the requirements of the National Curriculum and, for secondary schools, examination boards. While the implementation of the curriculum development plan remains the ultimate in-school responsibility of the senior management team, its practical application is of necessity delegated to curriculum teams and their leaders.

THE SCHOOL DEVELOPMENT REVIEW OR INSPECTION

This is a review of the school as an organisational and administrative unit, focusing primarily on the delivery of the school development plan. Additionally, school development reviews have in the past been collectively a central feature of the LEA's review of the effectiveness of its own organisational units, including the local inspectorate, support services and the education directorate.

With the advent of inspection by teams external to the LEA there will be fundamental changes. The traditional role of the LEA inspectorial or advisory service has been to inspect and support: to be concerned as the LEA watchdog with the maintenance of school standards, but also to be in a position to develop its strengths and diminish its weaknesses. It is, in our long experience as teachers and managers in a variety of schools, a role that has been discharged by many in the service with expertise and humanity. Most advisers with whom we have had dealings then, and since as consultants and trainers, have demonstrated that they know intimately their schools, the teachers in them and the governing bodies which they clerk or attend as professional advisers. Increasingly in recent years they have played a more proactive role in quality control: the inspectorial function has been strengthened by demands from central government, local government and, we suspect, by their own inclination. Yet the support function remains, even though the time for it has diminished.

By a stroke of the pen, the creation by Kenneth Clarke of the Office for Standards in Education (Ofsted), Her Majesty's Inspectorate (HMI) was removed from the arena of school inspection and that responsibility, from April 1993, placed in the hands of independent teams of inspectors. The residual role of HMI is to police the system through Ofsted, which now has the responsibility for training inspectors, assigning teams to schools and guaranteeing the quality of the process. It is worthy of note that the original concept that 'market-forces would prevail' and that governors would choose their team on whatever criteria they might wish to set up, including cost, has vanished without trace.

What has to be realised, and what government has so patently ignored, in ignorance or through political dogma, is that these inspections constitute only one element of quality control, and that unlikely to be the most important. In one visit every four years, by no means with any certainty of continuity since Ofsted will allocate schools in response to bids from teams, these teams may – or may not – make a rigorous but fair evaluation of a school's performance. What it will not do, since it is neither funded nor expected to, is to assist and support the school in remedying deficiencies that its external evaluation has revealed. That is a role that can only be discharged by local inspectors and advisers; but with educational cuts in real terms year on year and with local government itself under threat of massive reorganisation, we have to wonder whether there will be any organised professional group left to advise, assist and support. Hamlet without the Prince will be as nothing compared with quality control without the necessary support, for strong schools no less than weak ones.

THE BUSINESS PLAN

The business plan is a document that sets out in both words and figures a proposed business venture. It matters little whether that business venture is a factory, service industry, charity or educational establishment. In our case, the business is a school, which has the prime objective of educating children, usually and mainly those living within a given geographical locality.

For most schools the concept of the business plan is new; but, with local financial management in particular, many are seeing the need to think beyond the school development plan, linking their finance to both present and future pupil numbers in order that they may establish systematic control over staffing, resources, buildings and equipment – and the school's approach to marketing. It is this word 'marketing' that is the stumbling block for many in education. Increasingly schools are accepting, with reservations, the value of devising and routinely updating a business plan. The reservations come largely from observing the aggressive marketing approach of some schools which appear to be aping the worst features of the world of commerce. It may be that the term 'marketing' is unfortunate, for the business plan for a school has to apply to that term a specialised meaning that is only marginally present in commercial undertakings.

The school's main marketing concern lies in the management of external relations (Foskett, 1992). Most schools would rightly regard their key concern as that of internal relations, with its consumers, its pupils, and with their parents and guardians. Yet additionally and increasingly a school needs to accommodate relationships with those beyond its immediate domain: the neighbourhood, places of worship of whatever denomination, cultural, sporting and social clubs and organisations, local industry and commerce.

We have considered replacing the word *marketing* with the innocuous word *communication*. Communication is a crucial element of the business plan: the dissemination to the community at large of information about the school, and the means of receiving from the community – a much more difficult enterprise – their views and feelings about the school. Increasingly schools are having to distribute information by regulation. However much most of them dislike the distribution of league tables of results, at least that requirement gives them the occasion to convey more relevant and valuable information about the school. Yet we have come to the conclusion that the teaching profession cannot adapt and distort words to match their concept of what they ought to mean. Marketing, then, it is, with the understanding that educationists set their own parameters to what is professionally acceptable marketing behaviour and see it contextually within the business plan, itself a vital element in quality control.

HOW DOES APPRAISAL FIT IN?

For all teachers, whether their main focus is that of effective classroom practice or that of managerial competence, appraisal relates essentially to the school development plan. In the first place, as we have indicated in Chapter 4, the goals set for the individual teacher must be consonant with the aims and objectives of the school itself. However praiseworthy a teacher's intended goals may be in the abstract, they cannot exist in a vacuum. This must not be taken to imply that the school development plan is immutable, unable to take account of teacher initiatives and developments from the grassroots. There can be modification of the plan, particularly of its proposals for the second and third years, to take account of individual contributions, provided that these are in the interests of the staff, the pupils and the institution as a whole.

Goalsetting, then, provides the first structured opportunity for teacher involvement in fleshing out the development plan. Classroom observation provides the opportunity for teachers to look at the reality of their delivery of the curriculum. This is *focused quality control*, a crucial element of the management of schools today. If, for example, a number of these observations reveal that there are significant differences in the way teachers record pupil progress, this is less likely to reflect on the classroom teachers themselves than on the school management. It may be that agreed procedures have become obsolete or fallen into disuse because they have not been subjected to a periodic review. Again, there may be staff confusion about the delivery of some aspect of the National Curriculum, particularly when it is being subjected to repeated change; yet, in a busy school, even the best of curriculum leaders may not appreciate that there is an issue here for her attention.

The appraisal interviews themselves may well prove to be the most valuable of all these sources of information about school effectiveness derived from one-to-one communication with members of staff. Sadly, schools have in recent years had less and less opportunity for this vital activity as managerial and curricular tasks take up increasing amounts of teacher time. All three of the activities we have referred to – goalsetting, observation and the appraisal interview – have created opportunities for reintroducing that communication.

Yet it is one thing for these issues to be given the opportunity to surface and quite another for staff to find the time to do anything about them. The first requirement is that information deriving from appraisal that indicate organisational weaknesses as well as suggestions for improved management performance must be collated and communicated to those who are in a position to act on it. This is not in any way a breach of the confidentiality of the appraisal process. Appraisees are unlikely to stand in the way of opportunities for school improvement when the revealed shortcomings in no way reflect upon them. It may be that we have so far thought of staff development too much in terms of the individual and not enough in the collective. There will be occasions when, for staff to develop, the institution must take the initiative and put its own house in order.

Equally there are issues that are whole-school concerns that may quite properly be included on the appraisal interview agenda for each member of staff, thus enabling the senior management to have a perception of the way in which a particular innovation or development is taking hold. A secondary school, for example, may have included in its development plan a programme for the teaching of cross-curricular learning skills, not as a discrete subject area but as an integral part of all subject teaching. To introduce and monitor this programme will naturally feature in the goals of all members of staff, expressed differently according to the various levels of responsibility for the innovation. Information on the extent to which this goal has been achieved is vital to senior management if it is to monitor the innovation. The collation by the appraiser team of the achievements, concerns, criticisms, suggestions, of half the staff at the end of Year 1 will help the senior management team to make an interim evaluation of the progress of the innovation, and a similar activity a year later will enable the team to see the consequences of any modifications that were made as a result of the first year report.

A primary school may be concerned about inequalities in gender or race in its teaching materials and the staff may decide to nominate a working party to create a positive policy to examine and counter these. Again, this may lead to inclusion in the goals for all staff and will therefore be considered for the agenda of the appraisal interview. Up to half the staff in any one school year now have an opportunity to discuss with the appraisers their views on the achievements and shortcomings of the policy as they have been implementing it; and this gives the working party data for their internal evaluation of the progress of the policy.

We want to make two points in response to concerns that may be in the reader's mind. First, there is no breach of confidentiality involved. The appraisers are not making available to members of the senior management team in the first example, and the working party in the second, details from the appraisal statements of individual teachers. They are assisting in the compilation of a range of non-attributable views which, for long-term policy developments such as both of these, can contribute powerfully to successful implementation.

The second point is that this is not a substitute for other, more traditional methods of evaluation, but is complementary to them. However, there is much evidence that the use of the full staff meeting to assess how an innovation is progressing is the strategy most commonly employed, is the most economical of time, yet is also the least effective. The most persuasive expressions of support or the most strident voices in opposition may shut out the views of less vocal or less senior members of staff, regardless of how well a meeting is chaired. For gathering data the one-to-one interview is ideal as there is no likelihood of the views of the unobtrusive member of staff being overlooked. Yet it is also the most time-costly. In the appraisal interview, indeed, in the whole appraisal process from goalsetting to interview to follow up, there is a built-in opportunity to hear the views of all staff. Teacher appraisal is beginning to seem, in more ways than might originally have been thought, to have a major contribution to quality control, and particularly to quality control conceived not on a top-down model, but as a whole staff activity.

Is this then what appraisal is about? The very proper demands for teacher appraisal for staff development, argued by teachers' unions and most LEAs and now enshrined in the regulations, have tended to individualise appraisal outcomes. Occasionally we have even come to suspect that this emphasis on the individual may actually inhibit the natural evolution of schools towards collegial responsibility. Yet there are more roads to staff development than finding out individual needs for further training. The collective development of staff requires that senior management devise means to give all staff the opportunity to express their views and, where possible, to play a part in the decision-making process. Staff ownership of school policy makes a vital contribution to the health of the organisation, as writers on management have pointed out repeatedly. Teacher appraisal must contribute not merely to effective learning but also to effective management; both require the concerted efforts of classroom teachers and management.

There is evidence that the symbiotic relationship between staff development and school development is already well established in those schools which have had appraisal schemes up and running for some time. Schools more newly involved can benefit from this experiential learning and build it into their appraisal policies and practices, even in the demanding early stages. It is widely accepted that the school development plan review is not confined to external visitation, whether by LEA inspectors or the privatised inspectorial teams; any well-managed school will have its own methods of continuing oversight from within, including self-evaluation, a more powerful tool in quality control than is commonly recognised. In the same way, the appraisal interview is only part of a continuing process of staff support. There is a valuable mutuality to be developed between those two elements of oversight and support, as Handy and Aitken (1987) stressed in their excellent book *Understanding Schools as Organisations.*

ACCOUNTABILITY SYSTEMS v. GROWTH SYSTEMS

In the first edition of this book we wrote at length about the state of appraisal in the USA. It is worthy of note that there has been, even in that short period since we conducted our enquiry, the beginnings of a shift to what we would more readily recognise as teacher appraisal, that is a system which makes staff development central to the process. It is well known that, while federal government in the USA may call on all states to introduce teacher accountability, each state, and within certain constraints each district within the state, may implement that requirement as it sees fit.

There is evidence of a radical shift from an accountability system to a growth system, as they describe it, in two states at least, Washington and Oregon. Ken Madrell spent some time in early 1991 investigating systems of appraisal there. Oregon, he found, had a Professional Excellence Program which had two strands: an Accountability Program and a Professional Growth Program. The former is compulsory, and ensures that all teachers reach the Minimum Standards of Performance.

> The process involves four key stages: pre-evaluation conference, evaluation, post-evaluation conference and the teacher evaluation report. The evaluation involves at least two uninterrupted classroom observations, conducted by the principal, or, in the case of large high schools, the principal and vice principals. The teacher evaluation report is signed by both parties and is placed on the teacher's personnel file at the district office. Assuming no deficiencies are found, no further action will occur.
>
> (Madrell, 1991)

It is interesting to observe that the classroom observations are undertaken by the non-teaching managers of the institution, not by heads of faculty or others with a close knowledge of subject content. A study of the performance indicators in a number of states has led us to the conclusion that this is perfectly possible, since the criteria seem to have little subject specificity. The minimum criteria for effective teaching performance in Oklahoma, reprinted from Chapter 3 of the first edition in Appendix 3 of this edition, demonstrates that anyone with some training in accountability techniques – not necessarily anyone with teaching qualifications and experience – could use the indicators to evaluate the performance of the teacher of any subject.

It is worthy of note that this is an 'appraisal' process entirely imposed upon the teacher, with no opportunity for negotiation, self-appraisal or even, it would seem, for questioning the accuracy of the evaluation report. It is not, therefore, surprising that this accountability process was found to be 'a costly and ineffective method of quality assurance' and that Oregon found it necessary and wise to introduce the Professional Growth Program.

> This program recognises professional growth as a teacher's continuous personal commitment to the profession. It provides an opportunity for teachers interested in experimenting, researching and exploring avenues of professional growth in a supportive environment. [There is] a meeting early in the school year with the principal or vice principal at which goalsetting and timelines are developed. Training is provided in goalsetting and the Professional Growth Plans are shared informally with colleagues.
>
> (Madrell, 1991)

The scheme is voluntary but in the three years it has been operating two-thirds of the teaching force has taken part. There are 'no consequences for not reaching goals or carrying out the steps in the plan' and it is therefore understandable that the scheme's outcomes have included:

- a closer working relationship between teachers and principals
- a growth in understanding by management of what the classroom teacher is trying to achieve
- an increase in collegial interaction, between teachers and management and among teacher colleagues.

We have included this account partly because Oregon is only one of a number of states to move, however tentatively, from performance-rated appraisal to a model of appraisal that in broad outline, allowing for historical and cultural differences, matches that which we have so recently inaugurated in the United Kingdom. That accountability systems may have a place in school improvement we would not deny; but it is the institution which is accountable, primarily for the delivery of what it has itself determined to be appropriate to its own capacities and circumstances.

THE NETWORK OF MANAGEMENT AND DEVELOPMENT

Figure 15.1 on page 218 summarises the relationship between those elements described in the main part of this chapter which contribute to the management of our schools, and thence to control over the quality of their output.

Learning and management goals are shown as integral with the appraisal process, since they relate, and must be seen to relate, to the centrally placed, and in all respects central, school development plan. It would be unrealistic not to accept that both of these areas, development plan and appraisal, are 'dependencies' of whatever governmental regulations and guidelines may at any time be enforced. We have already witnessed repeated modifications to the National Curriculum that have imposed radical changes on schools' curriculum development plans; and there is every likelihood of the virtual destruction of the role of the LEA in promoting, monitoring and supporting the school development plan.

Between central government and the school, with responsibilities and roles introduced under the Education Reform Act (DES, 1988) the full implications of which are only now being appreciated, sits the school governing body. Whether or not the present Conservative government achieves its declared aim of having the majority of secondary schools, at least, under grant-maintained regulations by 1994 is largely irrelevant. With the diminution of the function and powers of the LEA, and the consolidation of local management of schools (LMS) and local financial management (LFM), the responsibilities of grant-maintained and LEA school governors are becoming broadly similar. Whether the governing body will seek to exert greater influence over school policy, or whether the traditional mutual respect of professionals and lay members will be maintained, remains to be seen. In his commentary on the Education Reform Act Leonard (1988) observed that 'the Act gives power to governors while leaving . . . the legal responsibilities firmly with the [LEA]'. If LEAs are to have only residual responsibilities, will this distinction still hold good? And where will be the safeguards for schools should governing bodies apply their own interpretations of regulations and the parameters of their legal powers? Some early warning signals on this have already been seen in the grant-maintained sector.

The figure indicates that there is at present only a tenuous relationship

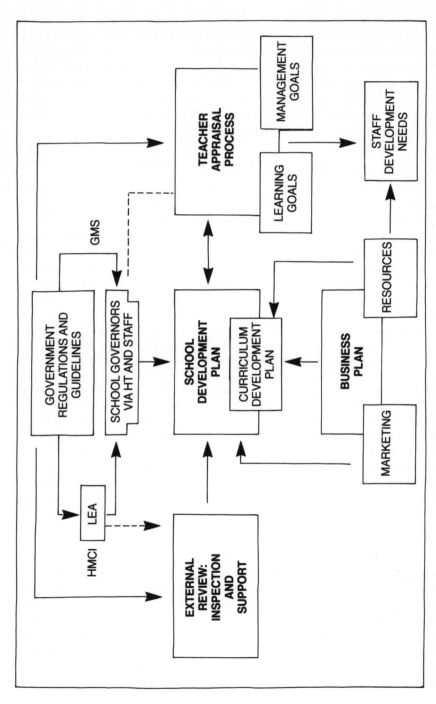

Figure 15.1 The network of management and development

between teacher appraisal and the responsibilities and role of the governing body. We trust that the broken line, which signifies the limitations currently placed on the information on the appraisal of individual teachers that may be made available to governors, will remain broken. This is not to imply that governors would necessarily abuse this information. What it does imply is that the high level of self-revelation and openness implicit in present arrangements for appraisal can only be sustained if the *collective* findings of appraisal are presented to governors, not those that will identify individuals. Quality control is a professional matter, and the role of the governing body is not to become directly involved, but to assure itself that every measure possible is being taken to improve the quality and performance of the teaching staff.

The business plan is certainly one element of the figure that many teachers may see as new, alien to their culture and even threatening. Yet all will readily appreciate the importance of that part of the box that refers to resources. How, ask our teachers today, is it possible to achieve high standards of quality in the absence of adequate resources?

This is not the place to debate why the resources are insufficient. Suffice that every teacher in an LEA school knows well that they are. The staff development needs that arise from appraisal cannot possibly be met from the current level of in-service funding, and equally the curriculum cannot be developed appropriately without a higher level of resourcing. It features in the business plan not only because its integration there acts as a counter to 'crisis spending', but also because there is hardly a school in the country that is not now dependent on the gaining of additional resources from non-statutory funding. That is unlikely to happen unless the school has paid attention to presenting within its business plan a clear indication of, on the one hand, the support it enjoys from the broad community including the students and their parents and, on the other, a precise indication of what any additional funding will achieve. Industrial and commercial concerns, trust funds and projects, will not in this day and age give handouts. They want value for money, to put it crudely, and they will wish to know that there is adequate quality control and that sound systems of review and evaluation are in place.

CONCLUSION

Although the years until 1995–6 may be well described as the proving ground for appraisal, its future will largely be determined by its successful introduction in the first two-year phase. If it is seen as an extraneous imposition, yet one more straw for the teacher-camel's back, then neither the first nor the second two-year phase is likely to be successful. What may happen then – and there is ample precedent for such a measure – is that appraisal for staff development will be replaced by a tick-sheet evaluation by management of a teacher's presumed worth. Negotiation and dialogue will play an insignificant part; self-appraisal will be a fruitless exercise. Goals will be determined not by staff, but for staff; and they will be framed to provide simple measuring rods, quantitative wherever possible, of the teacher's successes and failures.

These are the negative reasons why appraisal must be seen to succeed. The more positive reasons we hope we have made clear throughout this book, culminating in our view that appraisal is integral to quality control and the entire process of school improvement and effective management.

We are consultants, trainers and writers on education management. We can, of course, have our say and hope to have some influence. Ultimately it is up to teachers and education administrators to seek their alliances with those they most closely serve – the students and their parents – and those within the community who have an interest in the success of our educational system in general and the neighbourhood schools in particular. If ever there was a time when educationists must hold firm to their professional principles, and be seen to do so, it is now.

Guidance and code of practice on the collection of information for schoolteacher appraisal

1 This guidance and code of practice covers the collection of information for schoolteacher appraisal other than through classroom observation.

GENERAL PRINCIPLES

2 Information collection for the purpose of the appraisal of a schoolteacher should be designed to assist discussion in an appraisal interview having the purposes set out in §40 of the Circular.

3 Where it has been agreed that the appraisal should concentrate on specific aspects of the appraisee's job, the information collection should likewise concentrate on those aspects.

4 Appraisers should act with sensitivity to all concerned and should not exhibit any bias in collecting information.

5 Those giving information should not be put under any pressure save that of relevance and accuracy.

6 General comments should be supported by specific examples.

7 Interviews for the purpose of information collection should be held on a one-to-one basis.

8 Any information received anonymously should not be used.

9 Information which does not relate to the professional performance of a schoolteacher should not be sought or accepted.

10 Appraisees should not adopt an obstructive attitude to reasonable proposals for the collection of appropriate information.

11 Neither appraisers nor appraisees should act in any way that is likely to threaten the trust and confidence on both sides upon which successful appraisal depends.

BACKGROUND INFORMATION

Schoolteacher appraisal

12 The schoolteacher's appraiser must be familiar with relevant national and, in LEA-maintained schools, LEA policies and requirements. In grant-maintained schools, the appraiser must be familiar with the policies of the school's governing body.

13 The appraiser will also need to acquire a range of background information appropriate to the appraisee's wider professional responsibilities, for example, the school's statements of aims and objectives, pastoral arrangements, equal opportunities policies, or departmental policies.

14 The appraiser should obtain [a copy] of the schoolteacher's job description.

Headteacher appraisal

15 The headteacher's appraisers must be familiar with current national and, in LEA-maintained schools, LEA policies and requirements with regard to the curriculum, special needs, equal opportunities, staffing and cover, disciplinary and grievance procedures and other such matters relating to school management. In grant-maintained schools, the headteacher's appraisers should familiarise themselves with equivalent policies and requirements of the school's governing body.

16 They will also need a wide range of background information about the school and its context including:

- the school development plan
- curricular policies
- general organisation and deployment of staff
- composition and organisation of the governing body
- links with home, outside bodies and other schools
- the pattern of meetings with staff and with parents
- school activities and routines including assessment and recording systems, examination results, calendar of events
- staff appraisal and development arrangements and arrangement for induction
- financial and management systems.

This information will need to be assembled by appraisee heads, who may provide any supplementary information they wish.

17 The appraisers should obtain copies of the headteacher's job description.

Other guidance to the appraiser

18 The appraiser should aim to agree with the appraisee at the initial meeting

what information it would be appropriate to collect for the purpose of the appraisal, from what sources and by what methods.

19 When interviewing people providing information as part of an appraisal, the appraiser should explain the purpose of the interview and the way in which information will be treated.

20 Those giving information should be encouraged to make fair and considered comments which they are prepared to acknowledge and substantiate if required.

21 Any written submissions should remain confidential to the author, the appraiser and the appraisee.

22 Those offering significantly critical comments should be asked to discuss them directly with the appraisee before they are used as appraisal information.

23 Except where personal opinion is specifically sought (for example, where an appraiser is attempting to gauge staff reactions to a particular innovation), care should be taken to ensure that information is sought and presented in an objective way.

© Department For Education (DFE). Reprinted with permission

Appendix 2

Training videos

FOCUS IN EDUCATION

Focus in Education has produced a series of excellent videos drawing upon materials created in four of the six LEA pilot projects. They are highly professional in presentation, well packaged and each is accompanied by a booklet detailing the content, giving the running time for each section of the tape, and outlining the purpose of the compilation. There are three tapes from each of three LEAs, Newcastle-upon-Tyne, Cumbria and Suffolk, and four from Somerset. Tapes can be bought individually or in sets.

Awareness raising

Because these were the pilot projects, awareness raising permeates almost all the tapes. Specifically the first tape (FE19A) of the *Working Together* series (Newcastle) has an 18-minute sequence that promotes valuable discussion.

Into Appraisal (FE34) contains selected sequences from a number of the videos listed here and is a useful introduction to teacher appraisal.

Classroom observation

Let's Get It Right (Somerset) has a complete primary school observation sequence (FE15A), made up of a briefing session (7 minutes); the lesson, edited (13 minutes); and a very thorough debriefing cut with flashbacks to events in the lesson (15 minutes). FE15B is a secondary school English lesson, with the focus on group discussion.

What's In It For Me? (Suffolk) has on FE12B a complete Mathematics lesson with Year 2 pupils, followed by a discussion on the points raised; and on FE12C a secondary school Year 10 geography lesson, followed by discussion. Both run for just under an hour.

Working Together has a complete primary school PE lesson (FE19B) and a secondary school history lesson (FE19C) for Year 9 which focuses on the dynamics of group discussion. Each last for about 50 minutes.

FE36 consists of five tapes, compiled from the same sources, but specifically presented as a separate *Classroom Observation* series: FE36A is an overview, FE36B a middle school PE lesson, FE36C an early years mathematics lesson, FE36D a secondary school geography lesson, and FE36E a secondary school history lesson.

Headteacher appraisal

Two of the Somerset videos, FE15C and FE15D, cover the appraisal of a primary and a secondary headteacher respectively. FE13B from Cumbria presents the appraisal of a primary deputy headteacher. Each runs for up to an hour.

The address of Focus in Education is: Duke Street, Wisbech, Cambs PE13 2AE, tel: 0945 63441, fax: 0945 587361. Prices are available on request and flyers giving more details can be obtained. Video packs are sent on sale or return.

LEAP

The *LEAP management in education* project materials were produced by the BBC's Open University Production Centre and are obtainable through LEAs. Two modules provide useful background material for appraisal: module 2 on managing staff development and module 5 on accountability. Videos are included in the module materials.

Criteria for the management of effective learning

AUTHORS' INTRODUCTION

To achieve improvement in learning and teaching is a complex process, requiring purposeful planning and action and a regular and sustained programme of self-, peer and external evaluation. To this end indicators or criteria are essential, particularly in appraisal for staff development. In observing classroom performance, appraiser and appraisee must be in agreement on the nature of effective learning; and, similarly, within the school there must be common ground yet sufficient flexibility to allow for variations of emphasis according to the particular content under review. The indicators that follow, the Dudley LEA Task Group for Effective Learning makes clear, '[must] be flexible and cannot be . . . imposed from above. If [they] are to be useful, they have to be agreed and amended . . . by the people using them'.

The indicators are grouped in five areas: atmosphere (or ethos); the learning environment; resources; the role of the teacher as planner, deliverer and leader, and facilitator and guide; the role of the student.

ATMOSPHERE

Aim

The aim is to create or sustain an atmosphere of encouragement, acceptance, respect for achievement and sensitivity to individual need.

Indicators

- The teacher shows a personal interest in individual students beyond the needs of the immediate learning task.
- The teacher actively fosters a sense of group cohesion in work and discipline.
- The teacher is courteous to students and they reciprocate.

- The teacher makes frequent use of praise and encouragement, in a measured and sensitive way.
- The teacher frequently accepts or uses ideas expressed by a student.
- The students display a willingness to work cooperatively.
- The students feel free to signal their difficulties and to alert the teacher to organisational mistakes and problems and may sometimes express disagreement with a teacher's point of view.
- Students and teachers are mutually supportive.

THE LEARNING ENVIRONMENT

Aim

The aim is to create an environment where the classroom layout and appearance stimulate student–teacher interaction . . . flexible enough to allow adjustment to changing curricular needs. It is attractive and functional.

Indicators

- The teaching space is clean and tidy, and resources are stored in such a way as to permit quick retrieval.
- Displays are attractively arranged and are relevant to the current teaching and learning.
- Relevant reading, reference, writing and drawing materials are available to the students.
- The layout of furniture gives students as much work space as possible and allows for flexibility between individual work, small group work and class teaching.
- Adequate and appropriate audio-visual equipment and computers are easily accessible.
- There are clear policies, rules and procedures relating to the shared use of a room by several teachers.
- There is a set of 'house rules' governing students' use of the room and its facilities when teaching is not taking place.

RESOURCES

Aim

The aim is to provide easy access to resources (including IT) which are varied, attractive, available and appropriate, and well use by students.

Indicators

- Resources are differentiated to meet the needs of individual students, with particular regard to reading levels of printed materials.

- Quantities of resource items have been determined by the needs of the [learning] programme.
- Printed resources have design appeal, in addition to providing the necessary data and stimuli.
- Resources are classified and stored so as to help students find and use them.
- Resources are diverse so that students can learn through visual and aural experiences as well as through reading.
- The teacher has access to sources of information within both the school and the neighbourhood which will support the work.

THE TEACHER AS PLANNER

Aim

The aim is to plan work based on appropriate guidelines and to ensure that work is organised with clear purpose, targets and outcomes.

Indicators

- Detailed educational objectives have been derived from the broad statement of aims laid down by the programme of study.
- There is a detailed summary of the content of the programme.
- There is a description of the kinds of learning activity which are intended for each stage in the programme.
- Explicit arrangements have been made for the evaluation of the programme.
- Appropriate learning resources have been assembled and organised.
- The teacher has established procedures for the monitoring of each student's work.
- There is an efficient system for the continuous recording of each student's tasks, progress and achievements.

THE TEACHER AS DELIVERER/LEADER

Aim

The aim is to demonstrate personal attributes, technical competencies and subject knowledge that will promote students' learning in an atmosphere of respect and confidence

Indicators

- The teacher conveys an impression of self-confidence and self-control.
- The teacher shows flexibility and an ability to respond creatively to events.
- The teacher's instructions, descriptions and explanations are brief and clear.

- As a result of the teacher's skills as discussion leader, the students demonstrate a high level of participation.
- The teacher uses effective questioning techniques to raise the level of students' thinking.
- The teacher demonstrates a sound knowledge of the subject matter.

THE TEACHER AS FACILITATOR/GUIDE

Aim

The aim is to operate an efficient system of management and control which rests on firm arrangements and appropriate procedures so that the student does not rely on teacher direction and supervision all the time.

Indicators

- The teacher has established clear personal objectives and commitments for each student.
- The teacher gives clear directions on task procedures and encourages students to understand the structure of the lesson and the course.
- Simple and speedy procedures have been devised for tackling routine events and recurring problems.
- Students are encouraged to help in decision making about the organisation of the work and are given responsibilities and tasks that are within their competence.
- The teacher uses positive reinforcement: praise, incentives.
- The teacher maintains an appropriate balance in the use of time on supervisory, organisational and teaching activities.
- The teacher regularly reviews the conduct of lessons in terms of the effective use of time by both self and students.
- There are well organised opportunities for groups and/or individuals to report the outcomes of their work.
- Feedback is given to students in order that they can build up knowledge of their own performance.

THE ROLE OF STUDENTS

Aim

The aim is to ensure that they are aware of the purpose of the lesson and the criteria for success; when appropriate, to take an active part in the lessons at the planning, doing and reviewing stages, in order to demonstrate their developing sense of responsibility and independence; and to have the opportunity to work in small groups, as individuals and within the whole class.

Indicators

- When students arrive at the beginning of the lesson they take active steps to prepare for work.
- Students display initiative in finding the resources and equipment they need.
- Students frequently follow up classroom work and, when appropriate, homework, with further investigation in the school library and elsewhere.
- The teacher gives time to training the students in skills of personal organisation and learning.
- Students demonstrate their developing skills in group work by respecting the views of others and by engaging in debate without quarrelling.
- Students spend a high proportion of their time engaged on their learning tasks.
- Students experience success.

MINIMUM CRITERIA FOR EFFECTIVE TEACHING PERFORMANCE: OKLAHOMA

I PRACTICE

A Teacher management indicators

1 Preparation
   The teacher plans for delivery of the lesson relative to short-term and long-term objectives.
2 Routine
   The teacher uses minimum class time for non-instructional routines thus maximizing time on task.
3 Discipline
   The teacher clearly defines expected behaviour (encourages positive behaviour and controls negative behaviour).
4 Learning environment
   The teacher establishes rapport with students and provides a pleasant, safe and orderly climate conducive to learning.

B Teacher instructional indicators

1 Establishes objectives
   The teacher communicates the instructional objectives to students.
2 Stresses sequence
   The teacher shows how the present topic is related to those topics that have been taught or that will be taught.

3 Relates objectives
   The teacher relates subject topics to existing student experiences.
4 Involves all learners
   The teacher uses signalled responses, questioning techniques and/or guided practices to involve all students.
5 Explains content
   The teacher teaches the objectives through a variety of methods.
6 Explains directions
   The teacher gives directions that are clearly stated and related to the learning objectives.
7 Models
   The teacher demonstrates the desired skills.
8 Monitors
   The teacher checks to determine if students are progressing towards stated objectives.
9 Adjusts based on monitoring
   The teacher changes instruction based on the results of monitoring.
10 Guides practice
   The teacher requires all students to practise newly learned skills while under the direct supervision of the teacher.
11 Provides for independent practice
   The teacher requires students to practise newly learned skills without the direct supervision of the teacher.
12 Establishes closure
   The teacher summarises and fits into context what has been taught.

II PRODUCTS

A Teacher product indicators

1 Lesson plans
   The teacher writes daily lesson plans designed to achieve the identified objectives.
2 Student files
   The teacher maintains a written record of student progress.
3 Grading patterns
   The teacher utilises grading patterns that are fairly administered and based on identified criteria.

B Student achievement indicators

Students demonstrate mastery of the stated objectives through projects, daily assignments, performance and test scores.

© Routledge 1993

References

ACAS (1986) *Report of the Appraisal Training Working Group*, reprinted in HMSO (1989).

Barnard, C.I. (1938) *The Functions of the Executive*, Cambridge, Mass.: Harvard University Press.

Beare, H., Millikan, R. and Caldwell, B. (1989) *Creating an Excellent School*, London: Routledge.

Belbin, R.M. (1981) *Management Teams: Why they succeed or fail*, London: Heinemann.

Bunnell, S. and Stephens, E. (1984) 'Teacher appraisal: a democratic approach', *School Organisation* 4(4).

Burns, T. and Stalker, G.M. (1968) *The Management of Innovation*, London: Tavistock.

Davies, B. and Anderson L. (1992) *Opting for Self-Management*, London: Routledge.

De Board, R. (1983) *Counselling Skills*, Aldershot: Gower.

Dennison, W.F. and Shenton, K. (1987) *Challenges in Educational Management*, London: Routledge.

DES (1983) *Teaching Quality*, London: HMSO.

DES (1986a) *Education (No.2) Act*, London: HMSO.

DES (1986b) *Better Schools: Evaluation and Appraisal Conference*, London: HMSO.

DES (1988) *Education Reform Act*, London: HMSO.

DES (1989a) Circular letter 'Report of the National Steering Group and the Government's Response', 2 October 1989.

DES (1989b) *HMI Report: Developments in the Appraisal of Teachers*, London: DES.

DES (1992) *School Teachers' Pay and Conditions Document*, London: HMSO.

Dudley (1992) *The Management of Effective Learning*, Dudley, West Midlands: Dudley LEA.

Evertson, C.M. and Holley, F.M. (1981) 'Classroom observation', in J. Millman (ed.), *Handbook of Teacher Evaluation*, Beverley Hills, Calif.: Sage Publications.

Fisher, R. and Ury, W. (1981) *Getting to Yes*, London: Hutchinson.

Foskett, N. (ed.) (1992) *Managing External Relations in Schools*, London: Routledge.

Guardian, The (1992) 'Teachers head for a boycott', 20 April.

Hall, V., Morgan, C. and Mackay, H. (1985) 'Defining headship – an impossible task?' London: Secondary Heads' Association Review.

Handy, C. and Aitken, R. (1986) *Understanding Schools as Organisations*, Harmondsworth: Penguin.

Heywood, J. (1992) 'School teacher appraisal: for monetary reward, or professional development, or both?' in Tomlinson, H. (ed.), *Performance-related Pay in Education*, London: Routledge.

Herzberg, F.W. (1966) *Work and the Nature of Man*, London: Staples Press.

HMI (1985) *Quality in Schools: Evaluation and Appraisal*, London: HMSO.
HMSO (1989) *School Teacher Appraisal: A National Framework*, London: HMSO.
HMSO (1991) *The Education (School Teacher Appraisal) Regulations 1991*, London: HMSO.
Hughes, M. (1976) 'The professional as administrator: the case of the secondary school head' in R.S. Peters (ed.) (1976).
Joseph, K. (1984) Speech to the North of England Education Conference, January 1984, London: DES.
Kerley, R. (1989) 'Paying the price of opposing extremes', in *TSES*, 30 June 1989.
Leavitt, R.J. and Lipman-Brown, J. (1980) 'A case for the relational manager', *Organizational Dynamics*, Summer.
Leonard, J. (1991) *Teacher Performance Review: Recommendations for the NI Pilot Study*, Western ELB, Omar: DENI.
Leonard, M. (1988) *The 1988 Education Act: a Tactical Guide for Schools*, Oxford: Blackwell.
Macfarlane, E. (1992) *Education 16–19 in Transition*, London: Routledge.
McGregor, D.G. (1960) *The Human Side of Enterprise*, London: McGraw-Hill.
MacGregor, J. (1990a) 'Speech to the North of England Education Conference', *TES*, 12 January.
MacGregor, J. (1990b) Speech to the BEMAS Conference, September, London: DES.
Madrell, K. (1991) 'An ocean apart?', *Perspective*, July.
Maslow, A.H. (1959) *Motivation and Human Personality*, New York: Harper.
Mintzberg, H. (1979) *The Structuring of Organizations*, Englewood Cliffs, NJ: Prentice-Hall.
Montgomery, D. (1985) 'Teacher appraisal: a theory and practice for evaluation and enhancement', *Inspection and Advice* 21(1).
Morgan, M. (1990) 'Appraisal in a Cumbrian secondary school', in *Head Teachers Review*, Winter (1989/90), London: NAHT.
Morgan, C., Hall, V. and Mackay, H. (1983) *The Selection of Secondary Headteachers*, Milton Keynes: Open University Press.
Munn, P. (ed.) (1993) *Parents and Schools: Customers, Managers or Partners?*, London: Routledge.
NDC (1988) *Consortium of School Teacher Appraisal Pilot Schemes; Progress on Appraisal: an interim report*, Bristol: National Development Centre for School Management Training.
Newman, J. (1985) *Staff Appraisal Schemes in the South Midlands and the South West*, York: Centre for the Study of Comprehensive Schools.
Newton, C. and Tarrant, T. (1992) *Managing Change in Schools*, London: Routledge.
Peters, T.J. and Waterman, R.H. (1982) *In Search of Excellence: Lessons from America's Best-run Companies*, London: Harper and Row.
Peters, R.S. (ed.) (1976) *The Role of the Head*, London: Routledge & Kegan Paul.
Poster, C. D. (1976) *School Decision Making*, London: Heinemann.
Randall, G., Packard, P. and Slater, J. (1984) *Staff Appraisal: a First Step to Effective Leadership*, London: Institute of Personnel Management.
Robson, M. (ed.) (1984) *Quality Circles in Action*, Aldershot: Gower.
Scotsman, The (1991) 'Forsyth lifts threat of teacher appraisal plan', 13 November.
Suffolk LEA (1985) *Those Having Torches*, Ipswich: Suffolk Education Department.
TES (1991) 'Scotland gets four times more for appraisal', 4 January.
TES (1992) 'Harris CTC', *Times Educational Supplement*, 30 October 1992.
Tomlinson, H. (ed.) (1992) *Performance-Related Pay in Education*, London: Routledge.
TSES (1989a) 'SED claims a "general acceptance" of appraisal', 10 November.
TSES (1989b) 'Government to fund training for appraisal', 17 November.

TSES (1991) 'A positive marker for all teachers', 8 February.

Turner, G. and Clift, P. (1985) *A First Review and Register of School and College Based Teacher Appraisal Schemes*, Milton Keynes: Open University Press.

University of Wolverhampton (1993) *School Management Competences Project*, Wolverhampton: University of Wolverhampton.

Vroom, V.H. (1964) *Work and Motivation*, New York: Wiley.

Weber, M. (1947) *The Theory of Social and Economic Organisation*, New York: Free Press.

Wieck, K.E. (1976) 'Educational organizations as loosely coupled systems', *Administrative Science Quarterly* 21.

Wilkinson, C. and Cave, E. (1987) *Teaching and Managing: Inseparable Activities in Schools*, London: Routledge.

Wragg, E.C. (1987) *Teacher Appraisal: a Practical Guide*, Basingstoke: Macmillan.

Index